JOHN CHACKO

ECHOES OF PENTECOST

ECHOES OF PENTECOST

From the Upper Room to Your Living Room

The Spirit's Power for Everyday Faith

JOHN CHACKO

276 5th Avenue Suite 704 #944

New York, NY 10001

Copyright © 2025 John Chacko

ISBN (Paperback)

ISBN (Hardback)

ISBN (eBook)

All rights reserved

No part of this publication may be reproduced, stored in a retrieval system, copied in any form or by any means, electronic, mechanical, photocopying, recording or otherwise transmitted without written permission from the publisher. You must not circulate this book in any format.

Under no circumstances will any blame or legal responsibility be held against the publisher, or author, for any damages, reparation, or monetary loss due to the information contained within this book, either directly or indirectly.

DEDICATION

To Jesus,

My Lord, My Savior, My All.

This work, and all my work, is for you.

"He is the image of the invisible God, the firstborn over all creation. For by Him all things were created that are in heaven and that are on earth, visible and invisible, whether thrones, dominions, principalities, or powers. All things were created through Him and for Him. And He is before all things, and in Him all things consist. And He is the head of the body, the church, who is the beginning, the firstborn from the dead, that in all things He may have the preeminence."

Colossians 1:15-18

TABLE OF CONTENTS

PREFACE	1
BEFORE YOU BEGIN	5
INTRODUCTION	12

SECTION I , THE SPIRIT AND YOU: A BIBLICAL FOUNDATION	20
1. The Breath Of God	21
Chapter 1: The Spirit In Creation	24
Chapter 2: The Spirit In Everyday Life	36
Chapter 3: The God Who Chooses The Ordinary	43
2. Pentecost: More Than A Story	75
Chapter 1: The Event That Shook The World	78
Chapter 2: Beyond The Historical Moment	89
Chapter 3: From Routine To Alive	106
Chapter 4: The Time Is Now	135
SECTION II , LESSONS FROM THE CHURCH THROUGH HISTORY	140
3. Prayer That Changes The World	144
Chapter 1: The Birth Of A Prayer Movement	146
Chapter 2: The Supernatural Results	151
Chapter 3: The Secret Of Sustained Prayer	157
Chapter 4: Modern Prayer Movements	162
Chapter 5: Reflection: Deepening Your Prayer Life	169
4. Faith That Crosses Borders	181
Chapter 1: Paul - The Prototype Of Missionary Courage	183
Chapter 2: The Early Church	187
Chapter 3: Modern Global South Revivals	192
Chapter 4: Reflection: Where Is God Calling You?	201
5. Revival And Renewal	204
Chapter 1: Azusa Street And Charismatic Renewal	209
Chapter 2: Everyday Revival In Modern Life	218
Chapter 3: What Revival Could Look Like In Your Life	223
Chapter 4: Reflection: Your Revival Begins Now	228

SECTION III , LIVING SPIRIT-FILLED TODAY	**230**

6. Recognizing The Spirit's Voice — 235

Chapter 1: The Nature Of God's Voice — 237
Chapter 2: Discernment Patterns — 240
Chapter 3: Practical Ways To Listen In Prayer — 246
Chapter 4: Recognizing God's Voice In Daily Choices — 250
Chapter 5: Developing Confidence In Divine Communication — 255

7. Empowered For Healing And Wholeness — 260

Chapter 1: Understanding God's Heart For Wholeness — 262
Chapter 2: Physical Healing Through Ordinary Believers — 266
Chapter 3: Emotional And Relational Restoration — 270
Chapter 4: Words That Heal And Restore — 275
Chapter 5: Stepping Into Your Healing Calling — 280

8. Courage To Love And Lead — 285

Chapter 1: Understanding Spirit-Led Leadership — 286
Chapter 2: Leadership In The Family — 290
Chapter 3: Workplace Leadership Without Titles — 294
Chapter 4: Student Leadership And Academic Influence — 298
Chapter 5: Community Leadership And Civic Engagement — 302
Chapter 6: The Courage To Lead When It Costs — 306

9. Revival In The Everyday — 311

Chapter 1: The Spirit At The Dinner Table — 313
Chapter 2: The Sacred Workplace — 318
Chapter 3: Conversations That Transform — 323
Chapter 4: Supernatural Ordinary Moments — 328
Chapter 5: Creating Revival Culture — 333
Chapter 6: The Ripple Effect Of Ordinary Faithfulness — 339

SECTION IV , YOUR PENTECOST JOURNEY	**345**

10. The Echo Continues — 349

Chapter 1: Understanding Your Inheritance — 351
Chapter 2: Becoming A Modern-Day Witness — 356
Chapter 3: Living As A Pentecost Person — 362
Chapter 4: Your Personal Challenge — 367
Chapter 5: The Echo In Your Generation — 374

REFLECTION AND CLOSING PRAYER	**382**
REFERENCES	**388**

PREFACE

Every book is born out of a journey, and this one is no exception.

I did not set out to write a book about the Holy Spirit. In fact, if I am honest, I resisted the idea. I wondered, *Does the world really need another book about Pentecost?* Hasn't enough been written by theologians, pastors, and historians? What could I possibly add?

But as I prayed, the Spirit would not let me go. Time after time, the burden grew heavier. I began to see how many sincere Christians live with a faith that is good , but not full. Faithful , but not alive. Busy with religious activity , but rarely transformed by the breath of God.

And I recognized myself in them.

There were seasons when my faith was more duty than delight. I prayed, but my prayers rarely stretched beyond myself. I read the Bible, but the words often felt flat. I sang worship songs, but the fire in my heart flickered low. Outwardly, I looked faithful. Inwardly, I was hungry for something more.

It was in that season of dryness that God began to wake me up.

One Sunday, as I sat in church listening to a sermon on prayer, something unusual happened. The preacher's words seemed to carry a weight beyond themselves. It was as if every sentence unfolded in layers within me. I wasn't just listening to a man's voice , I was hearing the Spirit's whisper.

One question pierced me: *Why are you not praying for revival?*

I have prayed many prayers in my life. Prayers for my family, for my needs, for my church. But never for revival. Never for God to rend the heavens and pour out His Spirit on an entire people. Never for Him to move in power beyond the walls of the sanctuary, flooding communities, nations, and generations with His presence.

That question marked me. It shifted my prayer life from small circles of comfort to a wide-open cry for awakening. It wasn't just about asking for a blessing, it was about aligning with heaven's heartbeat.

Since that moment, I have come to see that revival is not merely a historic event or a church program. Revival is what happens when the Spirit of God breathes fresh life into weary hearts, awakening them to the reality of His love, power, and presence. Revival is when ordinary believers catch fire and become witnesses of extraordinary grace.

And I believe, with all my heart that this is not just for the past. It is for now.

Why This Book Matters

We live in a world aching for hope. Anxiety, division, cynicism, and fear run deep in our culture. Even within the church, many believers are weary. We know the language of faith, but we struggle to experience the life of faith. We go through motions, but our souls still whisper, there must be more.

The good news is, there is.

That "more" is not a new program, not another self-help strategy, not a clever idea. That "more" is the Spirit of the Living God.

This book is my humble attempt to put words around the echoes of Pentecost, those moments in Scripture, history, and even in my own story where the Spirit has broken in with fresh fire. My prayer is not that you would admire them as distant testimonies, but that you would encounter the same Spirit in your own walk with God.

I want you to know that Pentecost is not just a date on the church calendar. It is not a relic of the early church. Pentecost is an inheritance. It belongs to you, to me, to every believer who longs to walk in the fullness of God's presence.

The Spirit who empowered Peter to preach with boldness is the same Spirit who can empower you to speak courage into your workplace. The Spirit who comforted persecuted believers is the same Spirit who can comfort you in seasons of loss and confusion.

The Spirit who healed the broken and sent out missionaries across the world is the same Spirit who can bring healing and purpose into your everyday life.

A Personal Prayer for the Reader

As I write these words, I pray for you , the one holding this book. Perhaps you are young in faith and hungry to know God more. Perhaps you are seasoned in years yet weary in spirit.

Perhaps you are skeptical, unsure what to believe about the Holy Spirit. Or perhaps you are desperate , longing for God to breathe fresh fire into your soul.

Wherever you are, I want you to know: The Spirit sees you. He knows you. He loves you. And He is nearer than you think.

My prayer is that this book would not simply inform you but awaken you. That the stories within would not just inspire but invite. That you would find yourself leaning in, not to my voice, but to the Spirit's.

Because the Spirit still speaks.

A Word of Gratitude

I must also acknowledge that I do not write as a solitary voice. Countless saints before me have walked this path of Spirit-filled living, and I stand on their shoulders. From the apostles in Acts to the Moravians, from the revivalists of the Great Awakenings to the nameless intercessors in prayer closets around the world, their lives are living testimonies that God still moves when His people seek Him.

I also give thanks to those in my own life who modeled Spirit-filled faith , mentors who prayed with passion, friends who lived with courage, and communities that pressed me toward deeper surrender. Without their witness, I would not have had the courage to write these words.

An Invitation

So, dear reader, consider this book not as a manual but as a journey. A journey into the heart of God. A journey guided by the One Jesus promised would be with us forever: The Holy Spirit.

My invitation to you is simple: don't just read these pages. Pray through them. Pause. Listen. Respond. The Spirit may whisper something personal to you that I have not written. He will stir a hunger that no words of mine can satisfy. Let Him.

If you finish this book with more questions than answers, but with a deeper hunger for God's presence, then it will have fulfilled its purpose.

Because Pentecost is not about information.

It is about transformation.

And that transformation is for you.

With humility and hope,

John Chacko

BEFORE YOU BEGIN:
Your Greatest Journey

An Invitation to Eternal Life

Before you dive into the stories of supernatural transformation that fill these pages, before you read about the fire that fell on Pentecost and continues to fall today, before you discover your inheritance as a Spirit-filled believer, there is something far more important we must address: the foundation upon which everything else depends.

All the spiritual power, all the miraculous encounters, all the transformed lives you're about to read mean nothing if you haven't first experienced the greatest miracle of all, the miracle of salvation through Jesus Christ. The disciples couldn't be filled with the Holy Spirit until they first became followers of Jesus. The believers throughout history whose testimonies fill this book couldn't walk in supernatural power until they first walked through the door of salvation that Jesus opened for every person who has ever lived.

That door is open for you today. That same salvation is available to you right now, in this moment, before you turn another page.

The Problem We All Face

Every human being who has ever lived faces the same fundamental problem: we are separated from God by our sin. This isn't about being a "bad person" or failing to live up to certain moral standards. This is about the basic human condition that affects every one of us, regardless of our background, achievements, or good intentions.

The Bible declares with crystal clarity: "All have sinned and fall short of the glory of God" (Romans 3:23). This means you; this means me, this means every person who has ever drawn breath.

We have all chosen our own way instead of God's way. We have all fallen short of His perfect standard. We have all done things we shouldn't have and failed to do things we should have done.

But our problem goes deeper than just wrong actions, it's a problem of the wrong nature. We are born with a sinful nature that naturally rebels against God, naturally chooses selfishness over service, and naturally pursues our own desires instead of His will. This sin nature has infected every aspect of human existence and has separated us from the holy God who created us.

The consequence of this separation is devastating: "The wages of sin is death" (Romans 6:23). This death is not just physical death that everyone experiences, but spiritual death, eternal separation from God in a place the Bible calls hell. This is the destiny that awaits every person who dies in their sins, no matter how good they may have tried to be, no matter how many religious activities they may have participated in, no matter how sincere their efforts to live a moral life.

This is the most serious problem any human being can face, and it's a problem that no human being can solve through their own efforts. We cannot earn our way to heaven through good works. We cannot overcome our sin nature through willpower. We cannot bridge the gap between ourselves and God through religious activity or moral improvement.

The Solution Only God Could Provide

But here is the most amazing truth in the universe: what we could not do for ourselves, God did for us. The same God we had rebelled against, the same God whose holy nature our sin had offended, chose to provide the solution to our impossible problem.

"But God demonstrates His own love toward us, in that while we were still sinners, Christ died for us" (Romans 5:8). God didn't wait for us to clean up our lives or prove ourselves worthy of His love. While we were still in active rebellion against Him, while we were still choosing our way instead of His way, He sent His Son Jesus Christ to earth to live the perfect life we could never live and die the death we deserved to die.

Jesus Christ was not just a good teacher or a moral example, He was God in human flesh, the eternal Son of God who took on human nature so He could represent humanity before His Father. He lived a sinless life, perfectly fulfilling every requirement of God's holy law. Then He willingly went to the cross and took upon Himself the punishment that our sins deserved.

On that cross, Jesus became our substitute. He took our sin upon Himself so that we could receive His righteousness. He experienced the wrath of God against sin so that we could experience the love of God for sinners. He died the death that should have been ours so that we could live the life that should have been His.

But the story didn't end with His death. Three days later, Jesus rose from the dead, proving that He had conquered sin, death, and hell. His resurrection demonstrated that God had accepted His sacrifice as full payment for our sins and that eternal life was now available to everyone who would believe in Him.

This is the Gospel, the good news that God has provided salvation as a free gift to everyone who will receive it through faith in Jesus Christ.

Your Personal Invitation

Right now, in this moment, God is extending to you the same invitation He has extended to every person throughout history: *"Come unto Me, all you who labor and are heavy laden, and I will give you rest" (Matthew 11:28).*

Jesus Himself declared, "I am the way, the truth, and the life. No one comes to the Father except through Me" (John 14:6). He is not one of many ways to God, He is the only way to God. He is not one truth among many truths, He is the truth that sets people free. He is not offering one kind of life among many options, He is offering the abundant, eternal life that can only come from God.

This invitation requires a response from you. It's not enough to intellectually understand the Gospel or appreciate what Jesus did. You must personally receive Him as your Lord and Savior.

You must turn from your sin (Repent) and turn to Christ in faith, trusting Him alone for your salvation.

The Bible promises: "If you confess with your mouth the Lord Jesus and believe in your heart that God has raised Him from the dead, you will be saved. For with the heart one believes unto righteousness, and with the mouth confession is made unto salvation" (Romans 10:9-10).

Salvation is not earned through good works, religious ceremonies, or moral effort. It is received as a free gift through faith alone in Jesus Christ alone. *"For by grace you have been saved through faith, and that not of yourselves; it is the gift of God, not of works, lest anyone should boast" (Ephesians 2:8-9).*

The Most Important Prayer You Could Ever Pray

If you recognize your need for salvation and want to receive Jesus Christ as your Lord and Savior, you can do so right now through prayer. Prayer doesn't save you, only Jesus saves you, but prayer is how you express your faith in Him and receive the salvation He offers.

This is not a magical formula but a heartfelt expression of genuine faith. If you truly mean these words and are ready to turn from your sin and trust Jesus Christ for your salvation, pray this prayer from your heart:

Dear God,

I recognize that I am a sinner and that my sin has separated me from You. I acknowledge that I cannot save myself through my own efforts or good works. I deserve Your judgment for my rebellion against You.
But I believe that You love me and sent Your Son, Jesus Christ, to die on the cross for my sins. I believe that Jesus took the punishment I deserved and that He rose from the dead, conquering sin, and death.
Right now, I repent of my sins and turn to You. I receive Jesus Christ as my personal Lord and Savior. I trust in Him alone for my salvation and ask You to forgive all my sins.

Thank You for the gift of eternal life. Thank You for making me Your child. Thank You for the promise that I will spend eternity with You in heaven.

I commit my life to following Jesus and living for Your glory. Fill me with Your Holy Spirit and help me to grow in my relationship with You.

In Jesus' name I pray, Amen.

Since you prayed this prayer with genuine faith, the Bible declares that you are now a child of God: *"But as many as received Him, to them He gave the right to become children of God, to those who believe in His name" (John 1:12).*

Your sins have been forgiven. You have been given eternal life. You have been adopted into God's family. The Holy Spirit has come to live within you. You are a new creation in Christ, your old life has passed away, and a new life has begun.

Your New Beginning

Receiving Jesus Christ as your Savior is not the end of your spiritual journey, it's the beginning of the greatest adventure you could ever imagine. You are now ready to discover everything this book has to offer about living in the power of the Holy Spirit, experiencing God's supernatural presence, and becoming the person He created you to be.

As a new believer in Jesus Christ, you now have access to:

- *Forgiveness for all your sins (1 John 1:9)*
- *Eternal life in heaven (John 3:16)*
- *The Holy Spirit living within you (1 Corinthians 6:19)*
- *Power to live a victorious Christian life (Philippians 4:13)*
- *Direct access to God through prayer (Hebrews 4:16)*
- *The promises and guidance of God's Word (2 Timothy 3:16)*
- *Fellowship with other believers (1 John 1:7)*

The fire of Pentecost that you'll read about in the pages ahead is now available to you personally.

The supernatural transformation that has characterized Spirit-filled believers throughout history can now become your experience. The power that turned ordinary people into extraordinary witnesses of God's love can now work through your life.

But remember: your relationship with God must be built on the solid foundation of salvation through Jesus Christ. Everything else, spiritual gifts, supernatural experiences, miraculous encounters, flows from this fundamental relationship with God through His Son.

If you didn't pray the salvation prayer because you're not ready to make that commitment, I encourage you to continue reading with an open heart. The testimonies and truths in this book may help you understand more about God's love for you and His desire for a personal relationship with you. The same Holy Spirit who transforms believers is also working to draw unbelievers to salvation through Jesus Christ.

Moving Forward

Whether you just received Christ as your Savior or you've been a believer for years, you're now ready to discover the incredible inheritance that God has provided for every Christian. You're ready to learn about the fire that fell on Pentecost and continues to fall today. You're ready to explore what it means to live in supernatural power and become a Spirit-filled witness in your generation.

The journey from routine religion to authentic spiritual life begins with salvation and continues with the empowerment of the Holy Spirit. You've taken the first step by receiving Jesus Christ. Now you're ready to take the next steps toward experiencing everything God has made available to you as His child.

The fire is ready to fall on your life. The power is available to transform you. The adventure of Spirit-filled living awaits your faith and obedience.

Welcome to the family of God. Welcome to the life you were born again to live. Welcome to your personal Pentecost journey.

Turn the page and discover what God has prepared for those who love Him.

"Therefore, if anyone is in Christ, he is a new creation; old things have passed away; behold, all things have become new." - 2 Corinthians 5:17

Your new life begins now.

INTRODUCTION –
The Spirit Still Speaks

A Noisy, Hurried World

Our world has never been louder. From the moment we wake up, we are met not with silence, but with noise. The buzz of notifications. The glow of screens. The endless scroll of headlines, updates, opinions, and advertisements. Many of us start our mornings not with prayer, but with the news cycle or social media feed. Before our feet touch the ground, our minds are already being programmed to think, worry, or react in ways we never chose for ourselves.

Music lyrics whisper values. News anchors declare emergencies. Influencers tell us who to admire, what to buy, and how to think. Entertainment, often subtle and unnoticed, forms our view of identity, morality, and truth. All of it clamors for our hearts, competing for our devotion.

This isn't new. For centuries, humanity has been shaped by voices and stories. The difference is the speed and intensity of today's world. What once spread slowly through letters, papers, or word of mouth now multiplies instantly and globally. A single opinion can travel across continents in milliseconds. A cultural trend can influence millions before lunch.

And without realizing it, seeds are planted, grown, and we are shaped. We think we are choosing freely, but the truth is that much of what influences us was chosen for us. We live in a world that does not merely seek to inform us, it seeks to form us. To mold us into its image. To control how we think, feel, and act.

The Bubbled Culture

One of the most dangerous results of our noisy world is what I call a "bubbled culture", and you're likely trapped in one right now without knowing it.

Picture this: You're scrolling through your phone, and every click, every pause, every second you linger becomes data harvested by invisible watchers. Social media algorithms study your behavior like a predator stalking prey. Watch a political video for thirty seconds? Your feed floods with identical viewpoints. Pause on a particular preacher's sermon? Your recommendations transform into an echo chamber of voices saying exactly what you want to hear.

These digital puppeteers aren't trying to educate you, they're trying to addict you. The longer you stay online, the more money flows into their pockets. So they become dealers of comfort, feeding you a steady diet of agreement that creates a prison where every voice confirms what you already believe.

The spiritual consequences are catastrophic.

We stop seeking truth and start defending preferences. We surround ourselves with personalities who tickle our ears, books that stroke our biases, and podcasts that never challenge our assumptions. Like ancient Israel choosing false prophets over Jeremiah's painful honesty, we've traded spiritual growth for digital comfort food.

Here's the terrifying reality: when everyone around you agrees with you, you've stopped growing. You've stopped seeking. You've become a prisoner of your own preferences while calling it "staying informed." This bubble feels safe, even righteous. But it's spiritually lethal.

Why? Because truth is no longer pursued, it's assumed. When Pilate asked Jesus, "What is truth?" he was genuinely wrestling. Today, most people don't even pause to wonder. They already have their truth, their narrative, their comfortable conclusions. When a different truth appears, they dismiss it without consideration, like swatting away an annoying fly.

This isn't new. Ancient Israel chose soothing lies over Jeremiah's hard words. The wilderness generation preferred familiar Egyptian slavery over the risky promise of the Promised Land. The early church fractured into competing camps and ideological tribes. Bubbles are as old as human nature itself.

But never before have these bubbles been so sophisticated, so seductive, so perfectly crafted to our individual weaknesses. Modern algorithms don't just feed us what we like, they study our psychological patterns and serve up content engineered to keep us scrolling, clicking, consuming. We think we're making choices, but we're being shaped by invisible hands that profit from our spiritual stagnation.

The result? Our minds slam shut. Our hearts calcify. We transform from seekers of truth into defenders of comfort, from disciples into consumers, from pilgrims into prisoners.

But here is the good news that breaks every chain: The Holy Spirit is not confined by bubbles.

The Spirit: Breaker of Bubbles

On the day of Pentecost, the disciples were trapped in their own bubble. They were together in one room, afraid of the authorities, clinging to each other, unsure of the future. Their bubble was one of fear, tradition, and limitation.

Then the Spirit came. Wind filled the room. Fire rested on each head. Suddenly, they spoke in languages they had never learned, languages that burst the bubble of culture and carried the gospel across barriers of tribe, nation, and class. What had been a fearful group became a bold movement.

Pentecost shattered their bubble. And that is what the Spirit still does. He breaks us free from the false security of sameness. He calls us to embrace voices, cultures, and people different from ourselves. He loosens our grip on fear and comfort. He empowers us not to live in echo chambers, but to be the echo of heaven.

The Spirit is not just one more voice in the noise of our world. He is the Voice that silences lies.

He is the Guide who leads us into truth (John 16:13). He is the Comforter who frees us from fear and the Empowerer who sends us into mission.

Without the Spirit, our bubbles suffocate us. With the Spirit, our bubbles burst, and we breathe the fresh air of God's reality.

Why This Book Exists

This book was not written merely because I had free time or because I felt the need to add one more volume to the already overflowing shelves of Christian literature. It was written out of a deep conviction, born of prayer, tears, and many nights of wrestling with God.

I remember seasons when I felt spiritually dry, my prayers were more mechanical than heartfelt, my Bible reading more duty than delight. I was busy with life, with responsibilities, yet my soul longed for something more. Deep down, I knew I needed a fresh encounter with the living God.

It was in such a season that the Lord began to stir my heart to study revivals, not just as history, but as testimony. I wanted to know: What happens when heaven breaks into earth? What happens when ordinary men and women surrender themselves so completely that the Spirit of God sweeps through entire communities?

The more I read about the Moravians who prayed for a hundred years without ceasing, about the Great Awakenings that shook America, about the Azusa Street Revival where people of all nations and backgrounds came together under the outpouring of the Holy Spirit, the more I realized that revival is not a relic of the past. It is the heartbeat of God for every generation.

This book exists as both a testimony and an invitation. Testimony, because the history of revival bears witness that God is faithful to His promises. Invitation, because the Spirit is still calling us. He is calling us to wake from slumber, to shake off complacency, and to seek Him with all our hearts.

I have written these words not as a theologian who has mastered every doctrine, nor as a historian who has cataloged every detail, but as a fellow traveler, hungry for more of God.

This book exists because I need revival. And I suspect, if you are holding these pages in your hands, you do too.

A Night Heaven Touched Earth

He was only seventeen. Still fresh from the waters of baptism, the weight of that moment still rested on his shoulders like a holy mantle. The church he attended was small, wooden pews, a few ceiling fans turning lazily, and a sanctuary that could hold maybe a hundred people if every seat were filled. But what it lacked in grandeur, it carried in expectancy.

That night, the people were hungry. They sang, not for performance, but with longing. They prayed, not to be heard, but to touch heaven. As the first chords of worship began, he closed his eyes. He expected the usual, songs he had sung before, prayers he had prayed before. But this night was different. Something unseen pressed upon the room. Something heavier than air, yet lighter than breath.

The Holy Spirit descended.

At first, it was subtle, like a gentle wind rustling through the congregation. Then it grew stronger, undeniable, tangible. The boy felt his lips quiver. His chest tightened with a pressure that was not fear, but fire. His mouth opened, and suddenly, syllables he had never learned poured forth.

Tongues.

Confusion struck him. His mind fired questions: What are you saying? This makes no sense. People will think you're strange. Why embarrass yourself? The inner critic screamed. His reasons resisted. But deeper still, beneath the noise of self-consciousness, was another voice. Not condemning. Not mocking. Calling. Inviting. Urging. A holy nudge: Yield.

And so, he did. Trembling, uncertain, but willing, he yielded. He lent his vocal cords to the mystery. He stopped resisting and simply obeyed.

And in that moment, everything changed.

Strength coursed through his limbs. Energy surged through his body like electricity. His hands clapped without command. His voice grew louder, stronger, bolder. What had started as hesitant murmurs became a flood of sound. Then, something unexpected. One by one, others in the room began to join him. First, a woman in the back, then a man near the front, then a cluster in the middle. Soon the sanctuary filled with the sound of many voices speaking in heavenly languages.

The worship swelled. What had begun as a whisper became a wave. The boy stood. His legs shook, but not from fear. It was joy. Holy joy. He could not sit still. He clapped. He jumped. He moved to the aisle. Then, like David before the ark, he danced. Unrestrained. Unashamed. Up and down the aisle, his feet testified that heaven had invaded earth.

The congregation erupted. Men and women who had once been stoic now lifted their hands high. Those who had once sung softly now shouted praise. Some wept, others laughed, some fell to their knees. Worship turned wild. But it was not chaos. It was consecration.

For thirty minutes, perhaps more, the sanctuary pulsed with glory, with joy, with holy frenzy. The atmosphere was thick, like breathing liquid fire. To the natural eye, it might have looked unpolished, even foolish. But to those who had tasted it, it was heaven.

That night, heaven kissed earth. And a seventeen-year-old boy discovered a truth that would never leave him: when the Spirit speaks, it's not about understanding, it's about yielding.

Why This Story Matters

You may wonder why I share this memory here. I share it because revival is not first about nations, crowds, or movements. Revival begins with one person who says yes to the Spirit.

That boy could have resisted. He could have silenced the tongues, folded his arms, and waited for the feeling to pass. Many do. But by yielding, by giving voice to what the Spirit wanted to birth, he opened a door not only for himself but for the entire congregation. His obedience sparked obedience in others. His flame spread. And together, they became a bonfire of worship.

That night, I (for yes, I was that seventeen-year-old boy) learned something profound: God does not need my eloquence, my understanding, or my control. He only needs my surrender.

An Invitation for You

Perhaps you have never had a night like that. Perhaps you have sat in church, sung the songs, read the words, and still felt as though something vital is missing, some deeper life, some nearer God. Perhaps you long for heaven to touch earth, for God to break through your dryness, for something beyond routine.

You live in a world that screams for your attention, phones buzzing before your feet hit the floor, news cycles that demand outrage, feeds that curate only what you already think. We tuck ourselves inside comfortable bubbles of likeness and certainty, and the cost is that we stop being seekers of truth. We become defenders of preference.

But you were not made for noise. You were made for communion. You were made to hear the whisper of the Spirit, to walk in the presence of Jesus, to be a living temple of God.

Remember the boy in that small church: fresh from baptism, trembling with newness, unsure and self-conscious, yet when the Spirit came, he yielded. He spoke what he did not understand, and his yield became the spark that lit a room. What began with one yielding heart became a wave that swept an entire congregation.

If God could take a shy, uncertain teenager and kindle in him the fire of heaven, He can do the same for you. If God can turn an ordinary building into a meeting place between heaven and earth, He can make where you are holy ground.

So this is your invitation. Slow down. Lay aside, if only for a while, the endless stream of noise and opinion. Become a seeker again, ask What is truth? And be willing to listen. Hunger and thirst for righteousness with the audacity of one who believes God will fill them. Dare to expect that revival is not merely for "them" or "then"; it is a promise for your life.

Revival does not begin with movements; it begins with surrendered hearts. Perhaps yours. Bow low.

Yield the small things first, pride, comfort, the easy distractions, and make space for the Spirit to breathe. Read these pages slowly and prayerfully. Do not treat them as information to consume; treat them as an invitation to respond.

Will you accept this invitation? Will you risk being unsettled, humbled, and changed? If you will, read on with expectancy. The Spirit still speaks, and He may be calling you now.

A Simple Prayer

As we close this introduction, I want to leave you not with more words, but with a prayer. You may want to pause here, bow your head, and make these words your own.

> *Father in heaven, I praise Your Name and honor You. I come before You with hunger in my soul. The world is loud, and my heart is easily distracted, but I long for Your presence. I confess that I have too often lived on the surface, content with shallow faith. Forgive me, Lord. Awaken me again.*
>
> *Pour out Your Spirit upon me as You have upon generations before. Break down the walls of my pride and open my eyes to see Jesus afresh. Make me a seeker of truth, not just a consumer of noise. Teach me to hunger and thirst for righteousness until I am filled.*
>
> *Lord, start revival in me. Let it burn in my heart, in my family, in my church, in my nation. And let it all be for Your glory. In Jesus' name, Amen.*

If you prayed that prayer sincerely, you have already begun the journey. Revival is not something we wait passively to happen, it is something God births in those who are willing.

Turn the page not as a spectator, but as a participant. The same Spirit who hovered over the waters at creation, who fell in fire at Pentecost, who revived generations before us, that same Spirit is ready to breathe on you.

Let us begin.

I

THE SPIRIT AND YOU:
A Biblical Foundation

*"Before the world heard God's Word, the Spirit was His breath.
Let Him be yours."*

1. THE BREATH OF GOD

We all need to breathe to live, yet most of us rarely pause to think about it. Breathing is the most natural thing we do, the invisible rhythm that sustains our very existence. From that first piercing cry at birth until the final exhale at life's end, breath marks our days. It is constant, involuntary, taken for granted, until something interrupts it.

As a clinician, I have witnessed this interruption far too often. I have stood beside patients desperately struggling to fill their lungs with air, their chests rising and falling with tremendous effort, but never finding relief. They were breathing deeply yet not oxygenating adequately. Their bodies gasped for life-giving oxygen, but their lungs betrayed them. If you have ever tried breathing through a straw, you know the taste of this sensation, uncomfortable, then suffocating, then unbearable. Within moments, carbon dioxide builds in your blood, oxygen levels plummet, and your body panics. You cannot live long like this.

Breathing is a marvel of divine design. Inhalation is active work, your body creates negative pressure in the thoracic cavity, drawing air into your lungs as the diaphragm contracts. Yet its work we hardly notice, carried out in perfect rhythm thousands of times daily. Exhalation is passive. Once your lungs fill, elastic tissue recoils, and air flows back out. Even if you try holding your breath, you cannot hold it forever. Eventually, your body forces you to release. The cycle continues, breath by breath, until God calls you home.

This physical process is ventilation, air moving in and out of the lungs. But the real miracle happens deeper, at the microscopic level of the alveoli, where oxygen diffuses into the bloodstream and carbon dioxide is released. That is respiration, the true exchange of gases that sustains life. Without it, no breath would matter. Air alone cannot keep us alive unless it mingles with our blood, feeding every cell, every organ, every thought.

Here is the profound truth Scripture reveals: what is true in the body is also true in the spirit. Just as oxygen is necessary for physical life, the Spirit of God is necessary for spiritual life. Without Him, we are like lungs filled with air but no exchange, going through motions yet starving within.

Genesis tells us, *"The Lord God formed the man from the dust of the ground and breathed into his nostrils the breath of life, and the man became a living being" (Genesis 2:7).* It is one of the most intimate moments in all Scripture. The God who spoke stars into existence with a word chose instead to stoop down, shape humanity from dust, and breathe His very own breath into Adam's lungs. The Hebrew word for "breath" is ruach, which also means spirit or wind. In the Greek New Testament, the word is pneuma, carrying the same dual meaning. Breath and Spirit are inseparable.

Every inhale, then, is not just a biological function but a spiritual reminder: life is a gift, not a guarantee. We are not self-sustaining. We did not will ourselves into existence. We do not keep ourselves alive by sheer determination. Each breath is grace, given freely by the One who animates dust with His Spirit.

When we forget this, we live under an illusion that we are independent that we can survive on our own strength, that our lives are ours to control. But just as the body collapses without oxygen, the soul withers without the Spirit. The frightening reality is that it's possible to exist physically, lungs pumping, heart beating, yet be spiritually gasping, starved of God's breath.

Many live this way: active, busy, even religious, but without true respiration of the Spirit in their inner being.

Breathing illustrates dependence in its purest form. You cannot store it up. You cannot say, "I took a deep breath yesterday; I should be fine today." No, you must breathe again and again, unceasingly. In the same way, life with God is not sustained by one past encounter, no matter how powerful. We need Him continually. We need His Spirit to fill, renew, and empower us moment by moment. Paul understood this: *"Be filled with the Spirit" (Ephesians 5:18).* The verb tense implies ongoing action: keep on being filled. Just as breathing never ceases, neither should our openness to God's Spirit.

We cannot live without breath, and we cannot live without the Spirit. If we try, we faint spiritually just as surely as we would physically by breathing through a straw. Our worship becomes shallow, our prayers mechanical, our relationships strained. We may inhale doctrine, community, activity, but unless the Spirit brings true exchange, we remain lifeless.

Yet when the Spirit fills us, something extraordinary happens. The ordinary becomes alive with divine presence. Conversations take on weight. Work gains meaning. Decisions become guided. Suffering is endured with hope. Like oxygen saturating the blood, the Spirit saturates our lives with God's presence, carrying His life to every part of who we are.

The breath of God is more than metaphor, it is the very essence of life itself. To breathe is to live, and to live truly is to breathe of Him. The Spirit, the ruach of God, has been present from creation itself, moving through ordinary people in extraordinary ways, and still animating our lives today.

So pause for a moment. Notice your breathing. Inhale, exhale. Feel the rhythm. Each breath is testimony: you are alive, sustained not by your own power but by grace. As we step into the story of the Spirit, let us remember that what is most fundamental to our bodies is also most fundamental to our souls.

Without breath, no life. Without Spirit, no true life.

CHAPTER 1:
The Spirit in Creation

Breath. Wind. Spirit.

Three words that seem so ordinary in human language, yet in Scripture they carry eternity within them. In Hebrew, the word is ruach. In Greek, it is pneuma. Both words pulse with movement, force, and vitality. They mean air in motion, breath filling empty lungs, wind rushing across seas and deserts, Spirit stirring the depths of creation and the depths of the soul.

From the very first verses of the Bible, we are not introduced to God's Spirit as a theory, a metaphor, or an abstraction. We are introduced to Him as a living presence. He hovers. He moves. He breathes. He creates. He sustains. The Spirit is not simply something about God; He is God Himself in motion, God drawing near, God touching the world, God animating what was lifeless.

The Spirit is the breath of God. Not just a poetic phrase but the very force that makes existence possible. Without breath, dust remains dust. Without wind, seas remain stagnant. Without Spirit, the universe remains void and silent. But when the Spirit moves, life erupts, beauty unfolds, and order emerges from chaos.

The Spirit is life-giving. He is the unseen reason Adam opened his eyes in Eden. He is the force behind every inhale and every heartbeat you and I have taken today. Each breath we draw is a whisper of His sustaining grace.

The Spirit is order-bringing. Where there was formlessness, He hovered. Where there was chaos, He prepared the ground for God's Word to speak. The Spirit is never intimidated by confusion; He brings cosmos out of chaos, rhythm out of randomness, harmony out of havoc.

The Spirit is beauty-creating. The galaxies scattered like jewels across the sky, the intricate veins in a leaf, the endless hues of a sunset, all bear the fingerprint of His artistry. He does not simply make things exist; He makes them glorious.

If you want to understand the Spirit's work in your life, you cannot start with your own story; you must start with the story, the story of creation. For in the beginning, before man was formed, before history unfolded, before the first prayer was uttered, the Spirit was already there. Hovering. Moving. Preparing. And He has not stopped. The same Spirit who moved in Genesis still moves today. The same breath that gave Adam life gives you, life. The same wind that stirred the waters hovers over the chaos of your world.

To understand the Spirit's work in us, we must begin at the beginning, where breath, wind, and Spirit reveals God's presence as the source of all life.

The Spirit Hovering over the Waters (Genesis 1:2)

The Bible opens not with a neatly ordered universe but with a scene of unformed chaos. *"Now the earth was formless and empty, darkness was over the surface of the deep, and the Spirit of God was hovering over the waters" (Genesis 1:2).*

This verse, often passed over quickly, is one of the most profound portraits of the Spirit in all of Scripture. It sets the stage for everything that follows.

The picture is dramatic: the earth without form, void of structure, covered in deep and restless waters. Darkness stretched endlessly. No light, no landmarks, no life. A world uninhabited and unfinished, a place of potential yet untouched by purpose. And into this raw, unsettled scene enters the Spirit of God, not distant, not idle, but present, hovering.

Chaos and the Human Story

In many ways, this description mirrors the human condition. Just as the earth was formless and void, our lives apart from God lack true direction and substance. We may exist, but without the Spirit, we drift like vessels on dark waters, carried wherever the currents of culture and circumstance flow. Many people live this way, purposeless, untethered, merely surviving rather than living.

But Genesis 1 reveals a truth more dominant than the chaos. It reveals that the Spirit is already there. Before God spoke light into darkness, before form shaped the void, before beauty and life blossomed, the Spirit was present, hovering, waiting, preparing.

The same is true for us. Before you or I ever heard the Word of God, before we whispered the name of Jesus in faith, before we consciously turned toward the cross, the Spirit was already near. Scripture declares that we were chosen in Christ before the foundation of the world (Ephesians 1:4; 1 Peter 1:20). That means the Spirit was brooding over our lives long before we ever acknowledged Him, preparing, drawing, stirring, waiting for the moment when God's Word would break into our darkness.

The Meaning of "Hovering"

The Hebrew word translated "hovering" (rachaph) carries rich imagery. It conveys vibration, movement, a fluttering, or brooding presence. The word is used elsewhere in Scripture to describe an eagle stirring up its nest, fluttering over its young (Deuteronomy 32:11). The picture is both tender and moving: a parent bird hovering to protect, nurture, and awaken life in the nest.

This is how the Spirit is introduced to us, not as a static force but as a dynamic presence, alive with expectancy, ready to release order, beauty, and life. The Spirit hovers like a mother over her young, like an artist before a blank canvas, like a musician before the first note. Creation is not yet spoken into being, but the Spirit is already there, vibrating with potential, anticipating God's Word.

The Spirit in the Chaos

This reveals something profound about the nature of God's Spirit: He is present in the chaos. He does not wait for perfection to arrive before He moves. He does not shy away from darkness or disorder. Before there was light, the Spirit was there. Before there was order, the Spirit was hovering. Before there was beauty, the Spirit was brooding.

This is good news for us. Many of us look at our lives and see chaos: relationships tangled and strained, hearts burdened with grief, minds restless with fear, habits and sins that seem unshakable. We feel formless, empty, and void. Yet the Spirit does not abandon us to our confusion. He draws near to it. He hovers over the mess. He broods over the darkness. He waits for God's Word to be spoken into our situation so that light can pierce the night, and order can replace the void.

The Spirit is not repelled by the chaos of your life. He is drawn to it. He specializes in transforming darkness into dawn and disorder into design.

From Chaos to Creation

Genesis 1 reminds us that creation begins with chaos, but it does not end there. Where the Spirit hovers, life will come. Where the Spirit is present, transformation is inevitable. Chaos is not the final word; God's Word is. And when the Spirit and the Word work together, new creation always emerges.

This same truth unfolds across the pages of Scripture. In Ezekiel's vision of the dry bones, Israel was scattered, lifeless, and hopeless. Yet when the Spirit of God breathed upon them, they rose as a vast army (Ezekiel 37:9–10). In the New Testament, the disciples were fearful, uncertain, and hiding in an upper room. Yet when the Spirit came at Pentecost, they were filled with boldness, courage, and power (Acts 2).

The pattern is clear: the Spirit enters chaos, hovers over weakness, and releases life when God speaks.

Our Personal Application

So what does this mean for us today? It means that wherever you see chaos in your life, the Spirit is already hovering. That financial crisis that feels like deep water? The Spirit is near. That relationship fractured beyond repair? The Spirit is brooding. That anxious mind filled with confusion? The Spirit is present, anticipating the moment when God's Word will speak light and truth.

It also means that we are never beyond hope. As long as the Spirit hovers, there is potential for new creation. As long as He broods, the void is never final. As long as He breathes, life can always emerge.

Perhaps today you feel formless and void. Perhaps you look at your heart and see only darkness. Take courage: the same Spirit who hovered over the waters in Genesis hovers over you now.

And when God speaks into your life, through His Word, through His promises, through the gentle whisper of the Spirit, chaos will not have the last word. Creation will.

The Breath of Life (Genesis 2:7)

After six days of ordering, separating, and filling, God's masterpiece comes into focus:

Humanity. The crown jewel of creation. The Scriptures record,

"Then the Lord God formed the man from the dust of the ground and breathed into his nostrils the breath of life, and the man became a living being." (Genesis 2:7)

The contrast here is staggering. On one hand, man is formed from dust, common, overlooked, fragile, temporary. Not fashioned from diamonds or gold, but from dirt. The same dirt we sweep away, walk upon, and barely notice. Dirt has no glory in itself. It clings to shoes, cakes our skin, clouds our vision. Left alone, dirt is inert, lifeless, easily scattered by the wind.

And yet, God stoops. The eternal Creator kneels to the ground He Himself has made. With divine hands, He sculpts dust into form. Every curve, every joint, every muscle fiber shaped by His artistry.

But still, it lies motionless. No breath. No life. Dust shaped like a man but as silent as the grave.

Then, something extraordinary. God leans in, bends low, and breathes. The Almighty exhales

His own Spirit into Adam's nostrils. The infinite fills the finite. The eternal fills the temporal.

The divine fills the dust. And suddenly, clay quivers, eyes flutter open, and Adam inhales for the first time. Life has begun, not by accident, not by evolution, but by the intimate breath of God.

Dust animated by divinity. Clay infused with Spirit.

This moment is more than biology; it is theology. Humanity is not simply alive because lungs expand or hearts pump. We live because the breath of God sustains us. Our true essence, our consciousness, our capacity to love, to dream, to create, to worship, comes not from dust but from breath. This is what separates us from every other creature. Animals breathe, but only humanity carries within its lungs the direct breath of God.

And this truth redefines our worth. We are not cosmic accidents, not sophisticated animals, not dust left to its own devices. We are beings sculpted by God's hands and animated by His Spirit. Every inhale is a testimony that His breath still fills us. Every exhale is a confession that we remain utterly dependent on Him.

From Dust to Diamonds

Consider the dust again. When walking, we seldom notice what we tread upon. Dirt seems worthless, kicked, scattered, and ignored. But under pressure, dirt can yield diamonds. Hidden within what looks ordinary lies potential brilliance.

God sees what we cannot. When He stooped to the dust, He wasn't merely forming matter; He was calling forth destiny. From worthless earth, He made vessels of eternal value. From what the world disregards, God brings forth glory. That is the miracle of the breath, dust turned to living image-bearers of the Most High.

The First Breath and Every Breath

Long before hospitals, incubators, and ventilators, God was the first obstetrician. No sterile rooms, no monitors, no oxygen masks, just divine craftsmanship. He formed Adam, then leaned in. In the most intimate moment of creation, God breathed. No suction tubes, no medical interventions, only Spirit. Adam blinked, coughed, and drew his first breath. The belly rose, air filled the lungs, and for the first time in history, humanity said, "I am."

Fast forward through millennia to a delivery room today. A baby is born, tiny, wrinkled, silent. Not breathing. The doctor lifts the newborn gently, tilts the head, and clears the airways. For a suspended moment, the room holds its breath. Then, WAAHHH! The cry pierces the silence. Breath enters. Life begins. And somewhere in heaven, the Spirit smiles, for every first cry echoes Eden. Every new breath is a reminder: God still breathes, life still begins, and His Spirit still hovers over the chaos, ready to create.

Life is fragile, fleeting, utterly dependent on the Spirit of God. The breath in your lungs right now is borrowed. You did not create it. You cannot sustain it. Every inhale is grace. Every exhale is mercy. We are sustained, not self-sustaining.

The Spirit as Breath

Here lies a profound mystery: in both Hebrew (ruach) and Greek (pneuma), the word for Spirit is the same word for breath or wind. The Spirit is not merely like breath; He is the Breath of God.

Invisible yet undeniable. Untouchable yet essential. Breath cannot be held forever, nor can the Spirit be controlled. Breath must flow, must be inhaled and exhaled, just as the Spirit moves freely, filling, and empowering.

This changes everything. To live without the Spirit is as impossible as living without breath. A body without breath is a corpse; a soul without the Spirit is spiritually dead. We can busy ourselves, achieve success, or accumulate wealth, but without the Spirit, we are dust rearranged, animated only for a time, destined to wither.

But when God breathes into us, oh, the transformation! Dust becomes destiny. Clay becomes a carrier of glory. The ordinary becomes a vessel of the extraordinary.

Breath, Death, and Dependence

We take our breath for granted because it's constant, forgetting it is also fragile. We only notice this precious gift when it's threatened by sickness or fear. In the desperate gasp for air, we learn a humbling lesson: what we ignore in abundance, we treasure in its absence.

So too with the Spirit. We often move through life unaware of His presence, inhaling and exhaling without recognition. But the moment we try to live without Him, without prayer, without surrender, without yielding, we suffocate. Our souls faint. Anxiety chokes. Sin strangles. Only the Spirit can restore oxygen to the soul.

The Daily Gift

What if we saw every breath as worship? What if every inhale reminded us, God sustains me? What if every exhale whispered, I belong to Him? Then the mundane rhythm of breathing would become a symphony of praise. The ordinary act of living would become a continual reminder of our extraordinary dependence.

This is what Genesis 2:7 declares: we are dust, yes, but dust filled with divine breath. Every moment we live is Spirit-sustained. Every step we take is breath-enabled. Every heartbeat, every thought, every laugh, every tear, all carried by the Breath of God.

Inhale. Exhale. Live. Worship.

For the same God who stooped to breathe into Adam's nostrils bends low still, filling us with His Spirit, sustaining us in every breath, until the day He breathes us home.

The Spirit Sustaining Creation (Psalm 104:29–30)

The psalmist captures this dependence with poetic beauty:

> *"When you hide your face, they are terrified; When you take away their breath, they die and return to the dust. When you send your Spirit, they are created, and you renew the face of the ground."*
> *(Psalm 104:29–30)*

Here we see the ongoing work of the Spirit in creation. He is not only the initiator of life at the beginning but the sustainer of life in every moment. Without His breath, all creatures perish.

With His breath, new life springs forth.

This is not poetic exaggeration; it is spiritual reality. Every blade of grass, every bird in the sky, every human heart continues to exist because the Spirit breathes life into it. Without Him, creation collapses. With Him, creation flourishes.

Think about that for a moment. We often credit science with explaining how the world works, the laws of physics, the cycles of seasons, and the processes of ecosystems. These are real and wondrous, but behind them all is a deeper truth: The Spirit of God sustains it all. Science can describe the "how," but only faith recognizes the "who."

The Spirit is not an occasional visitor to creation but its constant sustainer. He is the breath in lungs, the rhythm in tides, the pulse in seasons. He renews the earth each spring, bringing life from barren ground. He feeds the creatures, provides rain for the land, and upholds the delicate balance of ecosystems. He is the hidden presence in all that lives.

And if this is true of creation, how much more of us? We live not by bread alone, nor by strength, nor by willpower, but by the Spirit who sustains us moment by moment. Every heartbeat is a gift. Every breath is grace.

The Spirit of Order, Beauty, and Creativity

Creation is not only functional; it is beautiful. Mountains rise in grandeur, oceans sparkle with light, flowers bloom in vibrant color, and stars scatter across the night sky. There is no reason for such beauty to exist if the world were merely an accident. Beauty exists because the Spirit of God delights in it.

From Genesis 1, we see not just raw creation but ordered creation. Light is separated from darkness, waters from land, day from night. The Spirit does not create chaos; He brings order to it. He is the architect of harmony, the composer of rhythm, the painter of detail.

This order is purposeful. A world of chaos cannot sustain life. But a world of order provides stability, balance, and flourishing. The Spirit ensures that the sun rises each morning, that seasons turn, and that ecosystems function in interdependence. His fingerprints are on the very fabric of creation's order.

But the Spirit is not only orderly, He is creative. He fills creation with diversity and wonder. No two snowflakes are alike. No two human fingerprints match. The world is not gray and uniform but bursting with color, shape, and sound. From the songs of birds to the fragrance of flowers, from the majesty of mountains to the intricacy of DNA, creation reveals the Spirit's artistry.

And He has imparted this creativity to us. As beings made in the image of God and animated by His breath, we too are creative. Whether in art, music, writing, gardening, problem-solving, or innovation, every act of human creativity reflects the Spirit's imprint. Our longing to create beauty, to bring order, to imagine what is not yet, the Creator's Spirit within us.

Application: The Spirit's Life, Order, and Creativity in Us

What does all of this mean for us today? It means the same Spirit who hovered over the waters, breathed life into Adam, and sustains creation is at work in our lives as well.

1. The Spirit Brings Life

Without the Spirit, we are dust. With the Spirit, we live. This is true physically, but it is also true spiritually. Sin leaves us lifeless, like dry bones scattered in a valley (Ezekiel 37). But when the Spirit breathes, the bones rattle, flesh forms, and life returns.

If you feel spiritually dry, lifeless, or numb, remember you are not beyond hope. The Spirit can breathe into you again. He can revive your weary soul, renew your joy, and awaken your love for God. The same breath that animated Adam can animate you.

2. The Spirit Brings Order

Just as He brought order to the chaos of creation, the Spirit brings order to the chaos of our lives. Many of us feel overwhelmed by confusion, pulled in a thousand directions, consumed by anxiety or fear. But the Spirit is not the author of confusion; He is the Spirit of peace and order.

When we yield to Him, He arranges our priorities, calms our fears, and gives us clarity. He brings order to our relationships, our inner thoughts, and our daily rhythms. He aligns us with God's will, bringing harmony where there was discord.

3. The Spirit Brings Creativity

The Spirit delights in beauty and creativity, and He invites us to participate in it. Perhaps you think of yourself as "not creative," but creativity takes many forms. Every time you solve a problem, imagine a better future, cook a meal, write a note of encouragement, or plan a project, you are engaging in creativity.

When we walk with the Spirit, our creativity becomes more than self-expression; it becomes God-expression. He inspires us to create things that reflect His beauty, order, and goodness. He may give you a song, a painting, a book, or a business idea. Or He may give you the creativity to restore a broken relationship, to design a ministry, to bring justice to a community.

Breathing the Breath of God

The Spirit in creation reveals who He is: the giver of life, the bringer of order, the source of beauty and creativity. From the chaos of the waters to the dust of the ground, from the psalmist's song to the wonder of ecosystems, the Spirit is present and active.

And He is still present and active today, in you, in me, in the world around us. Every breath we take is a reminder that we live by His Spirit. Every sunrise testifies to His order. Every act of creativity reflects His image in us.

So let us not live unaware. Let us pause and breathe deeply, remembering that the Spirit who hovered over the waters now hovers over our lives. The Spirit who breathed into Adam now breathes into us. The Spirit who sustains creation sustains us still.

Take a deep breath. Feel the air fill your lungs. That is grace. Now imagine the Spirit filling your soul with His life, His order, His creativity. That is the breath of God.

CHAPTER 2:
The Spirit in Everyday Life

The Misconception: Spirit Only for "Special" Moments

Many Christians associate the Holy Spirit with dramatic events: Pentecost's fire, tongues in the upper room, miraculous chains breaking, and prophets speaking with thunder. We often see the Spirit as a divine spotlight, appearing only for grand scenes in history and revival stories.

This view is limited. While the Spirit does move in extraordinary ways, He is also present in everyday life. The same Spirit who parted seas and raised the dead empowers a farmer planting seeds, a mother cradling her child at 3 a.m., a craftsman carving wood, a student studying for exams, and anyone simply getting through Monday.

The Spirit is not just for mountaintop moments but also a quiet companion in the valleys. He's not only for apostles, prophets, or priests but for ordinary people, sons, daughters, workers, and wanderers. He's not only the God of thunder but also of whispers.

And sometimes, He surprises us.

Consider Balaam's donkey (Numbers 22). Here's a perfect example of the Spirit in daily life: a talking animal. Balaam was so spiritually blind that God used his donkey to get his attention. Imagine Balaam beating his donkey when it turned around and essentially said, "Hey, buddy, what gives? Haven't I been a good donkey?" The donkey saw what Balaam couldn't: the angel of the Lord. Sometimes, God's Spirit uses the mundane, even humorous, to get our attention.

And it doesn't stop there. Think of Jonah sulking under a vine after Nineveh repented. The Spirit sends a worm to eat the plant, leaving Jonah hot, cranky, and exposed.

Imagine grumbling at God about a plant while a whole city revives. Talk about missing the point. Yet even then, God's Spirit taught Jonah, through a worm, shade, and discomfort, that His mercy extends beyond Jonah's narrow vision. The point is clear: The Spirit isn't just in burning bush moments. He works through donkeys, worms, vines, conversations, chores, and interruptions. Miss Him in the ordinary, and you miss Him most of the time.

Consider Jesus' ministry. Yes, there were miracles, blind eyes opened, storms calmed, dead raised. But much of His life was ordinary. He spent thirty years not preaching or walking on water but working as a carpenter. Do you think the Spirit was absent then? Hardly. The Spirit was in His patience with rough edges, in His conversations with neighbors, and in His obedience to Joseph and Mary. The same Spirit who descended on Him at the Jordan was present in Nazareth's workshop.

Rediscovering this truth sets you free. If the Spirit is only in the spectacular, then daily life, its rhythms, chores, conversations, and labors, seems untouched by His presence. But if the Spirit fills the ordinary, then no moment is wasted, and no act is too small to be sacred.

- Folding laundry with a prayerful heart becomes worship.
- Cooking dinner with gratitude becomes holy service.
- Writing an email with integrity becomes Spirit-led work.
- Changing diapers at midnight becomes discipleship in love.
- Laughing with friends becomes sacred joy.
- Even mowing the lawn can be an encounter with the God who turns chaos into beauty.

The Spirit is not far from your everyday life. He's not waiting for a revival conference to show up. He is as near as your next breath, as close as your next decision, as involved as your next conversation. He is the Lord of mountaintops, yes, but also the quiet Lord of Mondays.

The Spirit at Work in the Ordinary

Consider the hidden work of daily life.

- A farmer rises early, trusting the rain.
- A nurse adjusts an IV, offering medicine and compassion.
- A teacher writes on the chalkboard, shaping young minds.
- A student studies by lamplight, fueled by coffee and determination.
- A parent wipes away tears, prepares meals, or sits in exhaustion after a long day.

Is the Spirit absent from these moments? Scripture says no. From the beginning, God is intimately involved in the ordinary. Genesis shows the Spirit hovering over unformed waters, shaping and sustaining life.

We must train our eyes to see Him in unexpected places: the diligence of workers, the tenderness of caregivers, the creativity of artists, the endurance of those who persist without applause. The Spirit delights in the unseen as much as the celebrated.

Bezalel and the Spirit of Craftsmanship

This is beautifully illustrated in the story of Bezalel in Exodus 31:1–5.

"Then the Lord said to Moses, 'See, I have chosen Bezalel son of Uri, the son of Hur, of the tribe of Judah, and I have filled him with the Spirit of God, with wisdom, understanding, knowledge, and all kinds of skills, to make artistic designs for work in gold, silver, and bronze, to cut and set stones, to work in wood, and engage in all kinds of crafts."

Here, a surprising reality emerges: the first person explicitly "filled with the Spirit of God" is not a prophet, priest, or warrior, but an artist. A craftsman. A man called to hammer gold, carve wood, and design beauty for the tabernacle.

This is profound. The Spirit's filling isn't confined to "spiritual work." Preaching, praying, or prophesying aren't the only Spirit-filled tasks. The Spirit empowers creativity, craftsmanship, design, and artistry, enabling hands to shape material into reflections of divine glory.

Bezalel's chisels and hammers were holy instruments because the Spirit filled his work. His art was worshipful; his skill was Spirit-enabled.

This truth liberates us. If the Spirit can fill a craftsman's workshop, He can fill an office, classroom, kitchen, or hospital. Your spreadsheet, cooking, or caregiving can be Spirit-filled. With surrender and faithfulness, the ordinary becomes a dwelling place for God.

Spirit-Led Wisdom in Everyday Decisions

The Spirit's work extends to wisdom for daily choices. Isaiah 11:2 describes the Spirit as "the Spirit of wisdom and understanding, the Spirit of counsel and might, the Spirit of knowledge and the fear of the Lord."

Wisdom is practical. It guides us in handling work conflicts, disciplining children with love, balancing generosity with stewardship, and responding gracefully to insults.

The Spirit whispers in overlooked moments:

- "Be patient."
- "Speak gently."
- "Don't send that angry email."
- "Encourage her; she's weary."
- "Trust Me with this decision."

These aren't fireworks moments, but they are holy. They shape lives, relationships, and destinies. The Spirit guides us not only in great missions but in small conversations, commutes, grocery runs, and texts.

Relationships Shaped by the Spirit

The Spirit's presence is crucial in relationships. Paul's writings remind us that the Spirit's fruit, love, joy, peace, patience, kindness, goodness, faithfulness, gentleness, and self-control (Galatians 5:22-23), is expressed as relational virtues in how we treat each other.

The Spirit enables:

- A husband to love sacrificially.
- A wife to respect faithfully
- A child to honor parents.
- A parent to nurture children.

The Spirit softens tongues, heals wounds, and makes forgiveness possible. In the community, the Spirit helps us:

- Bear burdens
- Weep with those who weep.
- Rejoice with those who rejoice.

These aren't glamorous acts. They rarely make headlines but form the fabric of Spirit-filled living. The kingdom advances not just through preachers but through neighbors who love, friends who listen, and coworkers who serve humbly.

Application: Noticing God in the Ordinary

So how do we begin to live with this awareness, that the Spirit shows up not only in revivals and miracles but also in breakfasts, boardrooms, and bedtime routines?

1. Slow Down to Notice

Busyness blinds us to the Spirit's presence. The Israelites often missed God because they were grumbling or rushing ahead. Seeing the Spirit in the ordinary requires attentiveness.

Try a whispered prayer in the morning: *"Spirit, open my eyes today."*

Pause before a meeting:

"Lord, give me wisdom here." These small moments open the door to awareness.

2. Redefine "Spiritual Work"

Stop dividing life into sacred and secular. Washing dishes can be as holy as leading worship if you do it in the Spirit. Brother Lawrence, a 17th-century monk, discovered this truth in his small monastery kitchen. He learned to experience God's presence while scrubbing pots.

His testimony reminds us: no task is so small that it cannot be filled with God's presence.

3. Embrace the Hidden

Some of the Spirit's greatest works are unseen. A whispered encouragement. A meal prepared in love. A prayer prayed in secret.

These don't look spectacular, but they carry eternal weight. Heaven values what the world overlooks.

4. Depend on Every Detail

When you're overwhelmed, whisper: *"Spirit, help me."* When confused, pray: *"Spirit, guide me."* When joyful, celebrate: *"Thank You, Spirit."*

Every detail of life becomes a chance to depend on Him.

Ordinary Made Sacred

The Spirit isn't waiting for you only on Sundays or in revivals. He's with you on Mondays, in commutes, in laundry rooms, in classrooms, in conversations. He delights not only in grand stages but in hidden corners.

Bezalel's chisels, a mother's lullaby, a farmer's plow, a nurse's gentle touch, all can become holy instruments when surrendered to the Spirit.

And this changes everything. Life is no longer divided into sacred and secular, holy and ordinary. All of life, every breath, every task, every relationship, becomes a dwelling place for God's Spirit.

So, when you rise tomorrow, don't just watch for burning bushes or parted seas.

Look for the Spirit at your breakfast table, in your conversations, in your work, and in your silence.

The same Spirit who hovered over the waters and breathed life into Adam's lungs now hovers over your life, filling even the most ordinary moments with eternal glory.

CHAPTER 3:
The God Who Chooses the Ordinary

If you were given the task of changing the world, who would you choose? A wealthy monarch with armies at his disposal? A philosopher with unmatched wisdom? A speaker whose voice could command the multitudes?

God thinks differently. He delights in taking what seems small, weak, flawed, and overlooked, and breathing His Spirit into it until it becomes unstoppable.

Throughout Scripture, this is His unmistakable pattern. He doesn't scan the earth for the flawless, the polished, the self-sufficient. He looks for the ones the world ignores, the brother sold into slavery, the man who cannot speak clearly, the prophet who hides in fear, the fisherman who denies under pressure, the zealot who persecutes with rage.

Joseph. Moses. Elijah. Peter. Paul. Ordinary names. Ordinary people. And yet, extraordinary stories.

Why? Because when the Spirit fills the ordinary, the ordinary no longer stays ordinary. Dust becomes image-bearer. Stuttering lips confront kings. Shaking knees stand on mountaintops. Calloused fishermen speak with fire. A persecutor becomes a preacher.

We often disqualify ourselves before the race even begins. I'm not gifted enough. I've failed too many times. I don't have what it takes. But if Scripture teaches us anything, it's this: the Spirit of God doesn't wait for the perfect résumé. He specializes in taking weak vessels and filling them with His power.

This isn't just ancient history; it's present reality. The same Spirit who hovered over the waters, who raised Christ from the grave, now dwells in us. The God who chose Joseph in the pit, Moses in his fear, Elijah in his despair, Peter in his failure, and Paul in his rebellion is the same God who chooses you.

So as we step into these stories, let's do so with open hearts. Not as spectators marveling at ancient heroes, but as participants recognizing a holy pattern: God's Spirit takes ordinary lives and writes extraordinary chapters. And perhaps the next chapter is yours.

Joseph: From Pit to Palace

The story of Joseph is one of the most remarkable narratives in Scripture, not only because of its sweeping drama but because of how clearly the Spirit of God shines through the cracks of betrayal, injustice, and suffering. It's the story of a man who was betrayed by his brothers, enslaved by strangers, imprisoned by lies, and forgotten by those he helped, yet exalted to the highest office in Egypt. From pit to palace, Joseph's life is a living testimony that the Spirit of God specializes in taking what others mean for evil and turning it for good (Genesis 50:20).

Betrayal: The Pit of Rejection

Joseph's story begins not with triumph but with rejection. His brothers hated him. They resented his dreams, his father's favor, and the very presence of the Spirit that marked his life. That hatred gave birth to betrayal. When Joseph came to check on them in the fields, they conspired against him, threw him into a pit, and sold him to passing traders.

Imagine the terror of that moment. One day you're the favored son, wrapped in a multicolored robe; the next, you're stripped, bound, and carried off into the unknown. From the pit, Joseph must have cried out, but no one answered. From the caravan, he must have looked back at familiar hills disappearing behind him, wondering if he'd ever see his father's face again.

Here we see the first great truth: the Spirit of God does not abandon His chosen ones in the pit.

Though Joseph felt forsaken, heaven was not silent. The same Spirit who hovered over the waters in Genesis 1 now hovered over Joseph's life, brooding, waiting, preparing. What looked like the end of his story was only the beginning of God's.

Isn't that often our story too? The pit may look like betrayal, heartbreak, or disappointment, but the Spirit is not absent. He's preparing us for something greater than we can see.

Slavery: The House of Testing

Joseph is sold to Potiphar, captain of Pharaoh's guard. Outwardly, his life takes a humiliating turn: from beloved son to foreign slave. Yet Scripture emphasizes something stunning: "The Lord was with Joseph so that he prospered" (Genesis 39:2).

Even as a slave, Joseph's work bore the mark of God's Spirit. His diligence, integrity, and wisdom stood out so clearly that Potiphar entrusted him with everything in his house. Joseph was still in chains, but he was not in despair. His external status didn't define his internal reality.

But testing always comes. Potiphar's wife cast longing eyes on him and, when he resisted, falsely accused him of assault. Suddenly, Joseph found himself not only betrayed by family but also condemned by lies. From pit to slavery, from slavery to prison.

At each step downward, Joseph must have wondered: Lord, where are You? And yet, even here, the Spirit was shaping him. Integrity in Potiphar's house would one day prepare him to rule Pharaoh's palace. Faithfulness in hidden places was training for fruitfulness in public places.

Prison: The School of Waiting

Prison is not just a physical space; it is a spiritual test. To be locked away unjustly, forgotten by those you served, and seemingly cut off from your dreams, this is the ultimate test of trust. Yet in prison, Joseph's character deepened. Scripture again declares, "But while Joseph was there in the prison, the Lord was with him" (Genesis 39:20-21).

It was in prison that Joseph's gift began to shine more fully. When Pharaoh's cupbearer and baker had troubling dreams, Joseph, empowered by the Spirit, interpreted them with precision. Notice his words: *"Do not interpretations belong to God?" (Genesis 40:8).* Even in confinement, Joseph pointed others not to himself but to God.

And yet, when the cupbearer was restored, Joseph was forgotten. Two years passed in silence. Two years of waiting. Two years of wondering. But not two years wasted.

Here is a profound lesson: The Spirit often does His deepest work in seasons of waiting. We may feel forgotten, but God is building roots. We may feel delayed, but heaven is arranging details. For Joseph, the silence of two years would soon give way to the summons of a lifetime.

Palace: The Spirit's Wisdom

One night, Pharaoh had two troubling dreams that none of Egypt's wise men could interpret. Then the cupbearer remembered Joseph. Brought hurriedly from prison, Joseph stood before the most powerful man in the world.

Pharaoh recounted his dreams of fat and thin cows, healthy and scorched grain. And Joseph, still clothed in humility, declared: "I cannot do it, but God will give Pharaoh the answer he desires" (Genesis 41:16). The Spirit of God spoke through Joseph, giving him not only interpretation but also wisdom: seven years of abundance would be followed by seven years of famine, so Pharaoh should appoint someone discerning to prepare.

The response was immediate. Pharaoh turned to his officials and asked, *"Can we find anyone like this man, one in whom is the Spirit of God?" (Genesis 41:38).* The prisoner became prime minister, second only to Pharaoh himself. From the pit of betrayal to the palace of power,

Joseph's journey testified to one truth: when the Spirit of God is with a person, no circumstance can define their destiny.

The Larger Perspective: Spirit at Work in Suffering

Joseph's story could have ended with bitterness. He could have sought revenge on his brothers, cursed Potiphar's wife, or despised the cupbearer for forgetting him. But years later, when famine brought his brothers to Egypt, Joseph revealed the perspective that only the Spirit could give:

"You intended to harm me, but God intended it for good to accomplish what is now being done, the saving of many lives" (Genesis 50:20).

This is Spirit-given vision, the ability to look back at suffering and see God's fingerprints. Joseph recognized that the pit, the slavery, and the prison weren't detours but divine preparation. Each step downward was a step toward the purpose God had designed all along.

Application: The Spirit Who Redeems Our Stories

Joseph's life speaks to us today in profound ways:

1. The Spirit gives perspective in suffering.

Like Joseph, we face pits of betrayal, prisons of delay, and seasons of injustice. Yet the Spirit hovers even there. He doesn't waste our pain; He transforms it into preparation.

2. The Spirit gives wisdom in leadership.

Pharaoh recognized in Joseph something more than intelligence: The Spirit of God. In a world that prizes charisma, God prizes Spirit-filled wisdom. The Spirit equips us to lead not for self-promotion but for the service and salvation of others.

3. The Spirit shapes character in hidden places.

Before Joseph wore Pharaoh's signet ring, he wore shackles. Before he oversaw Egypt, he oversaw Potiphar's house. Faithfulness in obscurity is often the Spirit's training ground for fruitfulness in visibility.

4. The Spirit transforms our perspective.

Joseph could see what others couldn't, that behind human evil, God's hand was weaving redemption. Only the Spirit can give us such eyes: to see purpose in pain, hope in hardship, and God at work when others see only despair.

From Your Pit to God's Palace

Joseph's story isn't simply a tale of survival; it's a testimony of Spirit-filled transformation. Betrayed, enslaved, imprisoned, and forgotten, yet Joseph was never alone.

The Spirit of God carried him through every season, teaching him that power doesn't come from position but from presence.

And so, it is with us. Whatever pit you've known, whatever prison you endure, the Spirit of God hasn't abandoned you. He's preparing you for a purpose beyond your imagination. The God who turned Joseph's chains into a crown is the same God who works in your life today.

The Spirit specializes in raising ordinary people out of impossible places. From pit to palace, from pain to purpose, from despair to destiny, that's the story of Joseph. And by the Spirit, it can be your story too.

Moses: The Reluctant Prophet

If Joseph's story teaches us that the Spirit can lift us from pits and prisons, then Moses reminds us that the Spirit can use even the most reluctant, insecure, and fearful among us. Moses isn't introduced as a bold hero ready to lead. Instead, we meet a man hiding from his past, stammering over his words, and arguing with God about why he's the wrong choice. Yet this very man becomes the great deliverer of Israel. The key isn't his confidence but God's Spirit.

The Weight of Inadequacy

Moses' early years brimmed with promise. He was miraculously preserved as an infant, raised in Pharaoh's palace, and educated in all the wisdom of Egypt. By human standards, he seemed destined for greatness. Yet when Moses tried to act in his own strength, killing an Egyptian to defend his people, his plan backfired. Rejected by his fellow Hebrews and hunted by Pharaoh, he fled into the wilderness.

For forty years, Moses lived as a shepherd in Midian. Once a prince, now a wanderer. Once full of potential, now forgotten. He married, tended sheep, and likely settled into obscurity. Whatever dreams of deliverance he once carried had been buried under the weight of regret and the passage of time.

It's in this place, far from the halls of power, stripped of ambition, that God appeared. Because it's often in obscurity that God shapes His servants.

The Burning Bush Encounter

One ordinary day, Moses led his flock near Mount Horeb. There, a bush caught his eye, burning with fire, yet not consumed. As he turned aside to look, the voice of God called: *"Moses, Moses."* Trembling, Moses responded: *"Here I am."*

God revealed His plan: *"I have seen the misery of my people in Egypt... So now, go. I am sending you to Pharaoh to bring my people, the Israelites, out of Egypt" (Exodus 3:7, 10).*

Here was the divine assignment. The years of silence were over. The moment of destiny had arrived. And how did Moses respond? With reluctance.

Excuses, Fear, and Stammering

Moses offered excuse after excuse, each one exposing his insecurity:

1. *"Who am I that I should go?" (Ex. 3:11).* Moses saw only his weakness, forgetting the God who was sending him.
2. *"What if they do not believe me?" (Ex. 4:1).* Fear of rejection still haunted him from his failed attempt decades earlier.
3. *"I have never been eloquent... I am slow of speech and tongue." (Ex. 4:10).* Moses fixated on his stammer, convinced his weakness disqualified him.
4. *"Please send someone else." (Ex. 4:13)*

Eventually, all his excuses boiled down to simple resistance: I don't want to go. God met each protest with assurance: His presence, His power, His provision. He gave Moses signs, the staff that turned into a snake, the hand that became leprous and healed, and the promise of words placed in his mouth. Yet Moses still hesitated.

Here's the beauty: God doesn't dismiss the insecure. He doesn't choose leaders because they're eloquent or fearless. He chooses those who know their need and fills them with His Spirit.

Empowered by the Spirit

Despite Moses' reluctance, God sent him. And as Moses obeyed, however haltingly, the Spirit of God worked through him. Each confrontation with Pharaoh became not a display of Moses' eloquence but of God's power. The Nile turned to blood, frogs filled the land, hail fell from heaven, and darkness covered Egypt, not by Moses' skill but by God's Spirit.

When the Israelites were finally delivered and camped in the wilderness, Moses faced a new challenge: leadership. The burden of governing thousands overwhelmed him. Here, The Spirit's role expanded beyond Moses himself. God told him: *"I will take some of the power of the Spirit that is on you and put it on them (the seventy elders). They will share the burden of the people with you so that you will not have to carry it alone"* (Numbers 11:17).

The Spirit isn't a private possession but a shared gift. Leadership in God's kingdom is never about one hero; it's about a Spirit-filled community. Moses' stammering voice became part of a chorus empowered to shepherd God's people.

The God Who Works Through Weakness

Moses' story reveals a profound truth: God delights to work through weakness.

- Moses feared rejection, yet God made him the mouthpiece of deliverance.
- Moses doubted his speech, yet the words of the law flowed through him.
- Moses resisted leadership, yet God entrusted him with a nation.

His inadequacy wasn't an obstacle but the very stage for God's power. As Paul would later write, *"My grace is sufficient for you, for my power is made perfect in weakness"* (2 Corinthians 12:9).

Lessons for Us

Moses' journey isn't just ancient history, it's a mirror for us today.

1. God calls the reluctant.

Many of us, like Moses, feel inadequate. We fixate on our flaws, our lack of eloquence, our insecurities, our failures, and assume God can't use us. But God doesn't wait for perfect vessels. He fills cracked jars with His glory.

2. Obedience matters more than confidence.

Moses never became a polished orator. What mattered was that he went. God's power showed up not in Moses' eloquence but in his obedience.

3. The Spirit sustains leadership.

Moses couldn't bear the weight of Israel alone. Neither can we carry life's burdens alone. The Spirit doesn't just empower individuals, He shares His presence among communities, making leadership and service a shared calling.

4. Weakness invites God's strength.

Our stammer, our fear, our reluctance, these aren't disqualifiers. They're reminders that the mission depends on God, not us.

The Reluctant Prophet Transformed

Moses started as a reluctant prophet: stammering, excuse-laden, fearful. Yet through the Spirit, he became a deliverer, lawgiver, and friend of God. His story teaches us that the measure of a servant isn't their confidence but their surrender.

When you feel reluctant, remember Moses. When you fear rejection, recall his excuses. When you doubt your ability, recall his stammer. And when you wonder if God can use you, remember the burning bush.

The God who spoke through fire and empowered a stammering shepherd is the same God who fills us with His Spirit today. He still chooses the reluctant. He still strengthens the weak. And He still proves that His power is greater than our fear.

So, take heart: you don't have to be eloquent, fearless, or polished. You just have to be willing.

The Spirit will do the rest.

Elijah: A Man like Us

When we hear the name Elijah, it stirs images of fire from heaven, dramatic confrontations with kings, and miracles that defy nature. He stands among the greatest prophets of Israel, even appearing alongside Moses at the transfiguration of Jesus. Yet, James 5:17 reminds us: "Elijah was a man with a nature like ours." Behind the fiery prophet was a fragile human being, weak, weary, and often afraid. His story reveals not only God's power displayed through prayer but also the Spirit's gentle work of sustaining, encouraging, and recommissioning His exhausted servant.

Confronting Kings

Elijah's ministry begins abruptly in 1 Kings 17. Without genealogy or introduction, he appears before King Ahab with a startling declaration: "As the Lord, the God of Israel, lives, whom I serve, there will be neither dew nor rain in the next few years except at my word" (v. 1). It was a bold confrontation in a time when Baal, the supposed storm god, was worshiped as the giver of rain. Elijah stood as the lone voice against idolatry, pronouncing a drought that would devastate the land.

This act alone required remarkable courage. Ahab and Jezebel had already slaughtered prophets of the Lord. To speak truth to power was to risk death. But Elijah obeyed, and God sustained him through miraculous means, ravens feeding him in the wilderness, a widow's flour and oil never running dry, and even raising her son from death. Each provision demonstrated that the Spirit who called Elijah also upheld him.

Calling Down Fire

The pinnacle of Elijah's prophetic career came on Mount Carmel (1 Kings 18). After three years of drought, Elijah summoned Israel to a contest: the prophets of Baal versus the prophet of Yahweh. The challenge was simple, the god who answered by fire would be the true God.

The prophets of Baal raved, cut themselves, and cried out for hours, but no fire came. Then Elijah rebuilt the altar, drenched it with water, and prayed a simple prayer: *"Answer me, Lord, answer me, so these people will know that you, Lord, are God, and that you are turning their hearts back again" (v. 37).*

Immediately, fire fell from heaven, consuming the sacrifice, the wood, the stones, and even the water. The people fell to prostrate, crying, "The Lord, He is God! The Lord, He is God!" It was a decisive victory, one of the most dramatic demonstrations of divine power in the Old Testament.

Here, Elijah appears fearless, unwavering, and triumphant. Yet the story doesn't end with fire. It moves swiftly into fear.

Running in Fear

No sooner had Elijah confronted Baal's prophets than Jezebel threatened his life. You might expect Elijah, fresh from a fiery victory, to stand unshaken. Instead, he fled. *"Elijah was afraid and ran for his life" (1 Kings 19:3).*

This turn is striking. The prophet who called down fire now collapses under fear. The man who stood before a king now hides from a queen. The same Elijah who prayed boldly now prays for death: *"I have had enough, Lord. Take my life" (v. 4).*

Here is the human side James highlights: Elijah was a man like us. Victories don't make us invincible. Spiritual highs can be followed by crushing lows. Even prophets feel overwhelmed, exhausted, and depressed.

The God Who Sustains

In Elijah's despair, God didn't rebuke him. Instead, He ministered tenderly. As Elijah lay under a broom tree, an angel touched him and said, "Get up and eat." Twice, Elijah received food and drink, enough to strengthen him for a forty-day journey to Mount Horeb.

This detail is profound. Before Elijah could hear God's voice or receive a fresh commission, he needed rest and nourishment. God knows our human limits.

The Spirit who empowers us also cares for our physical weakness. Sometimes, the most spiritual thing we can do is eat, sleep, and recover.

At Mount Horeb, Elijah encountered God not in wind, earthquake, or fire, but in a gentle whisper. This wasn't only a rebuke to his expectations but also a reassurance. God's power isn't always displayed in dramatic spectacle. Often, it comes in the quiet presence of His Spirit.

Recommissioned for Service

After Elijah poured out his complaint, "I am the only one left," God reassured him: he wasn't alone. Seven thousand in Israel had not bowed to Baal. Elijah's despair had distorted reality; the Spirit corrected his perspective.

Then came the recommissioning. God gave Elijah new assignments: to anoint Hazael as king of Aram, Jehu as king of Israel, and Elisha as prophet in his place. The message was clear: Elijah's work wasn't finished. Though weary, he remained God's chosen servant. The Spirit who had sustained him would continue to guide him.

Prayer and Power

James draws on Elijah's story to illustrate the power of prayer: *"Elijah was a man with a nature like ours, and he prayed earnestly that it would not rain, and it did not rain on the land for three and a half years. Again, he prayed, and the heavens gave rain, and the earth produced its crops." (James 5:17–18).*

Notice the emphasis: Elijah was human, yet his prayers were effective. The point isn't Elijah's greatness but God's responsiveness. Prayer is effective not because we're extraordinary but because God is faithful.

Lessons for Us

Elijah's story carries enduring lessons for every follower of Christ.

1. Boldness comes from the Spirit, not personality. Elijah wasn't naturally fearless. His courage before Ahab and at Carmel came from God's Spirit. Likewise, we don't need to manufacture boldness; we need to rely on the Spirit.

2. Victories don't exempt us from weakness. Even after calling down fire, Elijah despaired. Spiritual highs don't prevent emotional lows. We shouldn't be surprised when exhaustion or fear follows great moments of triumph.

3. God meets us in our weakness with compassion. Under the broom tree, God didn't scold Elijah. He fed him, let him rest, and gently restored him. When we're exhausted or depressed, God's Spirit ministers with patience.

4. God's power is often quiet. Elijah expected God in the earthquake and fire, but found Him in a whisper. We, too, must learn to discern God's presence in the quiet nudges of the Spirit, not just in dramatic events.

5. Prayer is effective because God is faithful. Elijah's effectiveness wasn't about his stature, it was about God's willingness to act. Our prayers, offered in faith, are heard by that same God.

A Man like Us

Elijah stands as both a giant of faith and a mirror of frailty. He confronted kings, called down fire, and prayed for rain. Yet he also ran in fear, collapsed in despair, and wished for death. He was, as James says, a man like us.

Here's the comfort in Elijah's story: God doesn't discard His servants when they falter. He sustains them, encourages them, and recommissions them. The Spirit who fed Elijah under the broom tree and whispered at Horeb is the same Spirit who meets us in our weakness today.

So, take heart. If you feel exhausted, fearful, or inadequate, you're in good company. Elijah was a man like us, and the same God who empowered him empowers you.

Peter: From Denier to Preacher

The story of Peter is one of the most gripping transformations in all of Scripture. He's remembered as the disciple who denied Jesus three times, yet also as the preacher whose Spirit-filled words at Pentecost pierced three thousands hearts. He's the man who once cowered before a servant girl, yet later stood boldly before rulers and authorities proclaiming the risen Christ. His life testifies to what happens when the Holy Spirit takes a life marred by failure and breathes courage into it.

The Denial: A Rooster's Cry of Shame

Peter had promised loyalty. Hours before his collapse, he told Jesus with fiery conviction: *"Even if I have to die with you, I will never disown you" (Matthew 26:35).* But the test came swiftly.

In the courtyard of the high priest, while Jesus stood trial inside, Peter warmed himself by a fire. A servant girl noticed him. *"You were with Jesus of Galilee,"* she said. Fear surged. Peter denied it: *"I don't know what you're talking about."*

Another chance came. Another denial. The pressure mounted. A third voice confronted him: *"Surely you are one of them; your accent gives you away."* Peter swore an oath: *"I don't know the man!"*

At that moment, the rooster crowed. Luke's Gospel adds a piercing detail: *"The Lord turned and looked straight at Peter" (Luke 22:61).* That look undid him. He stumbled out, weeping bitterly.

Here is Peter's humanity laid bare. He wasn't fearless. He wasn't unshakable. He was weak, afraid, and ashamed. His bold promises gave way to trembling lips. And yet, through this man came the revelation, the unshakable rock on which Christ would build His Church.

Brokenness and Restoration

After the crucifixion, Peter lived in the shadow of his failure. He had denied the Lord he loved.

Though Jesus had risen, Peter's shame lingered.

Restoration came on the shore of Galilee, after a fruitless night of fishing. The risen Christ stood on the beach, fire crackling, fish cooking. Three times, He asked Peter the same question: "Do you love me?" Three denials were met with three affirmations of love. Each time, Jesus commissioned him: *"Feed my lambs.. Take care of my sheep.. Feed my sheep" (John 21:15-17).*

The symbolism was deliberate and healing. The fire on the beach recalled the fire in the courtyard. The threefold question mirrored the threefold denial. The shame of failure was met with the grace of restoration. Peter wasn't discarded, he was re-commissioned.

This is the gospel: Jesus doesn't define us by our lowest moment. The Spirit restores broken disciples, turning their wounds into channels of compassion and their failures into platforms for grace.

Pentecost: The Fire That Transforms

The true turning point came at Pentecost. Acts 2 describes the moment when the Spirit descended like tongues of fire, resting on each disciple. The timid group hiding in an upper room became a bold band of witnesses.

And who stood up to speak? Peter. The same man who had denied Christ weeks earlier now lifted his voice before a crowd. His sermon wasn't cautious or timid. It was piercing, direct, unapologetic: *"Let all Israel be assured of this: God has made this Jesus, whom you crucified, both Lord and Messiah" (Acts 2:36).*

The result was staggering. The people were "cut to the heart" and asked, *"What shall we do?"* Peter answered with clarity: *"Repent and be baptized, every one of you, in the name of Jesus Christ for the forgiveness of your sins. And you will receive the gift of the Holy Spirit" (v. 38).* That day, about three thousand people joined the church.

The rooster's cry of shame had been replaced by the trumpet's call of courage. The man who once denied knowing Jesus now proclaimed Him publicly with power. This transformation didn't come from a personality change or sheer willpower, it was the work of the Spirit.

Spirit-Filled Leadership

Peter's Spirit-filled boldness didn't fade after Pentecost. In Acts 3, he healed a lame beggar in Jesus' name, then preached again, declaring, *"Salvation is found in no one else, for there is no other name under heaven given to mankind by which we must be saved" (Acts 4:12).*

When the Sanhedrin threatened him, Peter didn't retreat. He replied, *"Which is right in God's eyes: to listen to you, or to him? You be the judges! As for us, we cannot help speaking about what we have seen and heard" (Acts 4:19-20).*

Later, he confronted Ananias and Sapphira's deception, guided the church through conflict, and even crossed cultural barriers to preach to Cornelius, a Gentile centurion. Each step revealed the Spirit's ongoing work, transforming Peter from an impulsive fisherman into a steady leader, from a fearful denier into a courageous shepherd.

Application: Spirit Transforms Shame into Courage

Peter's journey holds profound lessons for us today.

1. **Failure is not final.**

We often believe our mistakes disqualify us from God's purposes. But Peter shows otherwise. His greatest failure became the backdrop for God's greatest grace. The Spirit delights in taking broken, humbled people and lifting them into new service.

2. **Restoration precedes mission.**

Before Peter could preach, he had to be restored. Jesus met him in his shame, not with condemnation, but with love. Likewise, the Spirit doesn't bypass our wounds but heals them so we can serve with authenticity and humility.

3. Courage is Spirit-born, not self-made.

Peter's natural boldness failed him in the courtyard. But Spirit-given boldness sustained him before crowds and councils. Our courage in witness and leadership isn't something we muster, it's something God breathes into us.

4. Our voice matters.

On Pentecost, Peter stood up and spoke. He wasn't the most educated or eloquent, but he was available. The Spirit doesn't require polished perfection, only surrendered willingness. What matters isn't the strength of our words but the power of the Spirit behind them.

5. The Spirit redefines identity.

Peter the denier became Peter the preacher. His identity was no longer bound to his lowest moment but to the Spirit's work. The same is true for us. Whatever labels shame has given us, failure, coward, unworthy, the Spirit gives new names: forgiven, beloved, empowered.

From Rooster to Trumpet

The arc of Peter's life moves from denial to proclamation, from shame to boldness, from collapse to leadership. It's the story of grace multiplied through the Spirit.

Every believer carries the memory of a rooster's crow, the moment of failure, the season of fear, the word spoken in denial or silence. But the Spirit isn't finished with us there. He restores us through Christ's love, fills us with His presence, and transforms us into courageous witnesses.

The same Peter who wept bitterly also preached boldly. The same lips that once swore, "I don't know Him," declared with fire, "God has made this Jesus, whom you crucified, both Lord and Messiah."

This is the hope of the gospel: The Spirit specializes in rewriting stories. Where shame once reigned, courage now rises. Where failure seemed final, grace has the last word. Where weakness falters, the Spirit empowers.

Peter's life reminds us that no denial is too deep, no failure too final, no shame too strong for the Spirit to transform. And when He does, the sound of our lives shifts, from the cry of a rooster to the trumpet of good news.

Paul: The Persecutor Turned Preacher

Few figures in Scripture demonstrate the transforming power of the Holy Spirit more vividly than Paul. He began as Saul of Tarsus, the terror of the early church, a man whose very presence struck fear into the hearts of believers. Yet he ended as Paul the apostle, the boldest preacher of Christ, author of letters that still shape the church two millennia later. His story is living proof that no one, not even the fiercest opponent of God's work, is beyond the Spirit's reach.

Saul: Breathing Threats

Luke paints the picture starkly: "Saul was still breathing out murderous threats against the Lord's disciples" (Acts 9:1). The Greek phrase suggests that persecution wasn't just something Saul did, it was the very air he breathed. Like oxygen filling his lungs, hatred for Christ and His followers sustained him.

We meet Saul first in Acts 7, at the stoning of Stephen. While others hurled rocks at the Spirit-filled deacon, Saul stood nearby, watching, nodding in approval, guarding the cloaks of the executioners. That chilling image sets the tone: Saul wasn't a bystander but an accomplice. He saw the radiant face of Stephen as he forgave his murderers, yet his heart hardened even more.

From there, Saul became the church's chief hunter. He ravaged homes, dragged men and women into prison, and pursued believers even beyond Jerusalem. His zeal was unmatched, his mission clear: destroy this Jesus movement before it spread. If you had lived in those days, you might have prayed for God to stop Saul, perhaps even to strike him dead. Yet God had a different plan: to turn the enemy into an instrument, the persecutor into a preacher.

The Damascus Road Encounter

The turning point came on a dusty road. Saul had obtained letters from the high priest authorizing him to arrest Christians in Damascus. Armed with authority and rage, he set out, his mind filled with visions of dragging more followers of the Way back in chains.

But heaven interrupted.

"As he neared Damascus on his journey, suddenly a light from heaven flashed around him. He fell to the ground and heard a voice say to him, 'Saul, Saul, why do you persecute me?'" (Acts 9:3–4).

The irony cuts deep: the man who thought he was defending God's honor discovered he was fighting against God Himself. Notice the words: *"Why do you persecute me?"* Jesus identifies so closely with His people that attacking them means attacking Him.

Blinded and trembling, Saul asked the only question that mattered: *"Who are you, Lord?"* The answer shattered his world: *"I am Jesus, whom you are persecuting." (v5).*

In that moment, Saul's entire worldview collapsed. The crucified Jesus, whom he'd despised as a false Messiah, was alive, radiant, and Lord. The foundation of his life's mission crumbled into dust.

For three days, Saul sat blind, fasting, praying. The persecutor became helpless, dependent on the very disciples he'd come to arrest. Ananias, a reluctant believer, was sent by God to lay hands on him, calling him "Brother Saul." Scales fell from his eyes, and the Spirit filled him. The church's feared adversary became its greatest emissary.

From Church Destroyer to Church Planter

The transformation was immediate and radical. The same zeal that once fueled Saul's persecution now drove Paul's proclamation. Almost at once, he began preaching in Damascus:

"Jesus is the Son of God." (Acts 9:20). The hunter of Christians became their defender.

Over the years, Paul's Spirit-empowered ministry reshaped the world.

He planted churches across Asia Minor and Europe, wrote letters that form nearly half of the New Testament, and endured beatings, shipwrecks, imprisonment, and eventually martyrdom, all for the name he once hated.

Consider the irony:

- The man who once tried to silence the gospel became its loudest voice.
- The one who once dragged believers into prison spent years writing letters of encouragement from prison.
- The one who once stood by approving Stephen's death became the first to echo Stephen's forgiving spirit when facing his own execution.

This is the empowering work of the Spirit. He doesn't merely improve us; He remakes us. He turns enemies into family, persecutors into preachers, and destroyers into builders.

The Theology of Transformation

Paul never got over the wonder of his transformation. He called himself *"the least of the apostles" (1 Corinthians 15:9)* and *"the worst of sinners" (1 Timothy 1:15)*. Yet he became the loudest herald of grace: *"But by the grace of God I am what I am, and his grace to me was not without effect" (1 Corinthians 15:10)*.

Notice the progression:

- Saul, the zealous Pharisee, thought he was serving God but was actually blind.
- Then Saul the persecutor encountered Christ and was struck physically blind, revealing his spiritual blindness.
- Finally, Paul the preacher had his eyes opened by the Spirit and saw everything in the light of grace.

His theology flowed directly from his testimony. Paul's emphasis on salvation by grace through faith (Ephesians 2:8-9), his insistence that no one is beyond redemption, his conviction that the Spirit transforms hearts, none of it was mere theory. It was a lived reality. He knew firsthand that if God could save him, He could save anyone.

Application: No One Beyond Reach

Paul's story shouts a radical truth into our lives: No one is beyond the Spirit's reach.

We all have "Saul's" in our lives, people who seem hostile, hardened, unreachable. A spouse indifferent to faith. A child is rebellious against God. A coworker mocking Christianity. Or perhaps the "Saul" is within: our own shame, our own hostility toward grace, our own record of failure.

The Spirit's work in Paul reminds us:

- God's grace is stronger than our sin. If the Spirit could transform Saul the persecutor into Paul the apostle, He can transform anyone.

- No opposition is too fierce for the Spirit to overcome. Paul's zeal was unmatched, yet the Spirit redirected rather than destroyed it. The Spirit doesn't merely erase passion; He redeems it for God's purposes.

- Our past does not define our future. Saul's record was bloody, yet his future was fruitful. The Spirit rewrites stories.

What if we believed this with fresh faith? What if we prayed for the hardest hearts, not with despair but with hope? What if we looked at our own failures, not as final verdicts, but as raw material for God's grace?

A Revolutionary Call

Paul's transformation calls us to courage. If the Spirit could take a man like Saul and use him to carry the gospel across continents, what might He do with us? Our excuses fade in comparison.

We may feel ordinary, weak, or unworthy, but the Spirit specializes in unlikely vessels.

His transformation also calls us to humility. Paul never boasted about himself. He said, "We have this treasure in jars of clay to show that this all-surpassing power is from God and not from us." (2 Corinthians 4:7). His life proved that the power lay not in the vessel but in the Spirit, who filled it.

The Unstoppable Spirit

Saul of Tarsus breathed threats. Paul the apostle breathed grace. The hinge between them was the Spirit's encounter on the Damascus road. That same Spirit still moves today, interrupting journeys, shattering illusions, opening blind eyes, and rewriting stories.

No enemy is too far. No sinner too stained. No skeptic too hardened. No failure too final.

The Spirit who turned the persecutor into a preacher is the same Spirit who longs to work in us and through us. And when He does, the world takes notice.

The man who once scattered the church became the man who spread it. The man who once silenced voices for Christ became the man who gave the church its clearest voice. The persecutor became the preacher. And the glory belongs to the God whose Spirit always gets the last word.

The Spirit and the Ordinary You

The stories of Joseph, Moses, Elijah, Peter, and Paul aren't meant to be glass-encased relics of biblical history, admired from a distance but never touched. They're living testimonies, written into Scripture so that you and I might see ourselves reflected in their frailty, their doubts, their failures, and ultimately, in their Spirit-empowered victories.

The common thread is striking: God delights in choosing the ordinary, the flawed, the hesitant, and the broken. Why?

So that His power might be unmistakably displayed, and no one would mistake the vessel for the source of the treasure.

Why We Should Follow Their Example

You may never sit on a throne in Egypt like Joseph or March into Pharaoh's court with a staff in your hand like Moses. You may never call down fire on Mount Carmel like Elijah, preach to thousands at Pentecost like Peter, or cross the Mediterranean founding churches like Paul. But you will face betrayal, fear, fatigue, shame, and failure, just as they did. You will stand at a crossroads where obedience seems costly, courage feels impossible, and hope flickers dim.

That's precisely why their stories matter. They remind us that God's Spirit isn't looking for perfect résumés, eloquent speeches, or flawless track records. He's looking for surrendered hearts. Joseph's wisdom, Moses' courage, Elijah's persistence, Peter's boldness, and Paul's zeal weren't self-manufactured, they were Spirit-given. The same Spirit who hovered over the waters at creation and raised Jesus from the dead now dwells in you (Romans 8:11).

To ignore these examples is to believe the lie that God only works through "special" people. But to embrace them is to realize that your ordinary life is the very soil where the Spirit delights to plant extraordinary seeds.

Seeing Ourselves in Their Stories

Think about it:

- **Joseph** was betrayed by his own family, yet God turned the pit into a platform. Perhaps you know betrayal, rejection, or the sting of being misunderstood. The Spirit can transform your wounds into wisdom.
- **Moses** felt inadequate, tongue-tied, and terrified, yet God used him to liberate a nation. Perhaps you feel disqualified by weakness or lack of skill. The Spirit equips you to step into assignments greater than yourself.
- **Elijah** prayed with fiery faith but also collapsed in despair. Perhaps you, too, have days when exhaustion outweighs

courage. The Spirit doesn't abandon you in the cave; He whispers hope and recommissions you.

- **Peter** knew the bitter taste of failure, his denials echoing in his ears. Perhaps shame still clings to your soul. The Spirit is the voice of restoration, turning cowardice into courage.
- **Paul** carried a violent past; his hands stained with the blood of Christians. Perhaps you have regrets that seem beyond forgiveness. The Spirit declares that no one is beyond redemption, and no past is too dark for God's light.

Do you see it? Their stories are our stories. They aren't exceptions, they're patterns of how God works through broken clay jars, so His glory shines all the brighter.

The Encouragement We Need

Here's the staggering truth: The same Spirit who empowered them empowers us. This isn't rhetoric or religious hyperbole. At Pentecost, Peter declared that the promise of the Spirit was *"for you, for your children, and for all who are far off, for all whom the Lord our God will call" (Acts 2:39)*. That means us. That means now.

- When you face betrayal, cry out for Joseph's Spirit-given perspective.
- When you feel inadequate, lean into Moses' Spirit-driven courage.
- When you grow weary, pray Elijah's prayers and listen for God's gentle whisper.
- When you stumble, run to the same Jesus who restored Peter and wait for His Spirit to lift you again.
- When your past makes you feel disqualified, remember Paul, and dare to believe that the Spirit's power is stronger than your history.

You aren't excluded from this story. You're invited into it.

A Call to Courage

So, let's drop the excuse that "God cannot use someone like me." That phrase isn't humility, it's unbelief in disguise. The truth is that God always uses "someone like you." The Spirit doesn't wait until you're strong; He comes in your weakness. He doesn't demand perfection; He delights in surrender.

Imagine what might happen if ordinary believers like us truly lived as if the Spirit of the living God dwells within. Families would be healed. Workplaces would become mission fields.

Communities would glimpse Christ in the way we forgive, serve, and love. The world isn't transformed by flawless heroes but by Spirit-filled ordinary people who dare to believe that God can do the extraordinary through them.

Final Word

The question, then, isn't whether the Spirit still empowers ordinary people. The question is whether we'll believe it for ourselves. Will we dare to see our own stories reflected in Joseph, Moses, Elijah, Peter, and Paul? Will we open our hands, trembling though they are, and let the Spirit fill them with His power?

The Spirit specializes in this very thing: taking the insecure, the broken, the reluctant, and the flawed, and making them vessels of His glory. He has done it before. He's still doing it. And He longs to do it in you.

So today, rise from the pit, lift the staff, leave the cave, step out of denial, and turn from the past.

For the same Spirit who empowered them empowers you.

Closing Prayer

> *Spirit of the Living God, You hovered over the waters at creation, You whispered to prophets, You filled fishermen, shepherds, and tentmakers.*

Come breathe on us again. Take our weakness and clothe it with Your strength. Take our shame and turn it into boldness. Take our ordinary days and make them holy ground.

We are not Joseph, Moses, Elijah, Peter, or Paul, but we are Yours. And the same Spirit who filled them fills us now.

Do in us what only You can do. For Your glory and for the sake of the world, Amen.

Why Are These People Mentioned in Scripture?

The Bible could have been written very differently. God might have given us a clean theological manual, a book of rules and doctrines stripped of messy human stories. But instead, Scripture is full of lives: Joseph, Moses, Elijah, Peter, Paul, and countless others. They're there for a reason. Their stories aren't mere history but revelation, teaching us how God works, how His Spirit moves, and what it means to live as His people in a broken world.

When we look at Joseph, we see betrayal, slavery, false accusation, and prison. Yet we also see resilience, wisdom, and eventual honor. His story teaches us that God's Spirit isn't absent in suffering. The pit wasn't the end; the prison wasn't final. The Spirit gave Joseph the wisdom to interpret Pharaoh's dreams and the courage to lead Egypt through famine. Joseph shows us that the Spirit turns seasons of abandonment into platforms for influence.

Moses reminds us of human frailty. Here was a man who stammered, resisted his calling, and trembled before God at the burning bush. Yet the Spirit empowered him to stand before Pharaoh, confront injustice, and lead Israel out of slavery. The Spirit also shared Moses' burden by resting upon the seventy elders (Numbers 11:17), showing that God doesn't rely on flawless leaders but shares His Spirit to equip the weak. Moses shows us that reluctance doesn't disqualify us, God's Spirit fills those who admit their inadequacy.

Elijah, the fiery prophet, called down fire on Mount Carmel, confronted kings, and prayed droughts into existence. Yet James 5:17 reminds us: "Elijah was a man with a nature like ours."

He also ran in fear, hid in caves, and begged for death. His story teaches us that God's Spirit sustains us not only in triumph but also in exhaustion. The Spirit whispered to Elijah in the gentle breeze, not the earthquake or fire, reminding us that divine power often meets us in quiet, tender moments of despair. Elijah shows us that even the most broken and discouraged can be recommissioned by God's Spirit.

Peter represents us at our most fragile. He boasted loyalty but denied Jesus three times in His hour of need. Yet after his restoration, the Spirit filled Peter at Pentecost, transforming him into a bold preacher whose words pierced hearts and birthed the church. Peter shows us that shame and failure aren't the last word. The Spirit redeems weakness and empowers ordinary people to speak with divine authority.

Paul's story is perhaps the most dramatic: from persecutor to preacher, from enemy of Christ to ambassador of Christ. On the Damascus road, he encountered the risen Lord, and his life turned upside down. The Spirit turned his passion for destruction into zeal for proclamation, planting churches and writing letters that still shape us today. Paul shows us that no one is beyond the Spirit's reach, even the hardest heart can be transformed.

Why are these people in Scripture?

To remind us of who God is and how His Spirit works. God chooses the unlikely, dreamer, stammerer, prophets prone to despair, fishermen who falter, persecutors who rage, and fills them with His Spirit. Their stories are mirrors, reflecting both our frailty and God's faithfulness. They are testimonies, whispering across centuries: "If God could use us, He can use you."

The Bible isn't a gallery of perfect saints but a family album of Spirit-filled ordinary people.

Their inclusion is deliberate. God wants us to see ourselves in Joseph's resilience, in Moses' reluctance, in Elijah's despair, in Peter's restoration, in Paul's transformation. Their stories point us not to human greatness but to divine grace. They exist so we can believe, with conviction, that the Spirit who worked in them is the same Spirit at work in us.

Why It Matters for Us Today

Why do these stories matter for us today? Because we live ordinary lives, full of commutes, errands, jobs, meals, conversations, worries, and responsibilities. The temptation is to believe that God's Spirit is absent from these mundane spaces, reserved only for "spiritual giants" or "special callings." But these biblical lives shatter that illusion.

Joseph was a slave before he became a ruler. Moses tended sheep before he faced Pharaoh.

Elijah struggled with depression before he heard God's whisper. Peter was a fisherman before he became a preacher. Paul was a persecutor before he became an apostle. Their ordinariness isn't a liability, it's the very canvas where the Spirit painted God's glory.

The lesson for us is profound: we don't need to wait for a dramatic moment to be filled with the Spirit. The same Spirit who hovered over Joseph in prison, who emboldened Moses before Pharaoh, who whispered to Elijah in the cave, who restored Peter on the beach, and who blinded Paul on the Damascus Road is present in our daily lives right now.

So, here's the invitation:

- Where do I see God's Spirit in my ordinary days?
- Am I noticing, responding, yielding?

The Spirit is there in the breath that fills your lungs each morning. He's in the creativity that sparks a new idea at work, the patience that helps you endure, the courage that helps you speak truth in love. He's present in every conversation where you choose kindness over anger, in every nudge toward prayer, in every act of hidden service that no one sees but heaven.

These stories matter because they train us to see our own.

- Joseph's wisdom teaches us to trust the Spirit in suffering.
- Moses' reluctance teaches us to say yes even when we feel unqualified.

- Elijah's weakness teaches us to listen for God's whisper in exhaustion.
- Peter's restoration teaches us to let the Spirit turn shame into courage.
- Paul's transformation teaches us that no one is too far gone for grace.

And so, we're invited to change our lives. To surrender daily, to awaken to the Spirit's presence, to yield our ordinary to the extraordinary work of God. The Spirit who used them longs to use us.

Guided Reflection

- In my breath itself, do I recognize the Spirit's sustaining presence?
- In my creativity or problem-solving, do I see the Spirit's spark?
- In conversations and relationships, do I notice the Spirit guiding me toward love?
- In the quiet nudges to pray, to forgive, to serve, do I respond?

Invitation

Today, choose awareness. Choose surrender. Choose to see yourself in the great story of God's Spirit working through ordinary people. You're not just a spectator, you're part of the same unfolding narrative.

Closing Prayer

Spirit of God, open my eyes to see You in the ordinary. Open my ears to hear Your whispers in the noise. Open my heart to yield, even in small ways.

As You hovered over the waters, hover over my chaos. As You filled Joseph, Moses, Elijah, Peter, and Paul, fill me.

Take my ordinary life and make it Your dwelling place. Amen.

Living Spirit-Breathed Lives

The story of the Spirit isn't a subplot in Scripture, it's the very pulse of the Bible from Genesis to Revelation.

At creation, the Spirit hovered over the waters, brooding like a mother bird over unformed chaos, ready to bring light and order. At Pentecost, the Spirit came again, this time not over waters but over people, tongues of fire resting on men and women, filling them with life, courage, and power. The connection is unmistakable: the same Spirit who birthed the cosmos is the Spirit who births the church.

Pentecost wasn't an isolated eruption of divine activity. It was the continuation of a story that began when God first breathed life into Adam's lungs. It reminded us that humanity's existence has always depended on the Spirit's breath. Every inhale and exhale point us back to this truth: We live because God breathes. And we flourish because His Spirit fills.

But here's the wonder, we aren't merely biological beings sustained by oxygen; we're spiritual beings sustained by the Spirit. Just as a body suffocates without air, the soul suffocates without the Spirit. Pentecost is God's declaration that His breath isn't just for the beginning of life but for the transformation of life.

To live "Spirit-breathed" lives, then, is to recognize that ordinary existence, our conversations, chores, labors, and even our struggles, becomes extraordinary when filled with God's presence. Joseph interpreting Pharaoh's dream, Moses stammering before Pharaoh, Elijah praying in weakness, Peter preaching with fire, Paul planting churches, none of this was their own doing. It was Spirit-breathed living. Dust animated by divinity. Weakness clothed in power.

Spirit-breathed living means we no longer measure our days by visible outcomes alone. The Spirit may be at work in what feels unseen: a whisper of encouragement, a word spoken in love, an act of kindness that no one notices but heaven does.

The Spirit's work is as subtle as breath, as invisible as wind, and yet as influential as the fire at Pentecost.

It also means we learn to yield. Breath cannot be hoarded; it must be received moment by moment. Likewise, the Spirit is not a one-time experience but a continual filling. Paul's command to the Ephesians wasn't "be filled once" but "be continually filled with the Spirit" (Ephesians 5:18). Spirit-breathed lives are lives of surrender, daily dependence, moment-by-moment openness to the One who sustains us.

And this has practical implications. To be Spirit-breathed isn't to escape the world but to engage it differently:

- To speak truth when silence feels easier.
- To extend forgiveness when resentment feels safer.
- To persevere when quitting feels more logical.
- To serve in hidden places without applause, knowing heaven sees.
- To dream God-sized dreams when circumstances scream impossibility.

The Spirit takes the ordinary and infuses it with divine purpose. A carpenter builds a tabernacle.

A fisherman becomes a preacher. A persecutor becomes a missionary. A mother's whispered prayer shapes generations. A worker's integrity transforms an office. A student's quiet faithfulness inspires peers.

We often wait for the spectacular, but the Spirit delights in breathing into the simple. Yes, Pentecost was dramatic, but its purpose was practical. The Spirit came so that ordinary people could live extraordinary lives of witness in their world.

So, the question isn't whether the Spirit is breathing. The question is whether we are yielding. Are we allowing Him to shape our choices, guide our words, ignite our creativity, and sustain our courage? Or are we holding our breath, insisting on self-sufficiency, forgetting that without Him we return to dust?

Today, the invitation is simple yet groundbreaking: live Spirit-breathed. Receive afresh the breath of God.

Let Him turn your daily rhythms into sacred spaces. Let Him hover over your chaos, breathe into your dust, and set fire to your ordinary. For the same Spirit who hovered at creation and burned at Pentecost is breathing still. And He longs to breathe through you.

2. PENTECOST: MORE THAN A STORY

The Day Everything Changed

There are moments in history when the very fabric of reality seems to tear open, allowing the divine to break through in ways that forever alter the course of human existence. Some of these moments are recorded in Scripture, while others have echoed throughout the centuries in revivals, renewals, and awakenings. Yet none stand quite as central to the Christian faith as the day of Pentecost, recorded in Acts chapter 2, a day when heaven touched earth with such power that its reverberations continue to shake lives and transform hearts more than two thousand years later.

On that day, the world was forever changed. What the prophets had promised, and Jesus had foreshadowed suddenly became reality. Tongues of fire rested on ordinary men and women, and the rushing wind of God filled the room. Words unknown to the speakers poured from their mouths, declaring the wonders of God in languages they had never studied. Fear dissolved into boldness. Confusion gave way to clarity. The weak became strong, and the timid became fearless witnesses. From that upper room, the gospel burst forth into the streets of Jerusalem and ultimately to the ends of the earth. Pentecost was not simply an event; it was the birth of the Church, the empowerment of God's people, and the unveiling of a new era in human history.

And yet, for many believers today, Pentecost has become little more than a historical footnote, a story relegated to Sunday school flannel boards and theological textbooks. We read about it, nod our heads in acknowledgment, and then quietly return to our comfortable, predictable faith routines. We've taken the wild, untamable fire of God and domesticated it, turning it into a manageable narrative that fits neatly within our controlled spiritual expectations.

The Spirit who once turned the world upside down is too often treated as a gentle breeze we can enjoy when convenient, rather than the consuming wind of heaven that disrupts and transforms.

But what if Pentecost was never meant to be just a story we admire from afar? What if it were intended to be a pattern, a blueprint, a living reality that every follower of Jesus can and should experience? What if the same Spirit that fell on that first gathering in Jerusalem is still falling today, still transforming ordinary people into extraordinary vessels of God's power and love?

This book isn't written merely to inform your mind but to ignite your soul. It's a call to awakening, a summons to move beyond the safety of routine religion into the dangerous, exhilarating territory of authentic spiritual life. It's an invitation to experience your own personal Pentecost, to let the fire of God consume everything in your life that's merely religious form without genuine spiritual power.

The men and women in that upper room weren't remarkable by human standards. They were fishermen and tax collectors, tradesmen, and homemakers. Some had denied Jesus, others had doubted Him, and nearly all had abandoned Him in His hour of need. They were flawed, fragile, and fearful, people just like us, confused and uncertain, desperately needing something greater than themselves. Yet when the Spirit came, everything changed.

The same Spirit that raised Jesus from the dead came to dwell within them. That reality transformed them from spiritual infants into spiritual giants, from hesitant followers into courageous leaders, from people who hid behind locked doors into witnesses who turned the world upside down. The timid became bold. The silent became preachers. The powerless became conduits of supernatural power. Pentecost turned ordinary people into history-shapers.

That same transformation is available to you today. The question isn't whether God desires to move powerfully in your life, He absolutely does. The question is whether you're willing to move beyond the comfortable confines of predictable faith into the wild, wonderful, and sometimes unsettling world of authentic spiritual encounter. Pentecost isn't about religious spectacle; it's about divine empowerment for holy living and bold witness.

It's about being filled to overflowing with God's presence so that His love, truth, and power spill out of you wherever you go.

As we journey together through this exploration, we'll examine not just what happened on that first Pentecost but why it matters for us now. We'll see that Pentecost was never meant to remain locked in history as a one-time event. It was the inauguration of a new way of living, a new covenant, a new intimacy between God and His people, and a new mission empowered by heaven itself. That same Spirit hasn't retired, diminished, or disappeared. He's still moving, still filling, still empowering, still calling ordinary men and women to do extraordinary things for the glory of God.

If you allow Him, this study could be the doorway to a new season in your life. Your understanding will be challenged. Your faith will be stretched. Your heart will be ignited. This is not merely an examination of ancient history; it's a roadmap to spiritual revolution in your own walk with God. The Spirit who filled that upper room still longs to fill yours. The fire that fell in Jerusalem still longs to fall upon you.

The question is simple but urgent: are you ready?

The fire is still falling. The invitation is still open. Pentecost is not over, it has only just begun.

CHAPTER 1:
The Event That Shook the World

The Upper Room Encounter

The stage was set in the most unremarkable of places. No grand cathedral, no magnificent temple, no elaborate religious ceremony, just an upper room in Jerusalem where 120 believers had gathered in obedience to Jesus' final instructions. They had been told to wait, and so they waited. But what they were waiting for would exceed their wildest expectations and change the world forever.

To understand the magnitude of what happened on Pentecost, we must first grasp the context of this waiting period. Jesus had ascended into heaven just days before, leaving His followers in anxious anticipation. They had witnessed His resurrection, heard His final teachings, and received His Great Commission. Yet they were still, in many ways, spiritual children, full of enthusiasm but lacking the power to fulfill their calling.

The disciples had already tasted failure. During Jesus' crucifixion, they scattered in fear. Peter denied knowing Jesus three times. Thomas doubted the resurrection. These were not spiritual giants; they were ordinary people who had been touched by an extraordinary Savior but still struggled with very human limitations.

This is profoundly encouraging for us today. God doesn't wait for us to achieve spiritual perfection before He moves in our lives. He doesn't require us to have our theology perfectly sorted or our character flawlessly developed. He meets us in our weakness, in our doubt, in our fear, and transforms us by His power.

The upper room represents a place of surrender and expectation. The disciples weren't just passing time; they were preparing their hearts.

Acts 1:14 tells us they "all continued with one accord in prayer and supplication." They were united in purpose, aligned in expectation, and committed to seeking God together.

This unity was crucial. The Spirit of God moves most powerfully in environments of harmony and shared faith. When believers come together with one heart and one mind, they create a spiritual atmosphere that invites divine intervention. The disciples had learned to set aside their petty differences and personal ambitions to focus on their common calling.

But they were also wrestling with uncertainty. Jesus had spoken of a Comforter who would come, a Helper who would empower them for ministry. Yet they couldn't have imagined what this would actually look like. They were expecting something, but they had no framework for understanding the magnitude of what God was preparing to do.

This is often how God works in our lives. He gives us promises and instructions that stretch beyond our current understanding. He calls us to wait in faith, to prepare our hearts, to align ourselves with His purposes even when we can't see the full picture. The upper room experience teaches us that transformation often begins in the place of patient expectation.

The disciples were also navigating the tension between the already and the not yet. Jesus had already accomplished salvation through His death and resurrection. The kingdom of God had already been inaugurated. Yet something was still missing, the power to live out this new reality in transformative ways.

This same tension exists in every believer's life. We have been saved, we have been forgiven, we have been adopted into God's family. Yet many of us still feel powerless to live the victorious Christian life we read about in Scripture. We believe in God's power intellectually, but we haven't experienced it personally in ways that revolutionize our daily existence.

The upper room was about to become a collision point between heaven and earth, a place where the promises of God would be fulfilled in ways that would forever change human history. But it started with ordinary people doing ordinary things, praying, waiting, seeking God together.

As we consider our own lives, we must ask: Where is our upper room? Where do we go to wait on God, to seek His face, to align our hearts with His purposes? Do we have spaces in our lives dedicated to expectant prayer and spiritual preparation?

The disciples didn't know it, but they were about to experience the most significant outpouring of God's Spirit in human history. They thought they were simply being obedient to Jesus' instructions to wait. In reality, they were positioning themselves to become the launching pad for the greatest spiritual revolution the world has ever known.

This teaches us that our obedience in the ordinary moments, our faithfulness in prayer, our commitment to spiritual disciplines, our willingness to wait on God even when nothing seems to be happening, is often the preparation for extraordinary breakthroughs. God is always working, even when we can't see it. He's preparing us, positioning us, and getting ready to move in ways that will surpass our understanding.

The upper room wasn't just a physical location; it was a spiritual posture. It represented hearts that were open, unified, expectant, and surrendered. It was a place where human limitation met divine possibility, where earthly weakness encountered heavenly power, and where ordinary believers were about to become extraordinary ministers of God's grace.

Are you living with an upper-room mentality? Are you positioned for God to move in your life in unprecedented ways? The same Spirit that was preparing to fall on those first disciples is available to you today. The question is whether you're creating the spiritual atmosphere that invites His presence and power.

The stage was set. The players were in position. The promises were about to be fulfilled. But none of them could have imagined what was about to unfold on that day that would forever be remembered as Pentecost.

Wind, Fire, and Tongues

When the day of Pentecost arrived, it came not with whispered subtlety but with unmistakable divine drama. Acts 2:1-4 records:

"When the day of Pentecost had fully come, they were all with one accord in one place. And suddenly there came a sound from heaven, as of a rushing mighty wind, and it filled the whole house where they were sitting. Then there appeared to them divided tongues, as of fire, and one sat upon each of them. And they were all filled with the Holy Spirit and began to speak with other tongues, as the Spirit gave them utterance."

The word "suddenly" is crucial here. This wasn't a gradual development or a slowly building experience. In an instant, the atmosphere of the upper room shattered under the invasion of the divine. The God of the universe chose to announce His arrival with unmistakable signs that would forever be etched in the memory of those present and recorded for all generations to follow.

The first sign was the sound of the wind. But this wasn't a gentle breeze or even a strong gust, it was described as a "rushing mighty wind" that filled the entire house. The Greek word used here is "pnoe," which can refer to breath or wind, the same route from which we get "pneumatic." This connects directly to the Hebrew concept of "ruach," the Spirit of God that moved upon the waters at creation and breathed life into Adam's nostrils.

The wind was more than symbolic; it was the audible announcement that the breath of God was about to animate His people in a completely new way. Throughout Scripture, wind represents the Spirit of God in His power to create, give life, and bring change. Jesus Himself told Nicodemus that the Spirit moves like the wind, you can't see it, but you can certainly see its effects.

This wind filled the house completely. There was no escaping it, no corner where its presence wasn't felt. When God moves, He doesn't do it partially or halfway. His presence permeates every space, touches every life, and transforms every situation. The disciples weren't getting a small taste of God's power; they were being completely immersed in it.

Then came the fire, not as a single flame, but as "divided tongues, as of fire" that sat upon each person. Fire in Scripture always represents the presence and power of God.

It was fire that appeared to Moses in the burning bush, fire that led the Israelites through the wilderness, fire that consumed Elijah's sacrifice on Mount Carmel. Fire purifies, empowers, illuminates, and consumes.

The fact that these tongues of fire were "divided" and that one sat upon each person is profoundly significant. This wasn't only a corporate experience; it was also deeply personal. Every individual believer was touched by the fire of God. No one was left out. No one was considered too ordinary or too insignificant. The same fire that touched the apostles also touched the unknown believers, the women, the young, and the old.

This speaks vigorously to us today. God's fire isn't reserved for the spiritual elite, the ministry professionals, or the super-saints. It's available to every believer who opens their heart to receive it. The housewife in suburbia can experience the same fire that touched Peter. The businessman struggling with his faith can receive the same empowerment that transformed John. The teenager questioning their purpose can encounter the same God who revolutionized the lives of those first disciples.

The fire "sat upon" each of them, indicating both a settling presence and a continuing reality. This wasn't a momentary flash but an abiding anointing. The fire represented the permanent indwelling of the Holy Spirit, the fulfillment of Jesus' promise that the Helper wouldn't just visit but would remain with them forever.

The immediate result of this wind and fire was that "they were all filled with the Holy Spirit and began to speak with other tongues, as the Spirit gave them utterance." The filling was complete, and the response was immediate. They didn't have to work up the courage to speak; the Spirit gave them the words. They didn't have to overcome their fear of public speaking; the power of God overwhelmed their natural limitations.

The speaking in tongues was miraculous on multiple levels. First, it was supernatural, these were languages they had never learned, words flowing from their mouths by divine inspiration. Second, it was purposeful, each language spoken was recognized by people present from various nations who had come to Jerusalem for the feast.

This wasn't meaningless babbling but coherent communication in known languages that served a specific evangelistic purpose.

The significance goes even deeper. At the Tower of Babel, God confused the languages of mankind as judgment for their pride and rebellion. At Pentecost, He reversed this curse, using multiple languages not to divide but to unite people from every nation under the banner of the Gospel. What Satan intended for division; God transformed into a tool for evangelism.

The tongues also fulfilled the prophecy of Isaiah 28:11, which Paul later references in 1 Corinthians 14: "For with stammering lips and another tongue He will speak to these people." God was doing something entirely new, speaking to His people in ways they had never experienced before.

For many modern believers, the supernatural elements of Pentecost, the wind, the fire, the tongues, seem foreign or even frightening. We've been conditioned to expect a tame, predictable God who works within the boundaries of our comfort zones. But the God of Pentecost is not tame. He is wild, wonderful, and wonderfully unpredictable. He doesn't ask permission to move in supernatural ways; He simply moves.

This doesn't mean we should expect the exact same manifestations in every spiritual encounter. God is creative in how He reveals Himself. But we should expect Him to move powerfully, to break into our ordinary experiences with extraordinary reality, and to make His presence known in ways that leave no doubt He is real and active in our lives.

The question for us today isn't whether these things really happened, the historical evidence is clear. The question is whether we believe the same God who moved on that first Pentecost is still moving today. Do we expect Him to fill us with His Spirit? Are we open to supernatural encounters that might stretch our understanding and challenge our preconceptions?

The wind, fire, and tongues of Pentecost weren't just one-time phenomena; they were the inaugural demonstration of a new covenant reality. The Spirit who came that day is the same Spirit who lives within every believer today. The power that transformed those first disciples is the same power available to transform us.

But power requires faith to release it. Miracles require expectation to manifest them. Supernatural encounters require hearts open to supernatural possibilities. The disciples received what they were prepared to receive. They experienced what they were positioned to experience. They encountered what they were expecting to encounter.

Are you positioned for your own wind, fire, and tongues experience? Are you prepared for God to move in your life in ways that exceed your current understanding? The same Spirit that fell on Pentecost is hovering over your life today, waiting for you to create the spiritual atmosphere that invites His great presence.

Peter's Transformation

Perhaps no single person embodies the transformative power of Pentecost more dramatically than Simon Peter. The man who stood before thousands on the day of Pentecost and preached with such power that three thousand people were converted was the same man who, just weeks earlier, had denied even knowing Jesus when confronted by a servant girl. This wasn't gradual character development; this was supernatural transformation.

To fully appreciate the magnitude of Peter's transformation, we must remember his pre-Pentecost track record. This was the disciple who walked on water until fear made him sink. He declared Jesus to be the Christ, then immediately rebuked Him for talking about crucifixion. He impulsively cut off the ear of the high priest's servant, then fled in terror when Jesus was arrested. Most painfully, he vehemently denied knowing Jesus three times during the crucifixion, even cursing to convince his accusers.

Peter was a study in contradictions, bold yet cowardly, faithful yet fickle, passionate yet unstable. He had a heart that loved Jesus deeply, but a nature that crumbled under pressure. He was, in many ways, a picture of all of us, believers who genuinely love God but struggle to bridge the gap between our spiritual aspirations and our human limitations.

Yet, on the day of Pentecost, something fundamental shifted in Peter's spiritual DNA.

When the crowd gathered in response to the supernatural manifestations occurring among the believers, Peter didn't hide in the shadows or defer to others. He stood up with the eleven, raised his voice, and delivered one of the most overwhelming sermons in human history.

The transformation was evident from his very first words: "Men of Judea and all who dwell in Jerusalem, let this be known to you, and heed my words" (Acts 2:14). This was not the voice of a man plagued by fear and insecurity. This was the voice of someone who had encountered divine power and been fundamentally changed by it. The Spirit of God had not only filled Peter; He had transformed him from the inside out.

Peter's Pentecost sermon reveals several key elements of his transformation that speak powerfully to our own spiritual journey:

Boldness in the Face of Opposition

The crowd that gathered was not entirely friendly. Many were confused, some were skeptical, and others were openly mocking, suggesting that the believers were drunk. Peter could have easily retreated, made excuses, or tried to downplay what was happening. Instead, he seized the moment as an opportunity to proclaim the Gospel with unprecedented boldness.

This boldness wasn't natural courage, it was supernatural empowerment. The Greek word for boldness in Acts is "Parrhesia," which means fearless confidence, especially when facing authority or opposition. This was exactly what Jesus promised when He said the Spirit would give them words to speak before rulers and authorities.

Scriptural Authority and Understanding

Peter's sermon revealed a depth of scriptural knowledge and understanding that hadn't been evident before Pentecost. He quoted extensively from the prophets Joel and David, weaving together Old Testament prophecies with their New Testament fulfillment in ways that showed supernatural insight.

This wasn't the result of seminary training or years of theological study.

This was the Spirit of God illuminating the Scriptures and giving Peter understanding that transcended his natural education. Jesus had promised the Spirit would teach them all things and remind them of everything He'd told them. Peter's sermon was a living demonstration of this promise.

Christ-Centered Focus

Throughout his sermon, Peter kept the focus squarely on Jesus, His life, death, resurrection, and lordship. He didn't talk about himself, his own experiences, or his personal transformation. He talked about Christ. This represented a fundamental shift from the self-focused Peter of the Gospels to the Christ-centered Peter of Acts.

The Spirit's filling always produces this effect, it magnifies Jesus and minimizes self. When we're truly filled with the Spirit, we become less concerned with our own reputation and more passionate about Christ's glory. Our conversations shift from being about us to being about Him.

Prophetic Insight and Revelation

Peter demonstrated prophetic insight as he interpreted the events of Pentecost through the lens of Old Testament prophecy. He understood that what they were experiencing wasn't just a random supernatural occurrence but the specific fulfillment of God's promises. He had the spiritual discernment to recognize the times and seasons of God's working.

This kind of prophetic insight is available to every Spirit-filled believer. We can understand what God is doing in our generation, discern His purposes and plans, and gain insight into how current events fit into His eternal purposes.

Evangelistic Passion and Power

Peter's sermon produced an unprecedented result, three thousand people were converted in a single day. This wasn't just good preaching technique; this was the power of God working through a yielded vessel. Peter had become a channel through which the Spirit could flow to convict, convert, and transform lives.

The man who had been too afraid to acknowledge Jesus before a servant girl was now boldly proclaiming Him before thousands. The disciple who had struggled with his own faith was now strengthening the faith of multitudes. The follower who had been unstable and unreliable had become a rock-solid foundation for the early church.

What Made the Difference?

The difference in Peter wasn't the result of human effort, education, or gradual maturation. It was the supernatural work of the Holy Spirit. When the Spirit filled Peter on Pentecost, He didn't just give him temporary power for that moment, He fundamentally rewired his spiritual circuitry.

This is what the Spirit wants to do in every believer's life. He doesn't just want to visit us occasionally or influence us marginally. He wants to fill us completely, transform us thoroughly, and use us effectively. The same Spirit that turned Peter from a coward into a champion is available to work the same transformation in our lives.

The Pattern for Every Believer

Peter's transformation establishes a pattern that's available to every believer:

1. **Surrender**: Peter had to come to the end of himself. His denials of Jesus and subsequent restoration had broken his self-confidence and created a heart ready to depend completely on God.

2. **Expectation**: Peter joined the other believers in the upper room, waiting expectantly for what Jesus had promised. He positioned himself to receive what God wanted to give.

3. **Filling**: When the Spirit came, Peter was completely filled. This wasn't a partial experience or a momentary touch, it was a total immersion in God's presence and power.

4. **Action**: The filling resulted in immediate action. Peter didn't wait until he felt ready or fully understood what was happening. He stepped out in faith and allowed the Spirit to work through him.

5. **Fruit**: The result was supernatural fruit, thousands of lives transformed, the church established, and the Gospel launched into the world with unprecedented power.

This same pattern can be replicated in our lives today. We can experience the same kind of transformation that turned Peter from an unstable follower into an effective leader. But it requires the same elements: surrender, expectation, filling, action, and faith to believe that God wants to work as powerfully through us as He did through those first disciples.

Peter's transformation on Pentecost wasn't just a historical event, it was a demonstration of what God wants to do in every believer's life. The question isn't whether God can transform us; Peter's example proves He can. The question is whether we're willing to be transformed, whether we're ready to step beyond our comfort zones into the realm of supernatural empowerment.

The same Spirit that filled Peter is available to fill you. The same power that transformed him is available to transform you. The same boldness that enabled him to preach with such impact is available to enable you to live with supernatural influence. Your Pentecost transformation is waiting. Are you ready to receive it?

CHAPTER 2:
Beyond the Historical Moment

The Birth of the Church

Pentecost was more than a spectacular supernatural event; it was the birth of the Church as a living, breathing organism powered by the Spirit of God. What happened in that upper room didn't stay in that upper room, it exploded onto the streets of Jerusalem and ultimately spread to the ends of the earth, creating a movement that would revolutionize human history.

The Church that was born on Pentecost was unlike anything the world had ever seen. It wasn't just another religious institution or social organization. It was a supernatural community where the life of God flowed through ordinary people, transforming them into extraordinary vessels of His love, power, and purpose.

Acts 2:41-47 gives us a picture of this newborn Church: "Then those who gladly received his word were baptized; and that day about three thousand souls were added to them. And they continued steadfastly in the apostles' doctrine and fellowship, in the breaking of bread, and in prayers. Then fear came upon every soul, and many wonders and signs were done through the apostles. Now all who believed were together, and had all things in common, and sold their possessions and goods, and divided them among all, as anyone had a need. So continuing daily with one accord in the temple, and breaking bread from house to house, they ate their food with gladness and simplicity of heart, praising God and having favor with all the people. And the Lord added to the church daily those who were being saved."

This description reveals several key characteristics of the Pentecost Church that should mark every authentic Christian community:

Explosive Growth Through Divine Power

The first church service after Pentecost resulted in three thousand converts. This wasn't the result of marketing strategies, entertainment, or psychological manipulation. It was the power of God working through Spirit-filled believers to convict hearts and transform lives. The Gospel was preached with such anointing that people were "cut to the heart" and cried out, "What shall we do?"

This kind of explosive growth is still possible today when churches operate in the power of the Spirit rather than relying solely on human methods and programs. When believers are truly filled with the Spirit and empowered for evangelism, the results are supernatural. People are drawn not just to our words but to the life of God they see flowing through us.

Devotion to Biblical Teaching

The new converts didn't just make emotional decisions and then go back to business as usual. They "continued steadfastly in the apostles' doctrine." They were hungry for truth, eager to learn, and committed to growing in their understanding of God's Word.

This devotion to Scripture is foundational to any authentic move of God. The Spirit who inspired the Word will never lead us away from the Word. True spiritual experiences always drive us deeper into biblical truth, not away from it. When churches begin to neglect or compromise biblical teaching, they inevitably lose the power and presence of God.

Authentic Fellowship and Community

The early believers weren't just attending services together; they were doing life together. They shared meals, possessions, and daily experiences. Their fellowship was marked by gladness, simplicity, and genuine care for one another's needs.

This kind of authentic community can only exist where the Spirit of God is truly present. Human nature tends toward selfishness, competition, and isolation. But the Spirit creates supernatural bonds of love that transcend natural barriers and create a genuine spiritual family.

Supernatural Signs and Wonders

"Fear came upon every soul, and many wonders and signs were done through the apostles." The Pentecost Church operated in the supernatural. Miracles were normal, not exceptional. The same power that filled the believers on Pentecost continued to flow through them in ongoing demonstrations of God's reality.

These signs and wonders served multiple purposes. They confirmed the truth of the Gospel message, demonstrated God's compassion for human need, and created a sense of awe and reverence that opened hearts to spiritual reality. They weren't performed for entertainment but as expressions of God's love and power.

Sacrificial Generosity

The believers "had all things in common, and sold their possessions and goods, and divided them among all, as anyone had need." This wasn't communism or socialism; it was supernatural love in action. The Spirit of God so filled their hearts with love for one another that material possessions became secondary to meeting the needs of their spiritual family.

This kind of radical generosity still marks authentic moves of God. When the Spirit truly fills believers, they become generous with their time, resources, and lives. They move from a mentality of "what's in it for me?" to "how can I serve others?"

Consistent Worship and Prayer

The early church was marked by continual worship and prayer. They met daily in the temple for public worship and in homes for intimate fellowship. Their lives were saturated with prayer, praise, and spiritual focus.

This wasn't a religious duty but a spiritual delight. When people are truly filled with the Spirit, worship becomes natural, prayer becomes a joy, and spiritual activities become life-giving rather than burdensome.

Ongoing Evangelistic Fruitfulness

"The Lord added to the church daily those who were being saved." The early church didn't have to organize evangelism campaigns or pressure people to witness. The life of God flowing through them was so attractive that people were drawn to Christ on a daily basis.

This is how evangelism is supposed to work. When believers are truly filled with the Spirit and living supernatural lives, they become magnets that draw people to Jesus. Their changed lives become the most influential evangelistic tool.

The Church as God's Strategy

What makes this description even more remarkable is that this Church became God's primary strategy for reaching the world. Within a few decades, the Gospel had spread throughout the Roman Empire. Within a few centuries, Christianity had become the dominant force in Western civilization. All of this started with 120 Spirit-filled believers in an upper room.

The Church wasn't Plan B after Israel rejected the Messiah. It was always God's strategy for the New Covenant era. The Church is not just a human organization; it's a divine organism, the Body of Christ on earth, the primary vehicle through which God expresses His love and advances His kingdom.

Why Many Churches Fall Short

If the Pentecost model is God's design for the Church, why do so many modern churches fall far short of this standard? Why do we see more programs than power, more entertainment than transformation, more activity than anointing?

The answer lies in our departure from the Pentecost pattern. Many churches have substituted human methods for divine power, professional ministry for Spirit-filled laity, and religious activity for authentic relationship with God. We've tried to build the Church on everything except the foundation that actually works, the power of the Holy Spirit flowing through Spirit-filled believers.

Recovering the Pentecost Pattern

The good news is that the Pentecost pattern can be recovered. The same Spirit that filled the early church is still available today. The same power that transformed that first generation of believers can transform us. But it requires returning to the fundamentals:

1. **Expecting God to Move**: We must believe that God wants to work powerfully in our generation, not just in biblical times.
2. **Seeking Spiritual Filling**: We must prioritize being filled with the Spirit over being filled with programs and activities.
3. **Creating Atmosphere for God**: We must cultivate environments of worship, prayer, and expectation where the Spirit feels welcome to move.
4. **Emphasizing Biblical Truth**: We must remain grounded in Scripture while being open to supernatural experiences.
5. **Living Supernaturally**: We must expect and actively seek for God to work miracles, signs, and wonders through us.
6. **Building Authentic Community**: We must prioritize real relationships over religious performance.

The Church born on Pentecost was not perfect, but it was effective. It was not sophisticated, but it was supernatural. It was not impressive by human standards, but it was irresistible by divine standards. People were drawn to it not because of what it offered them but because of the life of God they encountered there.

This is what the Church is supposed to look like. This is what God intends for every local body of believers. The Pentecost pattern isn't just ancient history; it's a blueprint for today. The question is whether we're willing to abandon our human methods long enough to experience God's supernatural power.

Your church can experience a Pentecostal awakening. Your community can be transformed by the power of God. But it starts with individuals, starting with you, who are willing to be filled with the Spirit and live in the reality of God's supernatural presence and power.

The Church was born in power on Pentecost. It's time for that same power to be reborn in our generation.

The Promise for All Generations

One of the most innovative aspects of Peter's Pentecost sermon was his declaration that what they were witnessing wasn't just a one-time event for a select group of disciples. Quoting from the prophet Joel, he proclaimed: "And it shall come to pass in the last days, says God, that I will pour out of My Spirit on all flesh; your sons and your daughters shall prophesy, your young men shall see visions, your old men shall dream dreams. And on My menservants and on My maidservants, I will pour out My Spirit in those days; and they shall prophesy" (Acts 2:17-18).

This wasn't just historical documentation; it was a prophetic declaration. Peter was announcing that the Spirit's outpouring on Pentecost was the beginning of a new era, the "last days", in which God's Spirit would be available to all people, regardless of age, gender, social status, or ethnic background. The exclusivity of the Old Covenant was giving way to the inclusivity of the New Covenant.

The Democratization of the Divine

Under the Old Covenant, the Spirit of God came upon selected individuals for specific purposes, prophets, priests, and kings. The average Israelite could not expect a personal encounter with God's Spirit. There was a clear hierarchy of spiritual access, with the high priest alone entering the Holy of Holies once a year on behalf of the entire nation.

Pentecost shattered this system forever. The veil in the temple had already been torn from top to bottom when Jesus died, symbolically opening access to God for everyone. But Pentecost made this access practical and experiential. Now every believer could be filled with the Spirit, every Christian could experience God's presence, and every follower of Jesus could be empowered for ministry. This was groundbreaking in the extreme. It meant that the housewife could prophesy with the same anointing as the prophet. The young person could receive visions from God just like the seasoned spiritual leader. The servant could be as filled with the Spirit as the master. Gender, age, social class, and ethnic background became irrelevant when it came to spiritual empowerment.

For Every Generation

Peter's proclamation that this promise was "for you and your children and to all who are afar off, as many as the Lord our God will call" (Acts 2:39) established the trans-generational nature of the Pentecost experience. This wasn't just for the apostolic generation; it was for their children, their grandchildren, and every generation that would follow until Christ's return.

This means that the same Spirit who fell on Pentecost is available to you today. The same power that transformed the disciples can transform you. The same signs and wonders that marked the early church can mark your life and ministry. The geographical and temporal distance between us and that first Pentecost doesn't diminish the promise one bit.

Too many believers have been taught that the supernatural gifts and experiences of Pentecost were only for the apostolic age, that miracles, prophecy, divine healing, and supernatural empowerment ended with the death of the last apostle. This teaching, known as 'Cessationism,' effectively closes the door on the very experiences that God promised would characterize the entire church age.

But Scripture does not indicate that these gifts were temporary. In fact, Paul specifically states that the gifts of the Spirit will continue "till we all come to the unity of the faith and of the knowledge of the Son of God, to a perfect man, to the measure of the stature of the fullness of Christ" (Ephesians 4:13). Since the church has clearly not yet reached this state of perfection and unity, the gifts must still be active.

The Promise Crosses All Barriers

The inclusivity of the Pentecost promise is breathtaking in its scope. Joel's prophecy, quoted by Peter, specifically mentions:

- **Sons and daughters**: Both male and female are included in God's outpouring. Gender is no barrier to spiritual empowerment.

- **Young men and old men**: Age doesn't disqualify anyone from receiving visions and dreams from God. The spiritually young and the spiritually mature can both experience divine encounters.
- **Servants and handmaidens**: Social status doesn't matter. The wealthy and the poor, the powerful and the powerless, all have equal access to God's Spirit.
- **All flesh**: This ultimately extends beyond ethnic Israel to include all humanity. The Gospel would go to every tribe, tongue, and nation.

This radical inclusivity was scandalous in the first century and remains challenging today. We still struggle with the idea that God might use someone we consider unqualified, too young, too old, the wrong gender, wrong background, insufficient education, or improper pedigree. But God delights in using the foolish things of the world to confound the wise, and the weak things to shame the strong.

Historical Validation

Church history validates the ongoing nature of the Pentecost promise. Every major revival and spiritual awakening has been marked by a fresh outpouring of God's Spirit accompanied by supernatural signs and wonders. The Montanist movement in the second century, the ministry of St. Martin of Tours in the fourth century, the Celtic revivals, the Protestant Reformation, the Great Awakenings, the Welsh Revival, the Azusa Street Revival, and countless other movements have all demonstrated that God continues to pour out His Spirit in prevailing ways.

These weren't aberrations or deceptions; they were fresh fulfillments of the same promise that was inaugurated on Pentecost. Each generation has the opportunity to experience its own Pentecost, its own fresh encounter with the living God, its own supernatural empowerment for ministry and mission.

The Promise and You

The most important question is, not whether this promise was valid for past generations, history clearly demonstrates that it was.

The critical question is whether you believe this promise is for you personally. Do you believe that God wants to fill you with His Spirit in the same way He filled the disciples on Pentecost? Do you expect to experience supernatural empowerment for Christian living and ministry?

Many believers live far below their spiritual inheritance. They've accepted a form of Christianity that includes salvation from sin but excludes empowerment for service. They believe in the forgiveness of sins but not in the gifts of the Spirit. They embrace justification but neglect the fullness of God's provision for the Christian life.

This represents a tragic truncation of the Gospel. God didn't save us just to get us to heaven someday; He saved us to fill us with His Spirit and use us effectively in His kingdom today. The same Jesus who died for our sins also promised to baptize us with the Holy Spirit and fire. The same God who forgives also empowers.

Receiving Your Inheritance

If you recognize that you haven't yet experienced the fullness of God's promise, how do you receive your spiritual inheritance? The pattern is clear throughout Scripture:

1. **Recognize Your Need**: You must honestly assess whether you're living in the fullness of God's provision or settling for something less. Are you experiencing the joy, power, boldness, and fruitfulness that marked the early believers?

2. **Believe God's Promise**: You must believe that God wants to fill you with His Spirit just as much as He wanted to fill the first disciples. His promises are not reserved for a spiritual elite; they're available to every believer.

3. **Ask in Faith**: Jesus said, "If you then, being evil, know how to give good gifts to your children, how much more will your heavenly Father give the Holy Spirit to those who ask Him!" (Luke 11:13). God wants to give you His Spirit more than you want to receive Him.

4. **Expect God to Move**: Approach God with expectation, not just hope. Expect Him to move in your life in supernatural ways. Create space in your life for Him to work.

5. **Yield Completely**: The Spirit fills vessels that are completely surrendered. Half-hearted commitment produces half-hearted results. Total surrender opens the door to total transformation.
6. **Step Out in Faith**: When God begins to move in your life, step out in faith. Don't wait until you feel completely ready or fully understand what's happening. Obedience in faith releases the fullness of God's power.

The Promise for Your Family

Remember that Peter specifically said this promise was for "you and your children." This means that God wants to work not just in your life but in your family. Your spouse can experience the same feeling. Your children can encounter God in supernatural ways. Your grandchildren can walk in the same power that marked the early church.

Don't settle for a generation gap in spiritual experience. Don't accept the lie that young people can't have authentic encounters with God or that older believers are too set in their ways to experience fresh outpourings of the Spirit. God's promise transcends generational boundaries.

The Promise for Your Community

The promise also extends to "all who are afar off." This includes your neighbors, your coworkers, your city, and your nation. God wants to pour out His Spirit not just on individuals but on communities. He wants to transform neighborhoods, workplaces, schools, and entire regions through the power of His Spirit working through Spirit-filled believers.

This should radically expand our vision and expectations. We shouldn't just pray for personal blessing; we should pray for community transformation. We shouldn't just seek individual encounters with God; we should believe for corporate revivals that impact entire regions.

Living in the Promise

The Pentecost promise isn't just about a one-time experience of being filled with the Spirit. It's about living in the ongoing reality of God's presence and power. It's about expecting Him to work supernaturally through you on a regular basis. It's about walking in the gifts of the Spirit, ministering in His power, and seeing His kingdom advance through your life and ministry.

This requires a fundamental shift in how we view the Christian life. Instead of seeing it as primarily about moral behavior and religious activity, we must see it as supernatural living enabled by divine power. Instead of trying to live for God in our own strength, we must learn to live from the overflow of His Spirit within us.

The promise of Pentecost is as valid today as it was two thousand years ago. The question is not whether God is willing to pour out His Spirit, He's already demonstrated His willingness. The question is whether we're willing to receive all that He wants to give us.

Your Pentecost is waiting. Your filling is available. Your empowerment is promised. The same Spirit who transformed fishermen into world-changers is ready to transform you. Will you receive your inheritance?

Signs and Wonders Today

The supernatural manifestations that accompanied Pentecost, divine healing, miraculous provision, supernatural knowledge, and powerful demonstrations of God's presence, were not meant to be historical curiosities but ongoing realities in the life of the Church. Yet many modern believers struggle with the concept that God still works miracles today with the same frequency and power that marked the apostolic age.

This skepticism often stems from one of several sources: bad theology that teaches miracles ceased with the apostles, negative experiences with false or manipulative ministries, a Western worldview that struggles with the supernatural, or simply a lack of personal experience with God's miraculous power.

However, neither Scripture nor church history supports the idea that God has withdrawn His supernatural power from the Church.

The Biblical Foundation for Contemporary Miracles

Jesus Himself established the expectation for ongoing supernatural ministry when He declared: "Most assuredly, I say to you, he who believes in Me, the works that I do he will do also; and greater works than these he will do, because I go to My Father" (John 14:12). This promise wasn't limited to the twelve apostles; it was given to anyone who believes in Jesus.

The phrase "greater works" doesn't necessarily mean more spectacular miracles, but rather a greater scope and scale of ministry enabled by the Holy Spirit's presence in the Church. While Jesus' earthly ministry was geographically limited to Palestine and chronologically limited to three and a half years, the Church filled with His Spirit would carry the Gospel to the ends of the earth and continue His works throughout history.

Paul reinforced this expectation when he wrote to the Corinthians: "Now concerning spiritual gifts, brethren, I do not want you to be ignorant" (1 Corinthians 12:1). He then proceeded to list nine manifestations of the Spirit, word of wisdom, word of knowledge, faith, gifts of healings, working of miracles, prophecy, discerning of spirits, different kinds of tongues, and interpretation of tongues, and made it clear that these gifts were meant to operate in the church for the common good.

Historical Evidence

Church history provides abundant evidence that miraculous signs and wonders have continued throughout the centuries. The early church fathers, including Justin Martyr, Irenaeus, and Origen, wrote extensively about miracles occurring in their time. Augustine, initially skeptical of contemporary miracles, later documented numerous healings and supernatural events in his own ministry.

Throughout the medieval period, countless accounts of miracles were recorded in the lives of saints and Christian leaders.

The Protestant Reformation, while challenging certain practices, didn't deny the possibility of miracles but rather emphasized that such gifts should be biblical and authentic.

The Great Awakenings in America were marked by remarkable supernatural phenomena, including healing miracles, prophetic utterances, and compelling conversions. The Welsh Revival of 1904-1905 saw extraordinary demonstrations of God's power that transformed entire communities.

The Pentecostal and Charismatic movements of the twentieth century witnessed a dramatic restoration of supernatural gifts to the mainstream Church. Millions of believers worldwide have experienced divine healing, prophetic revelation, and miraculous provision that cannot be explained by natural means.

Contemporary Testimonies

Today, reports of miracles continue to come from every continent and every branch of Christianity. Medical doctors document healings that defy scientific explanation. Missionaries report supernatural provision and protection in dangerous situations. Pastors witness lives transformed in ways that can only be attributed to divine intervention.

Dr. Craig Keener's comprehensive study "Miracles: The Credibility of the New Testament Accounts" documents hundreds of well-attested contemporary miracles, including medical healings verified by physicians, resurrections witnessed by multiple credible sources, and supernatural phenomena that cannot be explained by natural causes.

The Global South, particularly Africa, Asia, and Latin America, has experienced unprecedented church growth accompanied by widespread reports of miraculous signs and wonders. These aren't primitive peoples easily deceived by superstition; many are highly educated individuals who carefully examine and document supernatural events.

Why Some Don't See Miracles

If miracles are still available today, why don't more Western believers experience them? Several factors contribute to this gap:

Theological Bias: Many believers have been taught that miracles ceased with the apostolic age, creating a theological barrier that prevents them from expecting or seeking supernatural encounters.

Cultural Worldview: Western culture is heavily influenced by naturalistic materialism, which assumes that everything can be explained by natural causes. This worldview makes it difficult to recognize or accept supernatural intervention.

Lack of Faith: Jesus Himself was limited in His miracle-working power in His hometown because of unbelief (Matthew 13:58). Faith is not just mental assent but a confident expectation that God will act supernaturally.

Comfort and Self-Reliance: In societies with advanced medical care, social safety nets, and material prosperity, people may not feel desperate enough to seek God for miraculous intervention. Necessity often creates the spiritual atmosphere in which miracles flourish.

Fear of Deception: Past experiences with false miracles or manipulative ministries can create fear that prevents people from being open to authentic supernatural encounters.

Lack of Teaching and Modeling: Many churches don't teach about spiritual gifts or provide opportunities for believers to exercise them, creating ignorance and inexperience with the supernatural.

Keys to Experiencing Miracles Today

For believers who want to experience more of God's supernatural power in their lives, several principles can help open the door to miraculous encounters:

Study the Biblical Foundation: Immerse yourself in Scripture's teaching about spiritual gifts, divine healing, and supernatural ministry. Understanding what God has promised gives you faith to receive what He offers.

Seek the Giver, Not Just the Gifts: The goal is not to collect supernatural experiences but to draw closer to God. When we seek Him with all our hearts, the gifts often follow naturally.

Start with Small Steps: Don't wait for dramatic miracles before you begin to exercise faith. Pray for minor needs, ask God for supernatural insight in everyday situations, and step out in small acts of faith.

Find Faith-Building Community: Surround yourself with believers who expect God to work supernaturally and who can encourage and mentor you in developing spiritual gifts.

Minister to Others: Often, our own spiritual gifts are activated when we attempt to minister to others. Pray for the sick, speak prophetically to encourage fellow believers, and ask God to use you supernaturally in others' lives.

Maintain Biblical Balance: Test everything against Scripture, seek wise counsel, and remember that the fruit of the Spirit (love, joy, peace, patience, kindness, goodness, faithfulness, gentleness, and self-control) is more important than the gifts of the Spirit.

Persistent Prayer and Fasting: Many supernatural breakthroughs come through persistent prayer, often combined with fasting. Don't give up if you don't see immediate results.

Practical Applications

Here are specific ways you can begin to experience and minister in supernatural power:

Divine Healing: Begin praying for sick people with the expectation that God will heal them. Start with friends and family members, laying hands on them and asking God to demonstrate His healing power.

Prophetic Ministry: Ask God to give you encouraging words, biblical insights, or supernatural knowledge for other believers. Share these impressions appropriately and watch how God confirms His word.

Supernatural Provision: Trust God for financial needs, job opportunities, and material provision beyond what you can arrange through natural means.

Miraculous Protection: Expect God to protect you and your family in supernatural ways. Pray for traveling mercies, safety in dangerous situations, and divine intervention when needed.

Spiritual Discernment: Ask God to give you, insight into spiritual situations, the ability to recognize deception, and wisdom that goes beyond natural understanding.

Supernatural Evangelism: Expect God to arrange divine appointments, give you supernatural insight into people's needs, and demonstrate His reality through signs and wonders that confirm the Gospel.

The Purpose of Miracles

It's crucial to remember that miracles are not ends in themselves but means to greater ends. They serve several important purposes:

- **Glorifying God**: Miracles demonstrate God's power and love, bringing glory to His name.
- **Confirming the Gospel**: Signs and wonders validate the truth of the Gospel message and open hearts to receive Christ.
- **Meeting Human Need**: God works miracles because He loves people and wants to relieve their suffering.
- **Building Faith**: Supernatural experiences strengthen faith and encourage believers to trust God more completely.
- **Advancing the Kingdom**: Miracles help establish God's kingdom on earth and demonstrate that Jesus is Lord.

The same God who parted the Red Sea, raised the dead, and filled the disciples on Pentecost is still working today. He hasn't retired, gone on vacation, or decided that miracles are no longer needed. The supernatural power that marked the early Church is still available to the contemporary Church.

The question is not whether God can work miracles today, He can. The question is whether we believe He will work them through us. Your faith, expectations, and willingness to step out in supernatural ministry will largely determine how much of God's miracle-working power you experience.

Signs and wonders are not optional extras in the Christian life; they are normal expressions of the supernatural Gospel we proclaim.

When the Church operates in the fullness of God's power, the world takes notice, hearts are opened to the Gospel, and the kingdom of God advances with irresistible force.

Your miracle-working ministry begins with believing that God wants to use you supernaturally. It continues with stepping out in faith, expecting Him to move, and yielding yourself as a vessel through which His power can flow. The same Spirit who fell on Pentecost is ready to demonstrate His power through your life.

Will you make yourself available?

CHAPTER 3:
From Routine to Alive

Recognizing Spiritual Deadness

One of the most dangerous conditions in the Christian life is spiritual deadness that masquerades as spiritual health. It's possible to attend church regularly, read the Bible occasionally, pray perfunctory prayers, and maintain a respectable Christian reputation while being spiritually lifeless on the inside. This condition is particularly insidious because it feels safe, comfortable, and socially acceptable, yet it represents a tragic departure from the vibrant, powerful life that God intends for every believer.

The Church at Sardis provides a sobering example of this phenomenon. Jesus said to them: "I know your works, that you have a name that you are alive, but you are dead" (Revelation 3:1). They had all the external trappings of a healthy church, good reputation, active programs, faithful attendance, but they lacked the essential element that makes Christianity supernatural: the living presence and power of God.

This same condition affects countless individual believers and churches today. We've created elaborate substitutes for authentic spiritual life, developing sophisticated forms of religious activity that require no real faith, produce no supernatural fruit, and demand no genuine sacrifice. We've learned to function quite well without the Holy Spirit, thank you very much, and we've convinced ourselves that this is normal Christianity.

The Symptoms of Spiritual Deadness

Recognizing spiritual deadness in our own lives can be challenging because it often develops gradually and can coexist with outward religious activity.

However, several key symptoms can help us honestly assess our spiritual condition:

Lack of Spiritual Appetite

When we're spiritually alive, we hunger for God's Word, thirst for His presence, and crave spiritual fellowship. We look forward to times of prayer and worship. We're eager to learn more about God and grow in our relationship with Him.

Spiritual deadness, however, is marked by loss of appetite for spiritual things. The Bible becomes boring, prayer feels like a duty, and worship becomes routine. We find ourselves more excited about entertainment, sports, or hobbies than about spiritual activities. We can go days without thinking seriously about God or His purposes for our lives.

Prayer That Lacks Power and Passion

Vibrant spiritual life produces prayer that is passionate, specific, and expectant. We pray with confidence that God hears us and will answer according to His will. We intercede earnestly for others and actively look for answers to our prayers.

Dead religion produces prayer that is perfunctory, vague, and faithless. We pray because we're supposed to, not because we're compelled to. Our prayers lack specificity because we're not really expecting specific answers. We rarely see dramatic answers to prayer because we rarely pray with the kind of faith that moves mountains.

Absence of Spiritual Fruit

Jesus said, "By their fruits you will know them" (Matthew 7:20). Spiritual life produces spiritual fruit, both the character fruit of love, joy, peace, patience, kindness, goodness, faithfulness, gentleness, and self-control, and the ministry fruit of people being saved, healed, encouraged, and discipled through our influence.

Spiritual deadness is marked by a lack of genuine spiritual fruit. We may be nice people who don't cause trouble, but we don't see lives transformed through our influence.

People aren't drawn to Christ through our witness. We don't experience the supernatural joy and peace that should characterize Spirit-filled living.

Fear of Spiritual Risk

Living a spiritual life requires stepping out in faith, taking spiritual risks, and trusting God in situations where we can't control the outcome. Spiritually alive believers are willing to pray for the sick (even if they don't get healed), share their faith (even if people reject it), and obey God's promptings (even if they don't fully understand them).

Spiritual deadness seeks safety and predictability. We avoid situations that require genuine faith. We stay within our comfort zones spiritually. We prefer forms of Christianity that don't demand much of us or expose us to potential failure or embarrassment.

Comfort with Spiritual Mediocrity

When we're spiritually alive, we're constantly hungry for more of God. We're not satisfied with yesterday's spiritual experiences; we want fresh encounters with the living God. We have holy dissatisfaction with our current level of spiritual maturity and are always pressing forward.

Spiritual deadness is characterized by contentment with mediocrity. We compare ourselves to other lukewarm believers and feel satisfied that we're doing as well as they are. We've lost the hunger for spiritual growth and the dissatisfaction with spiritual immaturity that drives us to seek more of God.

Resistance to the Supernatural

Authentic Christianity is inherently supernatural. The Gospel itself is the story of God becoming man, dying for our sins, rising from the dead, and sending His Spirit to live within believers.

Everything about our faith should be permeated with the expectation of supernatural intervention. Spiritual deadness is suspicious of the supernatural. We explain away miracles, rationalize answered prayers, and find natural explanations for divine interventions.

We're more comfortable with a tame God who works within predictable boundaries than with a wild God who does impossible things.

Lack of Spiritual Sensitivity

Living believers are spiritually sensitive. They can sense God's presence, discern spiritual atmospheres, and recognize when the Holy Spirit is moving. They're alert to spiritual opportunities and responsive to divine promptings.

Spiritually dead believers are spiritually insensitive. They can sit through intense worship services unmoved, hear anointed preaching unaffected, and miss obvious opportunities for ministry or witness. They've lost the ability to distinguish between the sacred and the secular, the spiritual and the natural.

Why We Settle for Spiritual Deadness

Understanding why we tolerate spiritual deadness is crucial to overcoming it. Several factors contribute to our acceptance of religious mediocrity:

Cultural Christianity

In cultures where Christianity is socially acceptable or even expected, it's easy to adopt Christian identity and behavior without experiencing Christian transformation. We can learn to speak the language, follow the customs, and maintain the appearances of faith without ever having a genuine encounter with the living God.

Fear of Fanaticism

Many believers are terrified of being perceived as religious fanatics, so they maintain a safe distance from anything that seems too spiritual or supernatural. They prefer a respectable, rational, culturally acceptable form of Christianity that doesn't challenge social norms or make others uncomfortable.

Bad Examples

Negative experiences with hypocritical, manipulative, or emotionally unstable people who claimed to be Spirit-filled can create fear of authentic spiritual life. We throw out the baby with the bathwater, rejecting genuine spiritual experience because of exposure to counterfeits.

Theological Confusion

Incorrect teaching about the nature of the Christian life can create spiritual deadness. If we're taught that salvation is primarily about avoiding hell rather than experiencing an abundant life, or that spiritual gifts ended with the apostles, we'll have low expectations for our spiritual experience.

Comfort and Prosperity

Material comfort can breed spiritual complacency. When our physical needs are met and our lives are relatively comfortable, we may not feel desperate enough to seek God with the intensity that produces spiritual breakthroughs.

Busyness and Distraction

Modern life is filled with distractions that can crowd out spiritual priorities. Between work, family, entertainment, and social obligations, we can easily become too busy to cultivate the spiritual disciplines that maintain vibrant faith.

The Cost of Spiritual Aliveness

It's important to acknowledge that genuine spiritual life comes with a cost. Living Christianity is more demanding than dead religion:

- It requires genuine surrender, not just intellectual assent
- It demands ongoing spiritual discipline, not just Sunday attendance

- It involves spiritual warfare, not just peaceful coexistence
- It calls for sacrificial service, not just comfortable participation
- It expects supernatural results, not just natural outcomes

Many believers unconsciously choose spiritual deadness because it's easier, safer, and less costly than authentic spiritual life.

The Tragedy of Wasted Potential

The greatest tragedy of spiritual deadness is wasted potential. Every believer has been called to be a vessel of God's power, a demonstration of His love, and an agent of His kingdom. When we settle for spiritual mediocrity, we rob ourselves of the joy and purpose for which we were created, and we rob the world of the witness it desperately needs.

Think about what could happen if every believer lived in the fullness of God's Spirit:

- Every workplace could have someone operating in divine wisdom and supernatural love
- Every neighborhood could have someone praying with power and ministering with compassion
- Every school could have students and teachers who demonstrate the reality of God's presence
- Every family could experience the transforming power of authentic Christian living

But when believers are spiritually dead, the world sees religious activity without spiritual power, moral rules without transforming grace, and good advice without divine enablement.

The Call to Honest Assessment

Before we can experience spiritual revival, we must honestly assess our current spiritual condition. This requires courage to look beyond external religious activity to examine the reality of our inner spiritual life. Ask yourself these penetrating questions:

- When did I last experience God's presence in a way that left me changed?
- How long has it been since I saw a clear answer to prayer that could only be attributed to God?
- Do I have genuine hunger for God's Word and delight in His presence?
- Am I seeing spiritual fruit, both character transformation and ministry effectiveness, in my life?
- Would my life look substantially different if the Holy Spirit were not living within me?
- Do I expect God to work supernaturally through me on a regular basis?

Honest answers to these questions can reveal whether we're experiencing the abundant life Jesus promised or settling for a religious routine that substitutes activity for authenticity.

The good news is that spiritual deadness is not a permanent condition. The same God who breathed life into Adam's lifeless body, who raised Jesus from the dead, and who transformed the disciples on Pentecost is ready to breathe new life into our spiritual deadness. But He waits for us to recognize our need and cry out for His intervention.

Spiritual deadness is not God's intention for any believer. He saved us to fill us, redeemed us to empower us, and called us to live supernatural lives that demonstrate His reality to a watching world. If you recognize symptoms of spiritual deadness in your own life, don't despair, desperation is often the first step toward transformation.

The fire of God that fell on Pentecost is still available today. The same Spirit that transformed frightened disciples into fearless apostles wants to transform you from spiritual deadness to spiritual aliveness. But it begins with honest recognition of where you are spiritually and a sincere desire for where God wants to take you.

Your spiritual resurrection is possible. Your Pentecost is available. Your transformation from routine to being alive is waiting. The question is: Are you ready to acknowledge your spiritual deadness so that God can make you spiritually alive?

Opening Our Hearts to Divine Fire

The transition from spiritual deadness to spiritual aliveness doesn't happen automatically. It requires a deliberate opening of our hearts to receive what God wants to give us. Just as the disciples had to position themselves in the upper room with expectant hearts and unified purpose, we must create the spiritual conditions that invite God's transforming presence into our lives.

The divine fire that fell on Pentecost is still burning today, but fire only consumes what is prepared to burn. God's Spirit only fills hearts that are emptied of self and opened to His presence. The same power that transformed those first believers is available to us, but we must learn how to position ourselves to receive it.

The Prerequisites for Divine Encounter

Throughout Scripture, certain conditions consistently precede powerful encounters with God. These aren't requirements we must fulfill to earn God's favor, but postures of heart that position us to receive what He freely offers:

Desperation

Almost every biblical revival began with someone who became desperate for God. Moses spent forty days on the mountain because he was desperate to know God's glory. David cried out that, his soul thirsted for God like a deer pants for water. The disciples persevered in prayer because they were desperate for the promised Comforter.

Desperation is different from casual interest or wishful thinking. It's a holy dissatisfaction with your current spiritual condition that drives you to seek God with unprecedented intensity. It says, "I cannot continue living at this level of spiritual mediocrity. I must have more of God, whatever it costs."

Many believers never experience a spiritual breakthrough because they're not desperate enough to pay the price for it. They want spiritual improvement, but not at the cost of comfort.

They desire God's blessing but not at the expense of convenience.

True desperation burns through these barriers and pursues God regardless of the cost.

Humility

Pride is perhaps the greatest barrier to spiritual encounter. God resists the proud but gives grace to the humble. The Pharisees missed Jesus because they were too proud to admit their spiritual need. The publicans and sinners found Him because they knew they were desperate for grace.

Opening our hearts to divine fire requires brutal honesty about our spiritual condition. We must acknowledge that our best efforts at Christian living have fallen short of God's standard. We must admit that we need supernatural help to live the life He's called us to live. We must confess that religious activity is no substitute for spiritual power.

This kind of humility is threatening to our ego, but essential for spiritual breakthrough. God cannot fill what is already full of self. He cannot empower what insists on self-reliance. He cannot transform what is satisfied with its current condition.

Surrender

Half-hearted commitment produces half-hearted results in the spiritual realm. God's fire burns completely, and it can only fall on hearts that are completely surrendered. This means yielding every area of our lives to His lordship, our relationships, our careers, our finances, our dreams, our fears, our failures, our successes.

Many believers want God's power but not His authority. They want His blessing but not His lordship. They want Him to enhance their lives but not redirect them. This selective surrender prevents the kind of complete transformation that God desires to work in us.

True surrender says, "Not my will but Yours be done. Use me however You want to use me. Change whatever You want to change in me. Send me wherever You want to send me. I am completely Yours."

Expectation

Faith is expectation in action. It's not just believing that God can work; it's expecting that He will work. The disciples gathered in the upper room with expectant hearts because Jesus had specifically promised that the Comforter would come. They weren't just hoping something might happen; they were expecting something would happen.

Many believers pray without expectation, worship without anticipation, and seek God without confidence that He will respond. This lack of expectation becomes a ceiling that limits what God can do in our lives.

Expectant hearts create an atmosphere that invites divine intervention. When we approach God with confidence that He wants to work effectively in our lives, we position ourselves to receive breakthroughs that exceed our natural understanding.

Unity

The disciples were "with one accord in one place" when the Spirit fell on Pentecost. Unity creates spiritual synergy that multiplies the effect of individual faith. When believers come together with a unified purpose and aligned hearts, they create an environment where God's power can flow more freely.

This doesn't mean we must find perfect people or perfect churches before we can experience God's power. It means we must be willing to lay down our personal agendas, preferences, and prejudices to pursue God together with other hungry believers.

Unity often requires forgiveness, humility, and the willingness to prefer others over ourselves. But the spiritual breakthrough that results from genuine unity is worth the cost of achieving it.

Practical Steps to Opening Your Heart

Understanding the prerequisites is just the beginning. We must take practical steps to create the spiritual conditions that invite God's transforming presence:

Create Sacred Space

Designate specific times and places for seeking God with unusual intensity. This might mean getting up earlier for extended prayer, setting aside a day for fasting and seeking God, or finding a quiet place where you can pour out your heart without distraction.

The upper room wasn't just any room; it was a place specifically set aside for seeking God. We need similar sacred spaces in our lives, times and places that are dedicated exclusively to spiritual pursuit.

Engage in Intensive Prayer

Move beyond routine prayers to intensive seeking. Spend extended time in God's presence, not just talking to Him but listening for His voice. Pour out your heart honestly, confessing your spiritual hunger and your need for His power.

This kind of prayer often involves spiritual warfare. The enemy doesn't want you to experience the breakthrough, so he'll fight to distract you, discourage you, or convince you that intensive seeking is unnecessary.

Study Biographies of Revived Believers

Read accounts of believers who experienced dramatic spiritual transformation. Study the lives of revivalists, missionaries, and ordinary believers who encountered God's power in extraordinary ways. Let their testimonies increase your faith and expectation.

Books like "They Found the Secret" by Raymond Edman, "Revival" by Martyn Lloyd-Jones, and biographies of great spiritual leaders can ignite your own hunger for spiritual breakthrough.

Fast and Seek God

Fasting demonstrates the seriousness of your spiritual hunger. It's a way of saying to God, "I want You more than I want food, comfort, or convenience." Biblical fasting combined with prayer has historically preceded major spiritual breakthroughs.

Start with short fasts if you're inexperienced, but don't avoid this discipline altogether. The combination of fasting and prayer creates a spiritual intensity that positions your heart to receive from God in unusual ways.

Find Faith-Building Community

Surround yourself with believers who expect God to work supernaturally and who can encourage you in your spiritual pursuit. Avoid those who are content with spiritual mediocrity or who discourage supernatural expectation.

This might require finding a new church, joining a small group focused on spiritual growth, or developing friendships with believers who are hungry for more of God. Community provides accountability, encouragement, and corporate faith that strengthens individual seeking.

Remove Spiritual Hindrances

Honestly examine your life for anything that might be hindering God's work in your heart. This could include unconfessed sin, unforgiveness toward others, compromising entertainment, unhealthy relationships, or misplaced priorities.

The Holy Spirit is holy, and He will not fill what is knowingly defiled. Cleansing your life of spiritual hindrances is not legalism; it's preparation for divine encounter.

Practice Spiritual Disciplines Intensively

Engage in Bible reading, prayer, worship, and meditation with increased intensity and focus. Don't just go through the motions; approach these disciplines with expectant hearts, asking God to speak to you, transform you, and fill you with His presence through them.

Overcoming Common Obstacles

As you begin to open your heart more fully to God's transforming fire, you'll likely encounter obstacles that attempt to derail your spiritual pursuit:

The Obstacle of Doubt

Let's be clear: The whisper that you're not "spiritual enough" for the fire of God is a deception designed to keep you powerless. Demolish it. God is not a reluctant giver. He is a Father who delights in pouring out His Spirit on His children. There are no tiers of acceptance in His Kingdom, only an open invitation to all who are thirsty.

"On the last and greatest day of the festival, Jesus stood and said in a loud voice, 'Let anyone who is thirsty come to me and drink. Whoever believes in me, as Scripture has said, rivers of living water will flow from within them.' By this he meant the Spirit." , John 7:37-39 God is not holding back. The only thing stopping the flood is your hesitation to ask.

The Obstacle of Discouragement

When spiritual breakthrough doesn't come immediately, discouragement can tempt you to give up. Remember that the disciples waited and prayed for days before Pentecost came. Spiritual breakthrough often requires persistent seeking over time. Don't let the enemy convince you that God isn't hearing or responding to your prayers.

The Obstacle of Distraction

The moment you commit to intensely seeking God, expect a counter-attack. A conspiracy of the world, the flesh, and the devil will immediately unleash a storm of distractions to break your focus. Your phone will scream for attention, tasks you ignored will suddenly feel urgent, and your own body will rebel with exhaustion, restlessness, and sudden cravings. This is not a coincidence or bad timing; it is a calculated assault. See these interruptions for what they are: spiritual warfare designed to pull you from the very presence of God.

Therefore, you must become a warrior at the gate of your own heart. Refuse to surrender your sacred ground. The enemy fights you hardest when you draw near because he fears what is forged in that fire, the power, intimacy, and authority that dismantle his influence in your life. Let the world rage and the flesh complain. Anchor your focus, defend your communion with God, and hold the line.

The Obstacle of Fear

Many believers are secretly afraid of what might happen if they truly opened their hearts to God's transforming power. They fear losing control, being asked to do something uncomfortable, or experiencing something they don't understand. This fear keeps them from the very encounters they need most.

Remember that God is good and that He loves you more than you love yourself. He will never lead you into anything that is ultimately harmful or destructive. His fire purifies and empowers; it doesn't destroy what He wants to use for His glory.

Signs That Your Heart Is Opening

As you create conditions for divine encounter, you may notice several signs that your heart is becoming more open to God's transforming work:

Increased Spiritual Hunger

Instead of feeling satisfied with minimal spiritual input, you'll find yourself craving more time with God, more understanding of His Word, and more experience of His presence. This hunger is itself a gift from God and a sign that He's preparing you for greater things.

Heightened Spiritual Sensitivity

You'll become more aware of spiritual atmospheres, more sensitive to God's voice, and more discerning about spiritual matters. This increased sensitivity indicates that your spiritual eyes and ears are being opened.

Greater Boldness in Prayer

You'll find yourself praying with more confidence and specificity. Your prayers will become more passionate and expectant. You'll begin to ask God for things that previously seemed too bold or impossible.

Deeper Conviction of Sin

As God's holiness becomes more real to you, you'll become more aware of areas in your life that need cleansing. This isn't condemnation but preparation, God is preparing your heart to receive more of His presence by revealing what needs to be removed.

Supernatural Peace in Uncertainty

Even as you experience spiritual upheaval and change, you'll notice a deep peace that transcends your circumstances. This peace is evidence that God's Spirit is at work in your life, preparing you for greater things.

What to Expect

While every person's encounter with God's transforming fire is unique, certain common elements often characterize divine breakthrough:

A Sense of God's Overwhelming Presence

You may experience God's presence in ways that are almost tangible, feeling His love, sensing His power, or being aware of His glory in unprecedented ways. These encounters often leave you changed permanently.

Release from Spiritual Bondage

Areas of struggle, fear, or defeat that have plagued you for years may suddenly lose their power over you. The Spirit's fire burns away spiritual bondage and brings supernatural freedom.

Supernatural Boldness

Like Peter on Pentecost, you may discover a boldness to speak about spiritual things, pray for others, or take spiritual risks that previously would have terrified you. This boldness comes not from natural courage but from supernatural empowerment.

Increased Fruitfulness

Your prayers may become more effective, your witness more influential, and your service more fruitful. The Spirit's empowerment often manifests in increased effectiveness in kingdom work.

Fresh Joy and Peace

You may experience dimensions of joy and peace that transcend your circumstances. These are the fruits of the Spirit's deeper work in your heart.

Heightened Spiritual Awareness

You may receive dreams, visions, prophetic insights, or supernatural knowledge that helps you understand God's will more clearly. The Spirit often communicates with freshly opened hearts in supernatural ways.

The Ongoing Journey

Opening your heart to divine fire is not a one-time event but an ongoing lifestyle. The same principles that position you for initial breakthrough must continue to characterize your walk with God:

- Maintain your desperation for God even after experiencing His touch
- Continue in humility, knowing that you need fresh encounters regularly
- Keep surrendering new areas of your life as God reveals them
- Preserve your expectation that God wants to work powerfully through you
- Pursue unity with other believers who share your hunger for God's presence

Remember that God's desire to fill you with His Spirit exceeds your desire to be filled. He's more eager to transform you than you are to be transformed. He's waiting for hearts that are truly open, truly hungry, and truly surrendered to His will.

The fire is still falling. The same Spirit who transformed the disciples on Pentecost is hovering over your life today, waiting for you to create the conditions that invite His presence. Your heart can be a landing place for divine fire. Your life can be a demonstration of supernatural power.

Your ordinary existence can be transformed into an extraordinary ministry.

But it requires opening your heart completely, not just to God's comfort and blessing, but to His refining fire that burns away everything that hinders His purpose in your life.

Are you ready to pray with the psalmist, "Search me, O God, and know my heart; try me, and know my anxieties; and see if there is any wicked way in me, and lead me in the way everlasting" (Psalm 139:23-24)?

The divine fire that transformed Peter from denier to preacher that changed Paul from persecutor to apostle, and that turned fishermen into fishers of men is available to you today. Open your heart wide. Remove every barrier. Create sacred space. Seek with intensity. Expect with confidence.

Your Pentecost is coming. Your transformation from routine to alive is at hand. The divine fire is ready to fall. The question is: Is your heart ready to burn?

Living the Pentecost Life

The ultimate goal of experiencing personal Pentecost is not just to have a compelling spiritual encounter but to live continually in the reality of that encounter. The disciples didn't just experience the Spirit's filling on Pentecost and then return to business as usual. They were fundamentally transformed into people who lived supernatural lives powered by divine energy, guided by heavenly wisdom, and producing eternal fruit.

Living the Pentecost life means making the supernatural normal, the miraculous routine, and the eternal priority over the temporal. It's about learning to walk in the Spirit so consistently that supernatural living becomes your natural way of being. This doesn't mean living in emotional ecstasy all the time, but rather living in the conscious awareness that the God of the universe dwells within you and wants to express His life through you every day.

The Daily Reality of Spirit-Filled Living

The Pentecostal life is not primarily about dramatic supernatural experiences, though these may occur. It's about the daily reality of living in partnership with the Holy Spirit, allowing Him to guide your decisions, empower your service, and transform your character. This lifestyle has several key characteristics:

Constant Communion with God

Spirit-filled believers maintain ongoing dialogue with God throughout their day. This isn't just scheduled prayer times but continuous awareness of His presence and regular conversation with Him about everything from major decisions to minor details.

Paul instructed the Thessalonians to "pray without ceasing" (1 Thessalonians 5:17). This doesn't mean we walk around with our eyes closed and hands folded, but that we maintain spiritual awareness and communication with God as we go about our daily activities.

This constant communion allows the Spirit to guide us in real-time, warning us of dangers, providing wisdom for decisions, and prompting us to minister to others as opportunities arise.

Supernatural Sensitivity

Those living the Pentecost life develop heightened spiritual sensitivity. They become aware of spiritual atmospheres, discerning spiritual needs in others, and are responsive to divine promptings. They notice when the Spirit wants to work through them and are quick to cooperate with His leading.

This sensitivity enables them to be used by God in ways that seem coincidental to observers but are actually orchestrated by divine providence. They "happen" to meet someone who needs exactly what they can provide, they "sense" when someone needs prayer or encouragement, and they "know" things about people or situations that they couldn't know naturally.

Faith-Fueled Expectation

People living the Pentecostal life expect God to work supernaturally on a regular basis. They pray with confidence that God will answer. They step out in faith, believing that God will provide.

They minister to others, expecting that God will work through them to meet needs and transform lives.

This expectation isn't presumption or manipulation, but faith-filled anticipation based on God's promises and character.

They've learned that God delights to work through willing vessels and that He's more eager to move supernaturally than we are to experience His movement.

Kingdom Perspective

Those filled with the Spirit see everything through the lens of God's eternal kingdom rather than temporary earthly concerns. They make decisions based on eternal values rather than temporal benefits. They invest their time, energy, and resources in things that have lasting significance rather than things that will pass away.

This doesn't mean they're impractical or irresponsible about earthly matters, but that they prioritize heavenly concerns and trust God to take care of earthly needs as they seek first His kingdom and righteousness.

Love-Motivated Service

The Pentecost life is characterized by supernatural love that motivates sacrificial service. The same Spirit who is love dwelling within believers produces love for God and love for others that goes beyond natural human capacity.

This love compels them to serve others, share the Gospel, pray for the sick, encourage the discouraged, and invest in people's spiritual and physical well-being. It's not duty-driven religious activity but love-motivated ministry that flows naturally from the Spirit's presence within them.

Practical Guidelines for Daily Spirit-Filled Living

Living the Pentecost life requires intentional choices and practical disciplines that keep us aligned with the Spirit's leading:

Start Each Day with Intentional Surrender

Begin each morning by consciously yielding yourself to the Spirit's control.

Pray something like: "Holy Spirit, I surrender this day to Your will. Fill me afresh with Your presence and power.

Guide my steps, guard my words, and work through me to accomplish Your purposes today."

This daily surrender keeps you in position for the Spirit to work through you rather than trying to live the Christian life in your own strength.

Cultivate Listening Prayer

Develop the discipline of listening to prayer throughout your day. Ask the Spirit questions and wait for His guidance. "What do you want me to say to this person?" "How should I handle this situation?" "Where do you want me to focus my attention today?"

Learning to recognize the Spirit's voice takes practice, but He promises to guide us into all truth and will speak to those who learn to listen.

Step Out in Faith Regularly

Look for opportunities to exercise faith in small ways throughout your day. Pray for someone's headache. Ask God to provide a parking space. Trust Him for wisdom in a difficult conversation. These small steps of faith build your confidence and create opportunities for the Spirit to demonstrate His power.

Maintain Spiritual Alertness

Stay alert to spiritual opportunities around you. Notice when someone seems discouraged and needs encouragement. Be aware when the Spirit prompts you to pray for someone or share a word of encouragement. Watch for divine appointments that God orchestrates.

The Spirit is always working around us, but we often miss His activity because we're not paying attention. Spiritual alertness keeps us positioned to participate in what God is doing.

Practice the Presence of God

Throughout your day, remind yourself that God is with you. Talk to Him about what you're experiencing. Thank Him for His presence. Ask for His help with tasks and challenges. This practice keeps you conscious of His nearness and available to His leading.

Brother Lawrence called this "practicing the presence of God," and it transforms ordinary activities into opportunities for communion with the Divine.

Live Expectantly

Approach each day with the expectation that God will work supernaturally through you. Expect to see answers to prayer, divine appointments, opportunities for ministry, and demonstrations of God's power. This expectation positions you to recognize and participate in God's activity.

Common Challenges in Living the Pentecost Life

Maintaining a Spirit-filled lifestyle isn't always easy. Several common challenges can derail our attempts to live supernaturally:

The Pressure to Conform

Society pressures us to live "normal" lives that don't include supernatural expectations or spiritual priorities. Friends, family, and coworkers may not understand your commitment to Spirit-filled living and may subtly or overtly pressure you to tone down your spiritual intensity.

Resist this pressure by remembering that you're called to be in the world but not of the world. Your primary allegiance is to God's kingdom, not to human expectations or social conventions.

The Temptation to Rely on Natural Abilities

Because we live in physical bodies with natural abilities, it's easy to revert to self-reliance rather than Spirit-dependence. Success in natural endeavors can actually hinder spiritual growth if it makes us less dependent on God's power.

Combat this by consciously acknowledging your need for the Spirit's help even in areas where you're naturally gifted. Ask for His wisdom, power, and guidance in everything you do.

Discouragement from Unanswered Prayer

When prayers aren't answered the way you expect or when you don't see the supernatural results you're believing for, discouragement can tempt you to lower your expectations and revert to more "realistic" Christianity.

Remember that God's ways are higher than our ways and His timing is perfect. Continue praying and believing while trusting His wisdom about when and how to answer your prayers.

The Danger of Spiritual Pride

As you begin to see God work through you in supernatural ways, pride can subtly creep in, making you feel spiritually superior to other believers or taking credit for what God has done through you.

Combat pride by remembering that any spiritual fruit in your life is solely the result of God's grace and power working through you. Stay humble, give God all the credit, and remember that apart from Him you can do nothing.

Maintaining Balance

Some people swing from spiritual deadness to spiritual extremism, becoming so "spiritually minded" that they're no earthly good. The Pentecost life is balanced, supernatural yet practical, spiritual yet sensible, faith-filled yet responsible.

Jesus modeled this balance perfectly.

He was completely filled with the Spirit and operated in tremendous supernatural power, yet He also worked as a carpenter, paid taxes, and maintained healthy human relationships.

The Fruit of the Pentecost Life

When believers consistently live in the power of the Spirit, several kinds of fruit naturally result:

1 Personal Transformation

You'll experience ongoing character change as the Spirit produces His fruit in your life. Areas of struggle and defeat will be replaced by victory and growth. Your thoughts, attitudes, and behaviors will increasingly reflect the nature of Christ.

2 Effective Ministry

Whether you're in professional ministry or serving as a lay believer, your ministry will become more effective as the Spirit works through you. People will be drawn to Christ through your witness, encouraged by your prayers, and helped by your service.

3 Supernatural Provision

As you prioritize God's kingdom and trust Him for your needs, you'll experience supernatural provision that goes beyond what you could arrange through natural means. This doesn't mean you'll become wealthy, but that God will meet your needs in often surprising ways.

4 Spiritual Fruitfulness

Your prayers will become more effective, your faith will grow stronger, and your spiritual discernment will become more accurate. You'll see God working in and through your life in ways that clearly demonstrate His supernatural power.

5 Joy and Peace in Difficulty

Even when facing challenges and trials, you'll experience supernatural joy and peace that transcends your circumstances. The Spirit's presence within you will provide stability and strength that enables you to rejoice in difficult times.

6 The Long-term Vision

Living the Pentecost life isn't just about personal blessing or even personal transformation. It's about participating in God's plan to demonstrate His kingdom to the world and prepare for Christ's return. Every Spirit-filled believer is part of a worldwide movement of God that began on Pentecost and will continue until Jesus comes again.

Your supernatural life becomes part of God's testimony to a lost world that He is real, that He loves them, and that He offers them salvation and transformation. Your prayers contribute to the advancement of God's kingdom around the world. Your faithfulness in living the Spirit-filled life helps prepare the Church for whatever challenges and opportunities lie ahead.

7 Making the Commitment

Living the Pentecost life requires a fundamental commitment to prioritize spiritual reality over natural circumstances, eternal values over temporal concerns, and God's will over personal preferences. It's not a lifestyle that you can maintain through willpower or good intentions; it requires daily dependence on the Spirit's power and guidance.

Are you ready to make this commitment? Are you willing to live as a supernatural being in a natural world? Are you prepared to trust the Spirit to guide you, empower you, and work through you in ways that may stretch your faith and challenge your comfort zone?

The same Spirit who fell on Pentecost is available to fill you and live through you every day. The same power that transformed fishermen into apostles can transform your ordinary life into an extraordinary ministry. The same presence that turned the world upside down through the early Church wants to turn your world right-side up through your Spirit-filled living.

Your Pentecost life is waiting. The fire is ready to fall afresh. The Spirit is ready to work through you in supernatural ways. The question is: Are you ready to live the life you were truly born again to live?

The time for routine Christianity is over. The time for supernatural living is now. Step into your Pentecost life today.

Your Personal Pentecost

As we reach the end of this journey through the transformative power of Pentecost, we stand at a crossroads. You now understand what happened in that upper room two thousand years ago.

You've seen how it launched the greatest spiritual revolution in human history. You've examined why it matters for every believer today and how it can transform your faith from routine to alive. The question that remains is the most important one of all: What will you do with this knowledge?

The disciples in the upper room faced a similar moment of decision. They had spent three and a half years with Jesus, witnessed His death and resurrection, and received His promise of the coming Holy Spirit. But they still had to choose whether to wait expectantly for that promise or return to their old lives. They had to decide whether to position themselves for transformation or settle for the familiar.

You face the same choice today.

The Reality of Your Moment

Right now, as you read these words, the same Spirit who fell on Pentecost is present with you. He's not waiting in some distant heaven for you to become more spiritual or more worthy. He's here, ready to fill you, empower you, and transform you from the inside out. The only question is whether you're ready to receive Him.

Many people will read about Pentecost, be inspired by the stories of transformation, and then close the book and return to their routine Christian lives. They'll file this information away as interesting biblical history or inspiring spiritual content, but they won't position themselves to experience their own personal Pentecost.

Don't let that be your story.

The God who moved powerfully in biblical times hasn't changed. The Spirit who transformed cowards into champions hasn't diminished in power. The fire that fell on that first group of believers is still burning, still available, still ready to consume everything in your life that is merely a religious form without spiritual power.

Your Personal Invitation

This book is more than information; it's an invitation. You're invited to experience your own upper room encounter. You're invited to move beyond the safety of routine religion into the dangerous, exhilarating territory of authentic spiritual life. You're invited to discover what it means to live not just for God, but from God, filled with His Spirit, empowered by His presence, and used for His purposes in supernatural ways.

Your invitation includes:

- Freedom from spiritual deadness that masquerades as Christian maturity
- Power to live the victorious Christian life you've read about but haven't experienced
- Boldness to share your faith and see people drawn to Christ through your witness
- Supernatural wisdom and discernment that guides you in every decision
- Divine love that enables you to serve others with joy and sacrifice
- Miraculous provision that demonstrates God's faithfulness in practical ways
- Spiritual gifts that allow you to minister to others in supernatural power
- Joy and peace that transcend your circumstances and radiate God's presence

But invitations require responses. The most beautifully written invitation is meaningless unless someone accepts it and acts upon it.

What Your Response Looks Like

If you're ready to accept this invitation to your personal Pentecost, here's what your response should include:

Honest Assessment

Begin by honestly assessing your current spiritual condition. Are you living in the fullness of God's Spirit, or have you settled for something less? Are you experiencing the abundant life Jesus promised, or are you surviving on spiritual maintenance mode?

Don't be discouraged if your honest assessment reveals spiritual deadness or mediocrity. Recognition of need is the first step toward transformation. The disciples themselves were far from perfect when the Spirit fell on them. God specializes in using ordinary, flawed people who recognize their need for His power.

Sincere Repentance

Repentance isn't just about feeling sorry for your sins; it's about turning away from everything that has kept you from experiencing God's fullness. This might include:

- Religious pride that keeps you from admitting your need for more of God
- Comfort with spiritual mediocrity that prevents you from seeking transformation
- Fear of the supernatural that closes your heart to divine encounters
- Unforgiveness that creates barriers to God's presence in your life
- Compromise with worldly values that dilutes your spiritual sensitivity
- Busyness that crowds out time for intensive spiritual seeking

Desperate Hunger

Cultivate a holy dissatisfaction with your current spiritual condition.

Become desperate for more of God. The lukewarm will never experience the fire of God because they're content with tepid spiritual temperatures.

Ask God to give you a hunger that won't be satisfied with anything less than His presence and power. Pray for a spiritual appetite that craves intimate fellowship with Him and supernatural empowerment for service.

Complete Surrender

The Spirit fills vessels that are completely emptied of self. This means surrendering every area of your life to God's control, your relationships, career, finances, dreams, fears, and failures. It means saying with Jesus, "Not my will, but Yours be done."

This surrender isn't a one-time event but a daily posture of the heart. Each morning, yield yourself afresh to the Spirit's control and ask Him to live His life through you.

Expectant Faith

Approach God with a confident expectation that He wants to fill you with His Spirit. Base your faith not on your feelings or circumstances but on His promises. He has clearly stated that He gives His Spirit to those who ask Him.

Expect God to work supernaturally in your life. Expect to see answers to prayer, divine appointments, and demonstrations of His power. Your expectation creates an atmosphere that invites divine intervention.

Persistent Seeking

Don't give up if your breakthrough doesn't come immediately. The disciples waited and prayed for days before Pentecost came. Some spiritual battles require persistent pressing through until victory comes.

Set aside extended time for prayer, fasting, and seeking God. Create sacred space in your life for intensive spiritual pursuit. Join with other hungry believers who share your desire for more of God.

Immediate Obedience

When the Spirit begins to move in your life, respond with immediate obedience. Don't wait until you fully understand what's happening or feel completely ready. Step out in faith and allow the Spirit to work through you.

This might mean praying for someone who needs healing, sharing your faith with a coworker, speaking an encouraging word to someone who's discouraged, or simply obeying a divine prompting that seems unusual or challenging.

The Promise and the Process

Your personal Pentecost is both a promise and a process. The promise is that God wants to fill you with His Spirit more than you want to be filled. The process is learning to live daily in the reality of that filling.

Some people experience dramatic, instantaneous transformation that parallels the biblical account of Pentecost. Others experience more gradual filling as they consistently position themselves to receive more of God. Don't get caught up in comparing your experience to others or demanding that God work in a particular way.

The important thing is not how the Spirit fills you but that He fills you. Focus on the reality of spiritual transformation rather than the methodology of spiritual experience.

Your New Life Begins Now

Your personal Pentecost isn't just about having a deep spiritual experience; it's about beginning a new way of living. It's about moving from routine to alive, from ordinary to extraordinary, from natural to supernatural.

This new life will include:

- Daily awareness of God's presence and partnership with His Spirit
- Regular experiences of supernatural wisdom, power, and provision

- Ongoing transformation of your character to reflect Christ's nature
- Increasing effectiveness in ministry as the Spirit works through you
- Growing boldness to share your faith and trust God for impossible things
- Deepening intimacy with God that makes His presence more real than your circumstances

The Ripple Effect

Your personal Pentecost won't just transform you; it will create ripples of transformation that touch everyone around you. Your family will encounter God through your transformed life. Your coworkers will see authentic Christianity in action. Your friends will witness the reality of God's power demonstrated in practical ways.

You'll become part of what God is doing in your generation to demonstrate His reality to a world that desperately needs to encounter the living God. Your transformation contributes to the advancement of God's kingdom and the preparation of the Church for whatever lies ahead.

CHAPTER 4:
The Time Is Now

Do you feel it? The tremors running through the foundations of the world? Do not be numb to this moment. Do not be distracted by the noise. We are standing at the most critical juncture in human history, a convergence of unprecedented peril and unprecedented opportunity. The thin veneer of civilization is cracking, revealing a darkness and a delusion that human reason cannot explain, and human effort cannot fix. The spirit of the age is one of chaos, confusion, and a deep, gnawing despair that has left humanity staggering in the dark. This is the hour when the powers of hell are making their boldest advance, and it is a moment that demands a Church that is more than a social club, more than a moral institution, more than a Sunday morning tradition.

This is no time for a safe, manicured, business-as-usual faith. Anemic Christianity is an offense to the cross and utterly useless in this fight. The challenges we face will not bow to clever marketing, slick productions, or eloquent sermons that lack fire. They will only shatter and flee before the raw, untamed, supernatural power of the living God, demonstrated through His people. The Church was never meant to be a lion in a cage, pacified by comfort, and sedated by compromise. It was born in a blaze of Pentecostal fire to be a conquering, advancing, demon-stomping army. We do not need more members on a roster; we need an army of fire-baptized believers who walk in the crushing authority of the name of Jesus and live lives that are a living, breathing spectacle of the Gospel's reality.

This divine appointment is for you. Your generation has been chosen for such a time as this. You stand on the precipice of the Spiritual outpouring that has the potential to eclipse anything the world has ever witnessed, even the glories of the early Church. Do not doubt this! The same Holy Spirit who tore through that Upper Room, turning a handful of frightened fishermen into apostolic giants who turned the world upside down, is not a relic of history. He is a roaring fire, a rushing, violent wind, straining at the leash, waiting to be unleashed again, but this time with a global scope and a glorious fury that will shake the very foundations of nations.

He is scanning the earth, right now. His eyes are not searching for the perfect, the polished, or the religiously accomplished. He is looking for yielded vessels. He is searching for believers like you, who have come to the end of themselves, who are desperately hungry for the authentic, who are utterly broken over their own powerlessness, and who are willing to be completely consumed by His glory and completely used for His purposes, no matter the cost.

Your Prayer of Response.

If your heart is burning with a holy dissatisfaction for the ordinary, if the very idea of a powerless faith makes you sick, then this moment is your altar. The following is not just a prayer to be recited; it is a declaration of war on complacency, a covenant of surrender, a violent cry of faith that heaven will honor. Pray this from the depths of your soul, with an expectation that the God of fire will answer with fire. If you're ready to experience your personal Pentecost, pray this prayer with sincere faith:

"Heavenly Father, my eyes are open. I see it now with painful clarity. I have been living in the shallow end of a vast spiritual ocean, content with a fraction of the glorious inheritance You shed Your blood to give me. I confess my desperate, aching need for more of Your Spirit in my life. I repent, I turn my back on it all, my spiritual complacency, my dead religious routines, my fear of man, my love of comfort, and every compromise that has kept me from the holy inferno of Your fullness.

Today, the war within me ends. I surrender. I raise the white flag to Your will and Your ways. I surrender every single area of my life to Your absolute and total control. My plans, my ambitions, my relationships, my future, they are all Yours. Use me however You want. Change whatever You must. I humble myself, and fill me with Your Holy Spirit just as You filled the disciples on Pentecost. I am holding nothing back.

I am done with doubt. I cast it down. I fully and completely expect You to work supernaturally in my life, starting at this very moment. I am ready to step out in radical faith and become a conduit for Your untamed power. Make me a vessel of Your tangible presence, a weapon of Your power, a voice for Your truth in this generation.

Lord, fill me now. I am empty, and I am waiting. Transform me from routine to revival. Let Your fire fall fresh on my life. In the mighty, matchless name of Jesus, Amen."

Your New Beginning

The moment sincere faith met those words, a divine transaction was sealed in the courts of heaven. You have crossed a spiritual threshold from which there is no return. Your personal Pentecost, your own private Upper Room experience, has just begun. The same Spirit who shattered the chains of fear in the disciples, who unloosed their tongues with a heavenly language, who emboldened them to preach in the face of persecution, is now flooding the deepest recesses of your being. He is not just a guest; He is the new owner. He is not just visiting; He is taking up permanent residence to begin a divine renovation, empowering you and preparing to unleash His power through you in ways that will leave you absolutely breathless.

This is not the end of a prayer. This is the cataclysmic beginning of the greatest adventure of your life. You are now positioned to seize the abundant, overflowing life Jesus promised, a life that is not merely endured but distinctly lived. You are being commissioned to operate in the same supernatural ministry He modeled and to become a revolutionary in the spiritual awakening He launched on Pentecost.

The fire has fallen. The Spirit has come. Your transformation from routine to revival has begun.

Now, you must walk worthy of this holy calling. Live in the staggering, awe-inspiring power of your inheritance. Guard the flame. Fuel it with prayer. Feed it with the Word. Become a living, breathing demonstration of the reality of your God to a world that is starving for something real. Your personal Pentecost is no longer a distant dream or a theological concept, it is your new, burning, all-consuming reality.

Welcome to the supernatural life. Welcome to authentic, untamed Christianity. Welcome to the adventure that will cost you everything and give you more than you could ever imagine.

The world is waiting.

Heaven is watching.

What will God do through your Spirit-filled life?

II

Lessons From The Church Through History

The deepest answer to prayer isn't what we receive, it's who we find when we stop demanding and start desiring

Will You Be the Next Chapter or Just Another Reader?

The blood-stained pages of church history tell a story that will either ignite your faith or expose the poverty of your spiritual expectations. For two millennia, ordinary men and women have encountered the same fire that fell on Pentecost, and their lives have become blazing testimonies to the unchanging power of God. Their stories are not dusty relics from a bygone era, they are burning coals that can set your heart ablaze with possibility.

In the catacombs beneath Rome, believers chose death over denial, singing hymns as lions tore their flesh because the Spirit within them was stronger than the fear around them. In medieval monasteries, monks experienced visions of Christ so real that they bore physical marks of His crucifixion. In reformation fires, ordinary priests discovered ardent truths they split nations and changed the course of history. In frontier camp meetings, hardened pioneers fell on their faces as God's presence swept through crowds like wind through wheat fields.

Each generation thought they were living in ordinary times. Each group of believers assumed the age of miracles had passed. Yet again and again, heaven broke through, shattering their assumptions and demonstrating that the God of Pentecost had not retired, had not grown weary, had not decided that supernatural power was only for the apostolic age.

But here is what will either comfort or convict you: none of these world-changers began as spiritual giants. They were farmers and housewives, merchants and students, clergy and laypeople who shared one common characteristic, they refused to accept spiritual mediocrity as normal. They created atmospheres of desperate hunger for God that invited heaven's invasion of earth. They positioned themselves for encounters that transformed not only their lives but the trajectory of entire civilizations.

The Welsh coal miner Evan Roberts was just an ordinary young man until he cried out, "Lord, bend me!"

The resulting revival swept through Wales like wildfire, closing taverns and emptying jails as entire communities were transformed by God's presence. D.L. Moody was a poorly educated shoe salesman until two women began praying for him to be filled with the Spirit, the encounter that followed turned him into the most effective evangelist of his generation. Maria Woodworth-Etter was a simple farmwoman until she yielded to God's call, becoming a vessel through which thousands experienced divine healing and supernatural manifestations of God's power.

These were not exceptional people living in exceptional times. They were ordinary believers who discovered what happens when human desperation meets divine power, when earthly hunger encounters heavenly fire, when finite beings make themselves completely available to an infinite God.

Their testimonies form an unbroken chain of evidence that spans centuries, crosses denominations, and transcends cultures. From the desert fathers to the Moravian missionaries, from the Great Awakening to the Azusa Street Revival, from the healing evangelists of the twentieth century to the church planters transforming nations today, the pattern remains consistent. When believers create conditions of surrender, hunger, and expectation, God responds with demonstrations of power that leave no doubt about His reality and availability.

Yet these same historical accounts reveal a sobering truth that should shake every comfortable Christian to the core: for every believer who experienced their personal Pentecost, countless others remained content with religious routine. For every church that hosted a revival, dozens settled for programs without power. For every generation that experienced spiritual awakening, others lived and died without ever tasting the supernatural life that was their inheritance.

The tragedy is not that God was unwilling to move, history proves He was always ready to pour out His Spirit. The tragedy is that so many believers were unwilling to pay the price of desperation, surrender, and faith required to receive what He offered. They chose the safety of spiritual mediocrity over the risk of supernatural encounter. They preferred the predictability of religious routine over the adventure of an authentic relationship with the living God.

This is why these historical accounts matter for our lives today. They are not just inspiring stories from the past, they are prophetic blueprints for the future. They reveal that the same Spirit who transformed Augustine in his garden, Luther in his cell, Wesley at Aldersgate, and Finney in his law office is available to transform us in our circumstances today.

The fire that ignited the early church fathers still burns. The power that sustained martyrs through persecution still strengthens. The presence that overwhelmed revivalists still fills. The same God who split history into before and after Christ, who scattered the apostles to the ends of the earth, who preserved His people through dark ages and ignited them in great awakenings, is hovering over your life right now.

History's greatest lesson is this: every generation has access to the same power, but not every believer chooses to receive it. The question these testimonies pose to us is not whether God can work as effectively powerfully today as He did in centuries past, the evidence overwhelmingly proves He can. The question is whether we will create the conditions in our lives that invite His supernatural intervention, or whether we will settle for reading about others' encounters while remaining content with spiritual normalcy.

The same fire that has burned through twenty centuries of church history is waiting to consume our hearts. Will you be the next chapter in this glorious story of divine power demonstrated through yielded vessels?

3. PRAYER THAT CHANGES THE WORLD

The Moravians' Century of Prayer and the Modern Movements They Inspired

In the annals of church history, there are moments when heaven and earth seem to touch, when the prayers of ordinary believers create extraordinary results that reshape the spiritual landscape of entire generations. One such moment began on August 13, 1727, in a small German village called Herrnhut. There, a group of persecuted refugees from Moravia, welcomed onto the estate of Count Nicolaus von Zinzendorf, found themselves united in an unprecedented spiritual awakening. These men and women, weary from persecution and displacement, turned their desperation into determination. What began that summer was not a fleeting burst of devotion but the birth of something the world had never seen: a rhythm of continuous, unbroken prayer that would last for more than one hundred years.

Day and night, around the clock, believers took turns in prayer, ensuring that the flame on the altar never went out. Their prayers were not vague or casual; they were fervent cries for God's kingdom to come, for the nations to be reached with the gospel, and for revival to break out wherever the Spirit pleased. This century-long prayer watch became the heartbeat of a missionary movement that would send Moravian believers to the farthest corners of the globe.

Ordinary tradesmen, farmers, and women who had never traveled beyond their villages willingly boarded ships for distant lands. Some even sold themselves into slavery to reach those who otherwise would never hear the name of Jesus.

The ripple effects of Herrnhut's prayer movement were staggering. The Moravians influenced leaders like John Wesley, whose encounter with their steadfast faith helped ignite the Methodist revival that swept across England and America. Through their prayers and sacrificial service, the Moravians helped fan revival fires on multiple continents, demonstrating that persistent, unified intercession can literally alter the trajectory of history.

Yet this is far more than a fascinating episode from the past. The same Spirit who empowered the Moravians is still at work today. Around the world, modern believers are rediscovering the principles that sustained Herrnhut's prayer watch. Prayer rooms that never close, such as the International House of Prayer in Kansas City, have carried forward the torch of day-and-night intercession. Movements like 24-7 Prayer have created global networks of believers committed to unceasing prayer for revival, justice, and mission. Even online platforms now connect intercessors across continents, covering the earth in prayer at every hour of the day. The story of the Moravians reminds us that prayer is not passive. It is world-changing. It does not merely shape individual lives, it transforms families, churches, nations, and generations. What God did in Herrnhut, He longs to do again in our day through communities willing to give themselves wholly to the place of prayer.

CHAPTER 1:
The Birth Of A Prayer Movement

The Impossible Beginning

The story of the Moravian prayer movement begins in what seemed like an impossible situation. Count Nikolaus Ludwig von Zinzendorf, a twenty-two-year-old German nobleman, offered sanctuary on his estate to a group of persecuted Christians fleeing from Moravia (modern-day Czech Republic). These believers, spiritual descendants of the martyred reformer Jan Hus, had endured centuries of religious oppression and were desperately seeking a place where they could worship freely.

By 1727, over three hundred refugees had settled in Herrnhut ("the Lord's Watch"), but what should have been a haven of Christian fellowship had become a cauldron of conflict. Different theological traditions clashed, personalities feuded, and the community teetered on the brink of dissolution. Zinzendorf watched in dismay as the very people he had sought to help seemed unable to love one another, let alone impact the world for Christ.

The crisis came to a head in the summer of 1727. Zinzendorf called the community together and challenged them with words that would echo through the centuries: "We must learn to love one another, or we will destroy what God has given us." He proposed a radical solution, they would commit to seeking God together until He either healed their divisions or made His will clear about their future. What followed was a period of intensive prayer, confession, and reconciliation that culminated on August 13, 1727, during a communion service that participants would later describe as their "Pentecost." The presence of God fell so intensely upon the gathered believers that old animosities melted away, theological disputes were resolved in love, and the entire community was united in a way that seemed humanly impossible.

Christian David, one of the community's leaders, wrote: "We hardly knew whether we were in heaven or on earth. We spent the whole night in prayer and singing, and the Holy Spirit came upon us in such a manner that we could do nothing but weep for joy." The transformation was so complete and so obviously supernatural that no one who witnessed it could doubt that God Himself had intervened.

The Covenant That Changed History

But the real miracle was what happened next. Inspired by their encounter with God's presence, twenty-four men and twenty-four women made a covenant that would alter the course of Christian history. They committed themselves to maintaining continuous prayer, twenty-four hours a day, seven days a week, with each person taking responsibility for one hour. They called it "the Hourly Intercession," and it began on August 27, 1727.

None of them imagined that their prayer covenant would continue unbroken for over one hundred years. They thought they were making a temporary commitment to seek God through their immediate crisis. Instead, they were launching the longest recorded prayer meeting in Christian history and setting in motion spiritual forces that would transform the world.

The covenant they signed was simple but profound:

"Dear Savior, do Thou in Thy mercy help us all to come closer to Thee and to love Thee with all our hearts. Grant that we might be united in Thee and that nothing may separate us from Thy love. Let the fire of Thy love burn in our hearts and shine forth in our words and actions, so that others may see and be drawn to Thee."

What made this covenant extraordinary was not just its duration but its scope. The Moravians didn't pray only for their own community or even their own needs. From the beginning, their prayers encompassed the entire world. They prayed for unreached peoples they had never met, for countries they could barely locate on a map, and for the advancement of God's kingdom to the ends of the earth.

The Immediate Results

The effects of continuous prayer were immediate and undeniable. Within weeks of beginning the hourly intercession, the Herrnhut community was transformed. Visitors reported an atmosphere of love, joy, and spiritual power unlike anything they had experienced elsewhere. Believers were spontaneously reconciled with enemies, confessions of sin became commonplace, and a spirit of sacrificial service permeated the community.

More remarkably, reports began coming from surrounding villages of spontaneous revivals. People who had never visited Herrnhut were experiencing spiritual awakenings. Entire communities were being transformed as the prayers of the Moravians seemed to create spiritual breakthroughs far beyond their physical location.

Within two years of beginning the prayer vigil, the first Moravian missionaries were departing for the West Indies to minister to slaves in conditions so dangerous that they were selling themselves into slavery to reach the unreached. By 1760, the Moravians had sent out more missionaries per capita than any other Christian group in history, establishing what many consider to be the first truly global missions' movement.

The connection between their continuous prayer and unprecedented missionary fruitfulness was not coincidental. The same hours spent in intercession for unreached peoples created both the spiritual passion and the supernatural provision necessary to send and sustain missionaries in the most challenging fields on earth.

The Prayer Warriors Behind the Movement

While Count Zinzendorf provided leadership and vision, the prayer movement was sustained by ordinary believers whose names are largely forgotten by history but are undoubtedly remembered in heaven. These were farmers and craftsmen, mothers, and children, young and old, who understood that their hour of prayer each day was not a religious duty but a sacred responsibility to hold up the arms of those advancing God's kingdom worldwide.

Anna Nitschmann, a young woman who would later become a missionary leader, wrote in her diary:

"My hour of prayer has become the anchor of my day. Everything else I do flows from those sixty minutes when I remember that I am not just Anna from Herrnhut, but a warrior in God's army, fighting battles I cannot see for victories that will last forever."

Christian David, the carpenter who had led many of the refugees to Herrnhut, transformed his workshop into a place of prayer. He would rise before dawn to spend extra time interceding for the missionaries whose names were posted on his wall. His prayers were so fervent and specific that visitors often found him weeping over letters from distant mission fields, pleading with God for breakthrough in places he would never see.

Maria Spangenberg developed what she called "praying the map." During her prayer hour, she would spread out a world map and place her hands on different regions, asking God to reveal His heart for unreached peoples and then praying with holy boldness for spiritual breakthrough in those places. Her prayers were often followed by reports of unusual spiritual activity in the exact regions she had been interceding for.

The Generational Vision

What sustained the Moravian prayer movement for over a century was their understanding that prayer was not just about their immediate needs but about God's eternal purposes. They viewed themselves as part of a generational relay race, passing the baton of intercession from parent to child, ensuring that the prayers would continue long after the original participants had gone to heaven.

Children were taught from infancy that prayer was the most important work they could do. Families would gather each evening to pray for specific missionary families by name, for unreached people groups, and for spiritual awakening in their own community. These prayer times were not dutiful religious exercises but passionate encounters with the living God that shaped the children's worldview and priorities.

Johann Nitschmann, writing to his son who was preparing for missionary service, captured the heart of this generational vision:

"Remember, my son that you are not just going to the Caribbean islands as Johann Nitschmann. You go as the answer to ten thousand prayers prayed by believers who will never see those shores. You carry with you the intercessions of your mother, your grandparents, and believers whose names you do not even know. Your ministry is not your work alone, it is the fruit of our community's prayers made visible."

This understanding created a sense of sacred responsibility that kept the prayer movement alive through changes in leadership, persecution, economic hardship, and the natural human tendency toward spiritual complacency. Each generation understood that they were stewards of something far greater than their own spiritual experience, they were maintaining a prayer covering that was enabling God's kingdom to advance worldwide.

CHAPTER 2:
The Supernatural Results

Missionaries to the Ends of the Earth

The most visible fruit of the Moravian prayer movement was the unprecedented missionary expansion that followed. Between 1732 and 1760, the small community of Herrnhut sent out more missionaries than all of Protestant Christianity had sent in the previous two centuries combined. These were not professional ministers or trained theologians, but ordinary believers who had been so transformed by their community's prayer life that they were willing to go anywhere and do anything to reach the unreached.

The stories of these early Moravian missionaries read like chapters from the book of Acts. Leonard Dober and David Nitschmann sold themselves into slavery to reach slaves in the West Indies who were forbidden to hear the Gospel from free men. When they arrived in St. Thomas in 1732, they found slaves so brutalized by their conditions that many had given up hope of any salvation, earthly or eternal.

But the prayers of Herrnhut had gone before them. Within months, spontaneous revivals were breaking out among the slave populations. Masters who had forbidden Gospel preaching were mysteriously changing their policies. Slaves who had never heard of Jesus were having supernatural dreams that prepared their hearts for the missionaries' message.

Anna, a slave woman in St. John, described her conversion: "For three nights I dreamed of white men who spoke of a God who loved even slaves. I did not understand the dreams, but my heart burned within me. When the Moravian brothers came to our plantation, I knew immediately that they were the men from my dreams. Before they could speak, I fell on my knees and begged them to tell me about this God who loved me."

The Moravian missionaries to the West Indies saw over 13,000 slaves converted in the first thirty to fifty years of their work. But the breakthrough came not through their preaching abilities or missionary strategies, but through the prayers that had been lifted up for those slaves by name in Herrnhut for years before the missionaries ever arrived.

Greenland: Impossible Made Possible

Perhaps the most dramatic example of prayer-powered missions was the Moravian work in Greenland. In 1733, a group of Moravians felt called to minister to the Inuit people of Greenland, despite warnings that the climate was so harsh that survival was nearly impossible for Europeans.

Hans Egede, a Danish missionary who had labored in Greenland for ten years with minimal results, was discouraging about the prospects. "The people are unreachable," he told the Moravians. "They have no concept of sin, no understanding of eternal judgment, and no interest in spiritual matters. I have preached to them for a decade and have perhaps three genuine converts."

But the Moravians had been praying for the Inuit people specifically since 1730. They had received what they believed were prophetic insights about God's heart for the Arctic peoples and were convinced that a breakthrough was imminent. Three young men, Christian David (not the carpenter, but a younger man with the same name), Matthias Stach, and Christian Stach, volunteered for what everyone assumed would be a suicide mission.

The transformation that followed was so dramatic that even skeptical observers had to acknowledge supernatural intervention. The same Inuit people who had been resistant to Egede's ministry for ten years began experiencing mass conversions within months of the Moravians' arrival. Entire villages would gather to hear the Gospel, often weeping with conviction before the missionaries had finished their first sermon.

Kajarnak, an Inuit shaman who had opposed Egede's work, became one of the most mighty evangelists among his people after his conversion. He later wrote: "When the new white men came, it was different.

Before they spoke, something in my heart was already listening. Before they explained sin, I was already feeling guilt I had never felt. Before they told me about Jesus, I was already hungry for something I could not name. Later, I learned that believers far away had been praying for me by name for three years before I met them."

The Great Awakening Connection

The influence of Moravian prayer extended far beyond their own missionary efforts. When Count Zinzendorf visited America in the 1740s, he brought with him the spiritual atmosphere that had been cultivated by decades of continuous prayer. His meetings with other Christian leaders, including John Wesley and George Whitefield, created connections that would fuel the Great Awakening.

John Wesley's famous Aldersgate experience, where he felt his heart "strangely warmed" while listening to a reading of Luther's commentary on Romans, occurred at a Moravian meeting in London. Wesley later wrote that the faith he encountered among the Moravians was unlike anything he had experienced in the Anglican Church. "They pray as if God is listening," he observed. "They believe miracles are normal. They live as if heaven is already breaking into earth."

The prayers of Herrnhut had created a spiritual hunger that was contagious. Everywhere Moravians went, they carried with them an expectation for God's supernatural intervention that sparked revival fires in other communities. Their century of prayer had not only powered their own ministry but had created a spiritual atmosphere that made revival possible across denominational and geographic boundaries.

George Whitefield testified that some of his most influential preaching occurred immediately after spending time with Moravian communities. "Their prayers have done something to the spiritual atmosphere," he wrote to a friend. "When I preach after being with them, it is as if the sky is already open, and heaven is ready to fall."

Transformation of European Christianity

The ripple effects of the Moravian prayer movement extended throughout European Christianity. The testimonies of their missionaries, combined with the obvious spiritual power that accompanied their communities, challenged the religious formalism that had settled over much of European Protestantism.

Pietist movements across Germany and Scandinavia began adopting Moravian prayer practices. Prayer societies formed in major cities often meet in homes to intercede for missions and revival. The University of Halle became a center for mission training, largely influenced by the Moravian model of combining intensive prayer with practical preparation for cross-cultural ministry.

In England, the Moravian influence contributed to the formation of the first Protestant missionary societies. William Carey, often called the "father of modern missions," was deeply influenced by accounts of Moravian missionary work. His famous pamphlet "An Enquiry into the Obligations of Christians to Use Means for the Conversion of the Heathens" included extensive references to the success of Moravian missions and attributed their effectiveness to their sustained commitment to prayer.

The Moravian example also influenced the development of what would later be called "faith missions", missionary societies that depended on prayer and faith for financial support rather than guaranteed denominational funding. George Müller's work with orphans in Bristol, Hudson Taylor's China Inland Mission, and numerous other faith-based ministries traced their founding principles to the Moravian model of trusting God to provide through the prayers of His people.

The Invisible but Measurable Impact

While the visible statistics of the Moravian prayer movement, the number of missionaries, the continents reached, the churches planted, are staggering enough to silence any critic, they are merely the shadows cast by a far greater, unseen reality. The true, earth-shattering legacy of that 100-year prayer meeting was not forged in the physical world, but in the spiritual realm. Its most profound impact was invisible, the seismic shifting of spiritual atmospheres, the demolition of ancient demonic strongholds, and the radical transformation of hearts and regions that can only be attributed to the relentless, sustained power of intercession.

This was not polite, passive prayer. This was warfare. The intercessors of Herrnhut were a spiritual artillery unit, bombarding enemy-held territory from thousands of miles away. Their missionaries, then, were not the initial invasion force; they were the ground troops sent in to occupy territory where the primary spiritual battles had already been won. Time and again, their letters home told the same astonishing story: the most hardened, hostile, and spiritually desolate fields on earth would suddenly, inexplicably, begin to soften. Nations and tribes steeped in centuries of witchcraft, idolatry, and brutal tradition would become inexplicably hungry for the Gospel, their spiritual soil plowed and prepared by a force they could not see. The missionaries were consistently stepping into the aftermath of a victory that had been secured years, sometimes decades, earlier in a humble prayer room in Germany.

This is not spiritual fantasy or wishful thinking. The divine fingerprints are all over the historical and statistical data. When analysts and historians have examined the missionary work of the 18th and 19th centuries, a pattern emerges that is so clear, so undeniable, it defies all natural explanation. Regions that had been specifically named, targeted, and saturated in prayer by the Moravian intercessors experienced Gospel breakthrough at rates that obliterate statistical probability. We are talking about spiritual strongholds that had resisted every previous attempt at Gospel penetration for centuries, places where missionaries had been martyred or driven out, suddenly becoming fields of miraculous harvest. And in many cases, this spiritual awakening would begin before the missionaries had even set foot on the soil, a divine calling card announcing that God had already answered the prayers of His people.

The renowned church historian, Dr. Kenneth Scott Latourette, a man not given to hyperbole, was forced by the sheer weight of the evidence to abandon any purely natural explanation. After his exhaustive research, he concluded with academic certainty: "The Moravian contribution to Christian missions cannot be explained by natural factors alone. Their success rate in the most challenging fields, their ability to sustain long-term work in hostile environments, and the transformations that preceded their arrival in numerous locations suggest supernatural assistance that correlates directly with their prayer practices." This is the verdict of history: what happened was not humanly possible. It was a direct, measurable result of a people who had tapped into the power of heaven.

Modern missiologists, studying this phenomenon, have given it a name: "prayer-prepared harvest fields." This wasn't a theory to the Moravians; it was their entire operational strategy. They witnessed this divine reality unfold among the enslaved peoples of the Caribbean, who went from brutalized hopelessness to fervent faith. They saw it among the Inuit peoples of Greenland, a land of ice that became a beacon of warmth for the Gospel. It was documented in their work among Native American tribes, countless African communities, and resistant peoples across Asia. The map of their missions is a map of prayer-saturated ground.

What is most convicting is that the Moravians themselves were never impressed with their own success. They were utterly awestruck by the power of their God. They were meticulously careful to give all credit to prevailing prayer, not to human methodology. Their missionary instructions were not filled with clever strategies for contextualization or communication; they were filled with urgent pleas to remain dependent on the prayer covering from home. They understood that successful evangelism was not the result of superior technique, but the inevitable fruit of sustained intercession. Their letters from the field are breathtaking testaments to this truth, describing with awe how they could literally feel the prayers of Herrnhut. They wrote of a palpable spiritual shield in moments of danger, of a supernatural provision appearing at the last second, and of a sudden, inexplicable warmth and receptivity in the hearts of people they spoke to. They knew, without a doubt, that they were not fighting alone.

The Moravians demonstrated that when a people seeks not just to petition God but to be utterly engulfed by His presence, they alter the spiritual geography of the earth. The Spirit does not merely visit these prayer-saturated zones; He begins to inhabit them, leaving a holy residue that history itself is forced to record as miraculous.

CHAPTER 3:
The Secret Of Sustained Prayer

The Heart Behind the Hours

What enabled the Moravians to sustain continuous prayer for over a century when most prayer initiatives struggle to last a few months? The answer lies not in their organizational systems, though those were important, but in the heart transformation that made prayer feel less like a duty and more like a privilege.

The Moravians had discovered what many modern believers have forgotten: prayer is not primarily about getting things from God but about getting God Himself. Their hourly intercession was not a time of presenting wish lists to heaven but an appointment with the living God who desires intimate fellowship with His people.

Anna Nitschmann's prayer journal, preserved in the Moravian archives, reveals the secret: "I do not go to my prayer hour to pray. I go to meet with Jesus. The prayer is simply what happens when I am with Him, like conversation between lovers, like breathing between friends, like music between the musician and his instrument."

This understanding transformed the nature of their intercession. Instead of religious duty, prayer became spiritual romance. Instead of trying to convince a reluctant God to act, they were communing with a passionate God who was eager to reveal His heart for the world. Instead of mechanical repetition of requests, their prayers flowed from an intimate knowledge of God's character and desires.

Count Zinzendorf captured this heart attitude in one of his most famous quotes: "Preach the Gospel to every creature but do it on your knees." The Moravians understood that their external ministry was merely the overflow of their internal communion with God.

The power to change the world came not from human effort but from hearts that had been transformed through sustained fellowship with the Almighty.

The Discipline of Sustained Seeking

While heart transformation was essential, the Moravians also developed practical disciplines that enabled them to sustain their prayer commitment across multiple generations. These disciplines were not legalistic rules but wisdom principles that helped maintain the spiritual atmosphere necessary for long-term intercession.

First, they maintained diversity within unity. Rather than requiring everyone to pray exactly the same way, they encouraged each intercessor to develop their own style of communion with God while maintaining unity around their common objectives. Some prayed with written prayers, others interceded spontaneously. Some focused-on worship and adoration, others on specific missionary needs. Some prayed while walking, others while kneeling. The variety prevented boredom while the unity-maintained focus.

Second, they practiced accountability without condemnation. Prayer partners were assigned to encourage one another and ensure that every hour was covered, but the emphasis was on mutual support rather than performance pressure. When someone missed their prayer hour due to illness or emergency, others would gladly cover for them without judgment or criticism.

Third, they maintained a fresh vision through constant communication with the mission field. Letters from missionaries were read during prayer times, creating an emotional connection between the intercessors and those they were supporting. Maps were updated regularly, prayer requests were specific and current, and testimonies of answered prayer were shared frequently to maintain faith and enthusiasm.

Fourth, they integrated prayer with daily life rather than treating it as a separate religious activity. Craftsmen would pray while working, mothers would intercede while caring for children, and farmers would seek God while tending crops. This integration made prayer feel natural rather than burdensome and helped sustain the movement through busy seasons and changing life circumstances.

The Community That Prays Together

The Moravian prayer movement was not sustained by individual heroics but by community commitment. They understood that sustained intercession requires mutual support, shared vision, and collective responsibility. No single person could maintain the intensity necessary for world-changing prayer, but a community of believers could create a spiritual atmosphere that sustained extraordinary intercession over long periods.

Their community structure was organized around prayer rather than prayer being added to their community life. Housing assignments, work schedules, and social activities were all arranged to support and enhance their prayer commitment. Families were intentionally scattered across different prayer hours to ensure generational participation. Work assignments were rotated to prevent any single person from bearing too much practical responsibility that might interfere with prayer obligations.

The entire community understood that they were not just a group of individuals who happened to pray together, but a corporate priesthood called to stand in the gap for the world. This understanding created a sense of sacred responsibility that transcended personal preferences and maintained commitment through difficult seasons.

When visitors came to Herrnhut, they consistently commented on the atmosphere of expectation that permeated the community. Children played with a sense of joy that seemed supernatural.

Adults worked with an efficiency and peace that impressed even secular observers. Elderly believers-maintained alertness and energy that defied their physical age. The entire community seemed to be charged with spiritual electricity that came from continuous communion with God.

Prayer That Transforms the Prayers

One of the most remarkable aspects of the Moravian prayer movement was how the intercession transformed those who practiced it. The longer they prayed, the more they became like the God they were seeking.

Their characters were refined, their perspectives expanded, their love deepened, and their faith strengthened through sustained communion with the Almighty.

Christian David, the carpenter, wrote after twenty years of daily intercession: "I began praying for missionaries because I thought God needed my prayers. I continued praying for missionaries because I discovered that I needed to pray. The hour I spend seeking God for others has become the hour that God uses to transform me. I am not the same man who began this prayer journey twenty years ago."

The transformation was evident to outside observers. Visitors consistently remarked on the unusual spiritual maturity of even young believers in Herrnhut. Children demonstrated wisdom beyond their years, young adults showed unusual spiritual discernment, and elderly believers radiated a peace and joy that seemed to come from another world.

This transformation was not the result of human effort but the natural consequence of spending time in God's presence. The Moravians discovered what Moses learned on Mount Sinai, prolonged exposure to God's glory changes those who experience it. Their faces didn't physically shine like Moses', but their lives radiated a spiritual glow that drew people to God wherever they went.

The prayer movement also produced unprecedented spiritual gifts within the community. Prophecy became common, divine healing occurred regularly, and supernatural wisdom was available for both practical and spiritual decisions. These gifts were not sought for their own sake but emerged naturally from hearts that were saturated with God's presence through constant prayer.

The Global Vision That Sustained Local Prayer

What kept the Moravian prayer movement from becoming self-centered was their global vision. From the beginning, their intercession focused more on unreached peoples than on their own needs. This outward focus created a spiritual dynamic that sustained their prayer commitment across generations.

They developed what they called "praying the nations", systematic intercession for every known people group on earth. World maps covered the walls of their prayer rooms, with different regions assigned to different intercessors. As geographical knowledge expanded, their prayer coverage expanded as well. They were among the first Christians to pray specifically for people in the interior of Africa, the islands of the Pacific, and the tribes of the Americas.

This global focus prevented the prayer movement from becoming repetitive or self-absorbed. There was always something new to pray for, some unreached group to intercede for, some missionary challenge to lift up to God. The vastness of the world's spiritual needs created a sense of urgency that sustained their commitment through decades of faithful intercession.

More importantly, praying for the world expanded their hearts to match God's heart. The longer they interceded for unreached peoples, the more they loved those peoples. The more they prayed for different cultures, the more they appreciated the diversity of God's creation. The more they sought God for global breakthrough, the more they understood the breadth and depth of His love for all humanity.

This expanding love created a spiritual momentum that was self-sustaining. Love, unlike duty, does not grow weary. The more the Moravians loved the people they prayed for, the more they wanted to pray for them. The more they prayed for them, the more they loved them. This upward spiral of love and intercession created a dynamic that could be sustained indefinitely.

CHAPTER 4:
Modern Prayer Movements

The International House of Prayer: Continuous Worship and Intercession

In 1999, a young pastor named Mike Bickle felt called to establish something that hadn't existed since the Moravian prayer vigil ended in the 1800s, a house of continuous prayer that would operate twenty-four hours a day, seven days a week. The International House of Prayer (IHOP) in Kansas City, Missouri, began with a small group of intercessors and musicians who committed themselves to maintaining non-stop worship and prayer.

What started as an act of obedience has grown into a global movement that has sustained continuous prayer for over two decades. The prayer room in Kansas City has never been empty since September 19, 1999, and similar houses of prayer have been established on every continent, creating a network of intercession that literally surrounds the earth with prayer.

The IHOP model combines worship with intercession in a way that makes sustained prayer feel more like celebration than duty. Teams of musicians and singers rotate through two-hour sets, creating an atmosphere of worship that supports and enhances intercession. Intercessors pray both individually and corporately, covering everything from local needs to global crises to the spiritual preparation necessary for Christ's return.

Anna Thompson, who has participated in the Kansas City prayer room for fifteen years, describes the experience: "When I first heard about 24/7 prayer, I thought it sounded exhausting. But when I experienced it, I discovered it was energizing. There's something about continuous worship that creates a spiritual atmosphere where prayer feels effortless.

It's like swimming downstream instead of fighting against the current."

The influence of IHOP has extended far beyond Kansas City. Thousands of young people have been trained in their internship programs and have carried the vision for continuous prayer to cities around the world. Their conferences and training materials have equipped believers from over 100 nations to establish their own houses of prayer.

The 24-7 Prayer Movement: A Global Network

While IHOP was establishing continuous prayer in America, a parallel movement was emerging in Europe. The 24-7 Prayer movement began in 1999 when Pete Greig challenged a group of young adults in England to sustain prayer for just one month. What they discovered during those thirty days of non-stop intercession transformed their understanding of prayer and launched a global movement.

The original prayer room was set up in a converted shipping container, with prayer requests covering the walls and worship music playing continuously. Young people signed up for one-hour time slots, and many experienced encounters with God that redirected the course of their lives. By the end of the month, they were convinced that they had discovered something essential to authentic Christian living.

The movement spread virally, with new 24-7 prayer rooms opening across Europe and eventually worldwide. Unlike traditional denominational expansions, this growth was organic and voluntary, believers were starting prayer rooms simply because they had been transformed by the experience and wanted to share it with others.

What makes the 24-7 movement unique is its integration of prayer with social action. Prayer rooms regularly focus on specific community needs, homelessness, addiction, human trafficking, educational challenges, and then mobilize participants to address those needs practically. This combination of intercession and action has created a generation of believers who see prayer not as escape from the world but as engagement with God's heart for the world.

Sarah Chen, who helped establish a 24/7 prayer room in Singapore, explains the connection: "We discovered that the more we prayed for the poor in our city, the more we wanted to serve them. The more we interceded for drug addicts, the more we felt called to work with them.

Prayer didn't take us away from practical ministry, it prepared us for more effective ministry."

The Global Day of Prayer: Mobilizing Millions

While continuous prayer movements focus on sustaining long-term intercession, the Global Day of Prayer demonstrates the power of synchronized, worldwide prayer. Launched in 2001 by a group of South African pastors, the Global Day of Prayer now mobilizes tens of millions of believers to pray simultaneously on Pentecost Sunday each year.

The movement began when South African church leaders realized that their nation's transformation from apartheid to democracy had been preceded and accompanied by unprecedented prayer mobilization. They decided to call the global church to dedicate one day each year to seeking God together for transformation in their own nations.

The response exceeded all expectations. Within five years, believers from over 220 nations were participating, making it the largest annual prayer gathering in Christian history. The synchronized nature of the prayer creates a sense of global unity and demonstrates the worldwide scope of the Church.

Archbishop Thabo Makgoba of South Africa describes the impact: "When millions of believers pray together with one heart and one voice, something spiritual happens that transcends the sum of individual prayers. There's a release of spiritual power that creates a breakthrough not just in individual lives but in entire nations."

The Global Day of Prayer has been credited with contributing to political transformations, social reforms, and spiritual awakenings in numerous countries. Government leaders have acknowledged its influence, and secular media has documented correlations between prayer mobilization and positive social changes.

The World Prayer Assembly: Uniting Prayer Leaders

In 2018, prayer leaders from around the world gathered in Indonesia for the first World Prayer Assembly, bringing together representatives from dozens of prayer movements to pray together and coordinate global intercession. The assembly revealed the remarkable scope of contemporary prayer mobilization, millions of believers participating in organized intercession on every continent.

The assembly identified over 50,000 houses of prayer, prayer centers, and prayer networks operating worldwide. These range from small groups meeting weekly in homes to massive prayer movements involving hundreds of thousands of participants. The diversity is extraordinary, but the common thread is believers who have discovered that prayer is not just personal devotion but a force for global transformation.

Dr. Cindy Jacobs, who helped organize the assembly, observed: "We discovered that God has been raising up prayer movements simultaneously all over the world without human coordination. In nations where Christians have never heard of each other's prayer initiatives, the Holy Spirit has been inspiring similar visions and similar commitments. This suggests that we're living in a season when God is mobilizing His people for prayer on an unprecedented scale."

The assembly also revealed the growing sophistication of prayer mobilization. Modern technology allows prayer requests to be shared instantly across continents, enables virtual prayer rooms where believers from different time zones can pray together, and provides platforms for coordinating prayer coverage for global events and crises.

Prayer Walking and Spiritual Mapping

One of the most significant developments in modern prayer movements is the practice of prayer walking, systematically praying on location for specific neighborhoods, cities, or regions. This practice combines the mobility of modern transportation with the ancient understanding that prayer can be more effective when offered in the specific locations where breakthrough is needed.

Prayer walking movements have emerged on every continent, with believers organizing regular prayer journeys through their communities. These range from individuals who pray while jogging through their neighborhoods to organized groups that spend weeks walking through entire cities while interceding for spiritual breakthrough.

The practice has evolved to include spiritual mapping, researching the historical, cultural, and spiritual factors that may be hindering Gospel advancement in specific regions and then praying strategically to address those barriers. This approach has led to documented breakthroughs in areas that had been resistant to Christian witness for centuries.

Pastor John Robb, who has led prayer walking expeditions to over 50 nations, explains the methodology: "We don't just pray generally for a city or region. We research its history, identify specific spiritual strongholds, and then pray on location with informed intercession. This combination of research and prayer has opened doors that had been closed for generations."

Prayer walking has been particularly effective in unreached regions where traditional missionary methods have had limited success. Teams of intercessors will spend months prayer-walking through a region before evangelists arrive, often discovering that the spiritual atmosphere has been transformed, and people are unusually responsive to the Gospel.

Digital Prayer Networks

The internet age has revolutionized prayer mobilization by enabling believers from different continents to pray together in real time. Online prayer rooms, mobile prayer apps, and social media prayer networks have created possibilities for intercession that the Moravians could never have imagined.

The Global Prayer Network, launched in 2015, connects prayer requests from missionaries, pastors, and believers worldwide with intercessors who commit to pray for specific needs. The network processes thousands of prayer requests daily and has documented remarkable answers to prayer that have come through coordinated global intercession.

Prayer apps like 'PrayerMate' and Echo Prayer allow believers to receive curated prayer requests on their smartphones and join organized prayer campaigns with believers from around the world. These tools have made it possible for ordinary believers to participate in global intercession without traveling or joining formal prayer organizations.

The COVID-19 pandemic accelerated the adoption of digital prayer platforms as believers sought ways to maintain corporate prayer while physically separated. Virtual prayer rooms operated continuously throughout the pandemic, and many believers discovered that online prayer meetings could be just as effective as in-person gatherings.

The New Monasticism: Communities of Prayer and Service

A growing movement of young believers has been establishing intentional communities that combine intensive prayer with social action. These "new monastic" communities draw inspiration from traditional monasticism while adapting to contemporary urban environments and social challenges.

These communities typically maintain regular schedules of corporate prayer while actively engaging in service to the poor, the homeless, and the marginalized. They've discovered that prayer and service are not competing priorities but complementary aspects of authentic Christian living.

The Taizé Community in France has become a model for this movement, attracting hundreds of thousands of young people annually to experience life organized around prayer, simplicity, and service. Similar communities have been established in major cities worldwide, often focusing on specific social issues while maintaining strong commitments to intercession.

Shane Claiborne, founder of The Simple Way community in Philadelphia, describes the integration: "We've discovered that you can't serve the poor effectively without praying for the poor, and you can't pray for the poor authentically without serving them. Prayer and action aren't separate things, they're two expressions of the same love."

These communities are producing a generation of believers who see prayer as inseparable from social engagement and understand intercession as preparation for more effective ministry to human need.

CHAPTER 5:
Reflection: Deepening Your Prayer Life

Starting Where You Are

The stories of the Moravians and modern prayer movements can feel simultaneously inspiring and overwhelming. How do you bridge the gap between admiring century-long prayer vigils and struggling to maintain a consistent ten-minute daily prayer time? The answer lies in understanding that extraordinary prayer movements begin with ordinary believers who start where they are and allow God to expand their capacity over time.

Count Zinzendorf didn't begin with a vision for one hundred years of prayer. He started with desperate believers who needed God's help to love one another. The 24/7 Prayer movement didn't launch with a global strategy, it began with young adults who committed to one month of continuous prayer in a converted shipping container. The International House of Prayer started with a handful of people who felt called to seek God together in a rented building in Kansas City. Every world-changing prayer movement has the same humble beginning: someone who decides to pray more consistently than they have been praying. The key is not starting with heroic commitments that you can't sustain, but with small, consistent steps that create momentum toward a deeper prayer life.

Sarah Martinez, a working mother of three who eventually became a prayer leader in her city, describes her journey: "I used to feel guilty because I couldn't pray like the spiritual giants I read about. Then I realized that they didn't start as spiritual giants, they became giants by starting small and staying faithful. I began with five minutes of prayer while my coffee brewed each morning. Those five minutes became ten, then twenty, then an hour. But it started with just five minutes and one simple decision: I will meet with God every day, no matter how briefly."

The first step in deepening your prayer life is an honest assessment of your current reality, followed by a small but consistent commitment to grow. Don't compare your beginning to someone else's middle or end. Start where you are, use what you have, do what you can, and trust God to expand your capacity as you remain faithful.

Creating Sacred Space and Time

The Moravians understood that sustained prayer requires intentional structure. They didn't just pray when they felt like it, they created systems that enabled regular, focused communion with God. You can apply this wisdom by establishing your own sacred space and time for prayer, even if it looks different from their elaborate prayer schedules.

Sacred space doesn't require a separate room or elaborate setup. It means having a designated place where you regularly meet with God, a space that becomes associated in your mind and heart with divine encounter. This might be a corner of your bedroom, a chair in your living room, a bench in your backyard, or even a route you walk regularly while praying.

The key is consistency and intentionality. When you repeatedly use the same space for prayer, it becomes easier to transition into a spiritual mindset when you enter that space. Your heart learns to expect God's presence there, and distractions naturally diminish as the space becomes associated with focused communion with the divine.

Rachel Thompson, a nurse who works rotating shifts, explains her approach: "I couldn't have a consistent time for prayer because my schedule changes constantly, but I could have a consistent place. I set up a prayer corner in my bedroom with a comfortable chair, my Bible, a journal, and a world map. Whether I'm praying at 5 AM before a day shift or 11 PM after a night shift, that corner helps me transition quickly into prayer mode. My heart knows that when I sit in that chair, it's time to meet with God."

Sacred time is equally important. The most effective prayer lives are built around consistent timing rather than sporadic inspiration. This doesn't mean your prayer time must be the same length every day, but it does mean having a regular appointment with God that you protect from other activities.

Morning prayer has advantages because your mind is fresh, and the day hasn't yet been filled with distractions and responsibilities. Evening prayer provides an opportunity to process the day with God and seek His guidance for tomorrow. The specific time matters less than the consistency of meeting with God regularly.

Developing a Rhythm of Prayer

The Moravians sustained their prayer movement by developing rhythms rather than relying on emotional intensity. They understood that prayer is more like physical exercise than emotional experience, it requires regular practice regardless of how you feel on any given day.

A rhythm of prayer includes different types of prayer throughout the day rather than trying to accomplish everything in one session. This might include:

Morning Prayer: Beginning the day by surrendering it to God, asking for His guidance, and interceding for family and immediate responsibilities.

Noon Prayer: A brief pause in the middle of the day to reconnect with God, give thanks for His presence, and seek wisdom for afternoon activities.

Evening Prayer: Processing the day with God, confessing sins, expressing gratitude, and committing tomorrow to His care.

Spontaneous Prayer: Brief conversations with God throughout the day in response to situations, needs, and opportunities for thanksgiving.

This rhythm creates a framework for continuous communion with God without requiring large blocks of time that may be difficult to maintain consistently. It transforms prayer from an isolated activity into an integrated lifestyle.

Mark Chen, a business executive who travels frequently, describes his rhythm: "I used to think prayer meant long, uninterrupted sessions that were impossible with my schedule. Then I learned to create a rhythm that worked with my life rather than against it.

I pray for ten minutes each morning while drinking coffee, send brief prayers throughout the day while driving or walking between meetings, and spend fifteen minutes each evening processing the day with God. This rhythm has given me more consistent prayer time than I ever had when I was trying to pray for an hour once a week."

Expanding Your Prayer Focus

One reason many believers struggle with sustained prayer is that they focus primarily on their own needs, which creates a limited scope for intercession. The Moravians sustained century-long prayer by expanding their focus to include the entire world. You can deepen your prayer life by gradually expanding your prayer focus beyond personal concerns.

Start by praying for your immediate circle, family, friends, coworkers, neighbors. As this becomes natural, expand to include your church, your community, your nation, and eventually the world. This expansion creates an ever-widening scope for intercession that prevents prayer from becoming repetitive or self-centered.

Use tools to help expand your vision:

- Pray through a world map, asking God to show you His heart for different nations
- Subscribe to missionary newsletters and pray specifically for cross-cultural workers
- Read news with a prayer perspective, interceding for regions experiencing crisis or breakthrough
- Adopt unreached people groups and pray for them regularly by name
- Intercede for government leaders, educators, and other influential people in your community

Lisa Johnson, a retired teacher who has become a prayer warrior in her church, explains her journey: "I started by praying for my grandchildren each morning. Then I began praying for their teachers, their friends, their friends' families. Before long, I was praying for the entire school system in our city.

Now I spend two hours each morning interceding for everything from local schools to international missions.

The more I pray for others, the more I love them, and the more I love them, the more I want to pray for them."

Incorporating Different Types of Prayer

The Moravians understood that sustained prayer requires variety. They incorporated worship, intercession, confession, thanksgiving, and contemplation into their prayer times, preventing boredom and maintaining spiritual freshness. You can apply this wisdom by learning different approaches to prayer and rotating between them.

Adoration: Focusing on God's character, attributes, and perfection. This might involve reading through psalms of praise, meditating on the names of God, or simply expressing love and worship to God for who He is rather than what He does.

Confession: Honestly acknowledging sin and failure while receiving God's forgiveness and cleansing. This creates clean hearts that can receive more of God's presence and power.

Thanksgiving: Expressing gratitude for God's blessings, provisions, and faithfulness. Gratitude creates joy and faith that energizes other aspects of prayer.

Supplication: Making specific requests for yourself, others, and God's kingdom. This is the type of prayer most believers are familiar with, but it becomes more effective when combined with other prayer types.

Intercession: Standing in the gap for others, pleading their cause before God, and asking for His intervention in their lives and circumstances.

Contemplation: Quietly waiting in God's presence, listening for His voice, and allowing His peace and love to fill your heart.

Declaration: Proclaiming God's promises and truths over situations that need divine intervention, speaking faith into circumstances that appear hopeless.

Rotating between these different types of prayer keeps your prayer time fresh and addresses different aspects of your relationship with God.

It also develops different spiritual muscles, making you a more well-rounded intercessor.

Learning to Listen

One of the most important aspects of a mature prayer life is learning to listen for God's voice. The Moravians understood that prayer is conversation, not a monologue. They spent as much time listening as talking, which enabled them to receive divine guidance for their intercession and their lives.

Listening in prayer requires slowing down and creating space for God to speak. This might mean reading a passage of Scripture and asking God what He wants to say to you through it. It might mean sitting quietly and asking for His guidance about a decision you need to make. It might mean asking Him to show you how to pray for a specific person or situation.

Learning to recognize God's voice takes practice and patience. His voice is often quieter than our own thoughts, gentler than our emotions, and wiser than our natural understanding. It comes through Scripture, through gentle impressions in our hearts, through circumstances, and through the counsel of mature believers.

Jennifer Kim, a young mother who has developed a strong prayer life, describes her learning process: "At first, I did all the talking in prayer and wondered why it felt one-sided. Then I started asking questions and waiting for answers. I learned to distinguish between my own thoughts and God's gentle whispers. Now my prayer times often include long periods of just listening, and I've discovered that God has much more to say to me than I have to say to Him."

Praying Scripture

One of the most distinct ways to deepen your prayer life is to pray Scripture back to God. This practice ensures that your prayers align with God's will, provides rich content for intercession, and connects you with the same prayers that believers have prayed for thousands of years.

You can pray the Psalms as personal prayers, inserting your own name or the names of others into the verses.

You can pray through the prayers of Paul in the New Testament, asking God to accomplish in your life and the lives of others what Paul requested for the early churches. You can pray through the promises of God, asking Him to fulfill them in your generation.

Praying Scripture also provides structure for prayer times when you don't know what to say or how to pray. Instead of struggling to find words, you can use the inspired words of Scripture as a framework for your own prayers.

David Park, a seminary student who has been transformed by praying Scripture, explains the impact: "When I started praying the Bible instead of just reading it, everything changed.

Suddenly, I was praying with the same passion as the psalmists, the same vision as the prophets, and the same love as Jesus. Praying Scripture expanded my vocabulary for prayer and aligned my heart with God's heart in ways I never experienced when I only prayed my own words."

Building Community Around Prayer

While personal prayer is essential, the most prevailing prayer lives are sustained by the community. The Moravians understood this, which is why they made prayer a corporate commitment rather than just individual discipline. You can strengthen your prayer life by connecting with others who share your hunger for deeper intercession.

This might mean:

- Joining or starting a prayer group in your church
- Finding a prayer partner who will pray with you regularly and hold you accountable
- Participating in community prayer walks or prayer events
- Connecting with online prayer communities that match your interests and schedule
- Attending prayer conferences or training events to learn from experienced intercessors

The prayer community provides encouragement when your personal prayer life feels dry, accountability when you're tempted to give up, and corporate power that exceeds individual intercession.

It also provides opportunities to learn from others who have developed mature prayer lives.

Maria Santos, who leads a prayer ministry in her church, describes the importance of community: "I could never have sustained a deep prayer life on my own. There were too many times when I felt discouraged, distracted, or just plain tired. But when I joined with others who shared the same hunger for God, we strengthened each other. When I was weak, they carried me. When they struggled, I encouraged them. Together we accomplished things in prayer that none of us could have achieved alone."

Dealing with Common Obstacles

Every believer who attempts to deepen their prayer life encounters obstacles that threaten to derail their progress. Understanding these common challenges and having strategies to overcome them is essential for sustained growth in prayer.

The Obstacle of Dryness: There will be seasons when prayer feels mechanical, boring, or ineffective. This is normal and temporary. During dry seasons, focus on faithfulness rather than feelings. Continue praying even when you don't feel like it, trusting that God is working even when you can't sense His presence.

The Obstacle of Distraction: In our hyperconnected world, maintaining focus during prayer can be extremely challenging. Create barriers to distraction by turning off devices, praying in a quiet space, and using tools like written prayers or prayer guides to help maintain focus.

The Obstacle of Doubt: Sometimes you may wonder if your prayers are making any difference or if God is really listening. Combat doubt by keeping a prayer journal where you record requests and answers, by studying biblical promises about prayer, and by connecting with other believers who can testify to answered prayer.

The Obstacle of Busy Schedules: Modern life seems designed to crowd out prayer time. Protect your prayer time by treating it as non-negotiable, by starting small and building gradually, and by finding creative ways to pray throughout the day rather than only during formal prayer times.

The Obstacle of Spiritual Warfare: As you deepen your prayer life, you may experience increased spiritual opposition. This is actually a positive sign that your prayers are making a difference. Combat spiritual attacks through the armor of God described in Ephesians 6, through corporate prayer with other believers, and through persistent faith that doesn't give up when battles become intense.

Making Prayer Your Legacy

The Moravians understood that their prayer commitment was not just about their own generation but about creating a legacy of intercession that would benefit future generations. As you deepen your prayer life, consider how your prayers can create a positive impact that extends beyond your own lifetime.

This legacy thinking might include:

- Teaching your children to pray and involving them in your intercession
- Praying specifically for future generations and the challenges they will face
- Supporting and mentoring younger believers who are developing their prayer lives
- Participating in prayer movements that are building for long-term impact
- Recording your prayer insights and testimonies to encourage others

Your prayer life is not just about your personal spiritual development, it's about participating in God's eternal purposes and contributing to the advancement of His kingdom on earth. When you pray with this perspective, every prayer becomes significant, every intercession becomes part of a larger story, and your prayer life becomes a contribution to the great work that God is accomplishing through His people worldwide.

The prayer movement that began with the Moravians continues today through believers like you who are willing to commit themselves to deeper intercession. Your prayers can change your family, transform your community, and contribute to the spiritual breakthrough that your generation desperately needs.

The same fire that sustained the Moravians' century of prayer is available to ignite your heart for intercession. The same God who answered their prayers is waiting to respond to yours. The same power that transformed the world through their intercession is ready to work through your prayers to accomplish His purposes in your lifetime.

Your deepened prayer life begins with your next prayer. The journey of a thousand miles begins with a single step, and the journey toward prayer that changes the world begins with one believer who decides to seek God more consistently, more passionately, and more persistently than ever before.

That believer can be you. Your prayer legacy begins now.

The Fire Still Burns

As we stand at the conclusion of this journey through the history of world-changing prayer, we must ask ourselves a crucial question: What will we do with what we have learned? The testimonies we have examined, from the Moravians' century-long vigil to the global prayer movements of today, prove beyond doubt that prayer is not just personal devotion but a force capable of transforming individuals, communities, and entire nations.

The fire that fell on Pentecost and sustained the Moravians still burns today. The same Spirit who empowered their intercession is available to empower yours. The same God who answered their prayers with supernatural breakthrough is waiting to respond to your intercession with demonstrations of His power that will amaze you.

But fire only burns in hearts that are prepared to be consumed. Prayer only transforms the world through believers who are willing to be transformed first. The movements we have studied began with ordinary people who made extraordinary commitments to seek God with unprecedented desperation, consistency, and faith.

The question that history poses to you is not whether God can use your prayers to change the world, the evidence overwhelmingly proves He can. The question is whether you will position yourself to be part of what God is doing in your generation through the prayers of His people.

Somewhere in the world today, a new prayer movement is beginning. Perhaps it will start in a college dormitory where students commit to praying together every morning before classes.

Maybe it will emerge in a suburban neighborhood where neighbors begin gathering weekly to intercede for their community. It could begin in a workplace where believers start meeting for prayer during lunch breaks. Or it might start in your own heart as you read these words and feel the Holy Spirit stirring you to deeper intercession than you have ever experienced.

The Moravians didn't set out to sustain prayer for a hundred years, they just committed to pray until God answered their immediate need. The 24-7 Prayer movement didn't plan to become global, they just started with one month of continuous prayer in one converted shipping container. The International House of Prayer didn't envision worldwide influence, they simply obeyed God's call to maintain continuous worship and prayer in Kansas City.

Your prayer life may seem small and insignificant compared to these historical movements, but remember that every world-changing prayer movement began with one person who decided to pray more consistently than they had been praying. Your five-minute morning prayer could grow into the hour that transforms your family. Your weekly prayer group could become the community prayer meeting that sparks revival in your city. Your intercession for one unreached people group could be the prayer that opens an entire nation to the Gospel.

The same fire that has burned through twenty centuries of church history is ready to ignite your heart for intercession. The same power that sustained the Moravians through persecution and hardship is available to sustain your prayer life through every obstacle and discouragement. The same vision that sent missionaries to the ends of the earth is ready to expand your heart for the world's spiritual needs.

Your prayer legacy begins with your next prayer. The fire still burns. The Spirit still moves. The God who has been transforming the world through the prayers of His people for two thousand years is inviting you to join the greatest movement in human history.

Will you answer the call? Will you let the fire fall on your heart? Will you become part of the prayer that changes the world?

The choice is yours. The fire is waiting. The world is desperate for believers who will pay the price of intercession necessary to see God's kingdom advance with power in this generation.

Pray like the Moravians. Seek like the revivalists. Intercede like your generation depends on it.

Because it does.

4. FAITH THAT CROSSES BORDERS

The Courage to Cross

There is something in the heart of authentic faith that refuses to remain contained within comfortable boundaries. Like water breaking through a dam or fire leaping across barriers, a genuine encounter with the living God produces an unstoppable impulse to move outward. It cannot be bottled up or domesticated. It creates an irrepressible urge to cross every border, geographical, cultural, linguistic, economic, and social, to share the transforming reality of Christ with those who have never heard His name. Real faith is not satisfied with silent belief or private devotion; it longs to overflow into mission, service, and proclamation until the whole earth is filled with the knowledge of the glory of the Lord.

This is the story of faith that crosses borders. It is the account of ordinary believers who became extraordinary pioneers, men and women who left behind the familiar and the safe in order to carry the Gospel into hostile territories and among unreached peoples. Some set sail for distant lands, enduring storms, sickness, and separation from family. Others trekked on foot through deserts, jungles, and mountains to reach villages hidden from the world. Still others stepped into the dark corners of their own cities, ministering to the poor, the forgotten, and the despised.

Whether the distance was measured in miles or in cultural barriers, the motivation was always the same: love for Christ and love for those who had yet to encounter Him.

From the moment Jesus breathed His final commission, "Go into all the world and preach the Gospel to every creature," His followers have been compelled by divine love to venture beyond their comfort zones. They were drawn into the dangerous, exhilarating territory of cross-cultural ministry, often at tremendous personal cost. Many faced ridicule, imprisonment, persecution, and even death.

Yet the call of Christ proved stronger than the pull of fear, and His Spirit supplied the courage they lacked.

The courage required for this calling is not mere human bravery. On our own, we cling to security, shrink back from danger, and prefer what is familiar. But the resurrection power of Jesus transforms weakness into boldness. The same Spirit who empowered Peter to preach on Pentecost, who sent Paul across the Roman Empire, and who strengthened countless saints through the centuries, still equips believers today. It is this supernatural courage that turns cowards into champions, doubters into martyrs, and comfortable believers into world-changing missionaries.

For two thousand years, this holy fire has driven men and women across every conceivable barrier, and it continues to burn. In every generation, God raises believers who refuse to let borders, whether physical, cultural, or spiritual, contain their faith. They know that the love of Christ compels them, and they will not rest until every tribe, tongue, and nation has heard the good news.

CHAPTER 1:
Paul - The Prototype Of Missionary Courage

From Persecutor to Pioneer

The most dramatic example of missionary courage in Christian history begins with the most unlikely candidate imaginable. Saul of Tarsus was not just indifferent to Christianity, he was its most violent opponent. A highly educated Pharisee who could have enjoyed a prestigious life within the Jewish religious establishment, he instead made it his mission to destroy the early Church. He stood approving as Stephen was stoned to death. He dragged believers from their homes and threw them into prison. He breathed "threats and murder against the disciples of the Lord" (Acts 9:1).

But authentic missionary courage often begins in the most unexpected places. On the road to Damascus, this persecutor encountered the persecuted Christ and was transformed in an instant from Christianity's greatest enemy into its most effective advocate. The same passion that had driven him to destroy the Church now compelled him to build it. The same intelligence that had crafted arguments against Christianity now developed the theological framework that would sustain it for millennia.

Paul's transformation was so complete and so sudden that even the early Christians struggled to believe it was genuine. When he tried to join the believers in Jerusalem, "they were all afraid of him, and did not believe that he was a disciple" (Acts 9:26). This former enemy had to prove his conversion through years of suffering and service before the Church fully accepted his apostolic calling.

The Making of a Missionary

What transformed Paul from a comfortable religious leader into a boundary-crossing missionary was not human ambition but divine compulsion. He described his calling in terms that reveal the supernatural nature of missionary courage: "Woe is me if I do not preach the gospel!" (1 Corinthians 9:16). This was not a career choice but a spiritual necessity. The love of Christ had so overwhelmed him that keeping the Gospel to himself was impossible.

Paul's missionary preparation involved three years in the Arabian desert, where he encountered God in solitude and received direct revelation about his calling to the Gentiles. This wilderness experience was crucial, it established his relationship with Christ as the foundation for his ministry rather than human training or ecclesiastical approval. When he finally began his missionary career, he carried with him not just theological knowledge but personal intimacy with the risen Christ.

The scope of Paul's vision was breathtaking. While other apostles focused primarily on Jewish audiences, Paul felt called to carry the Gospel to "the ends of the earth" (Acts 13:47). He understood that the message of Christ was not just for one culture or ethnic group but for all humanity. This global vision required extraordinary courage because it meant venturing into territories where the name of Jesus was unknown and often unwelcome.

The Cost of Crossing Borders

Paul's missionary journeys read like an adventure novel, except the adventure was real, the stakes were eternal, and the courage required was supernatural. His ministry was marked by constant danger, persistent opposition, and repeated suffering that would have discouraged anyone operating in merely human strength.

In 2 Corinthians 11:23-28, Paul provides a catalog of his sufferings that reveals the true cost of missionary courage:

"In labors more abundant, in stripes above measure, in prisons more frequently, in deaths often. From the Jews, five times I received forty stripes minus one.

Three times I was beaten with rods; once I was stoned; three times I was shipwrecked; a night and a day I have been in the deep; in journeys often, in perils of waters, in perils of robbers, in perils of my own countrymen, in perils of the Gentiles, in perils in the city, in perils in the wilderness, in perils in the sea, in perils among false brethren; in weariness and toil, in sleeplessness often, in hunger and thirst, in Fastings often, in cold and nakedness, besides the other things, what comes upon me daily: my deep concern for all the churches."

This was not the career path of someone seeking comfort, security, or worldly success. Paul endured these hardships because his encounter with Christ had given him a perspective that transcended temporal concerns. He had seen the risen Lord, experienced the reality of eternal life, and understood that no earthly suffering could compare to the glory that would be revealed in those who believed.

Strategic Missionary Methodology

Paul's courage was not reckless but strategic. He developed missionary methods that maximized the spread of the Gospel while minimizing unnecessary risks. He typically began his ministry in each city by preaching in the Jewish synagogue, where he could build on existing knowledge of Scripture and monotheistic theology. When opposition arose, as it almost always did, he would turn to the Gentiles.

His strategy of establishing churches in major urban centers was brilliant. These cities served as communication hubs from which the Gospel could spread naturally through trade routes and social networks. Rather than trying to evangelize every village personally, Paul focused on training local leaders who could carry the ministry forward after his departure.

Paul also understood the importance of partnership in missionary work. His letters reveal an extensive network of co-workers who shared both his vision and his courage. Barnabas, Silas, Timothy, Luke, Priscilla, Aquila, and dozens of others risked their lives alongside Paul to establish churches throughout the Roman Empire. This team approach multiplied both the effectiveness and the sustainability of his ministry.

The Fruit of Faithful Courage

The results of Paul's missionary courage were extraordinary by any measure. Within thirty years of his conversion, he had established thriving churches throughout Asia Minor, Macedonia, and Greece. These weren't just small groups of believers but organized communities that provided leadership, financial support, and spiritual nurture for converts from diverse cultural backgrounds.

More importantly, Paul's theological writings became the foundation for Christian doctrine and practice. His letters to these missionary churches addressed practical questions about cross-cultural ministry, church organization, and Christian living that continue to guide believers today. Without Paul's missionary courage, we wouldn't have Romans, 1 and 2 Corinthians, Galatians, Ephesians, Philippians, Colossians, or 1 and 2 Thessalonians.

Paul's influence extended far beyond his lifetime. The churches he established became launching points for further missionary expansion. The leaders he trained carried the Gospel into regions he never visited. The theological framework he developed enabled Christianity to adapt to different cultures while maintaining its essential message.

CHAPTER 2:
The Early Church - Courage Becomes Contagious

From Jerusalem to the Ends of the Earth

While Paul's missionary journeys are the most documented examples of early Christian courage, he was not alone in crossing borders for the Gospel. The entire early Church was characterized by a missionary boldness that compelled believers to carry Christ's message far beyond their comfort zones.

The book of Acts records that within days of Pentecost, the Gospel had begun to spread beyond Jerusalem's boundaries. The persecution that scattered believers after Stephen's martyrdom, intended to destroy the Church, actually multiplied its influence. As Acts 8:4 records, "those who were scattered went everywhere preaching the word."

This wasn't an organized missionary strategy but spontaneous missionary courage. Ordinary believers who fled persecution didn't hide their faith in new locations, they proclaimed it. They understood instinctively that their salvation was too precious to keep secret and their Savior too wonderful to remain unknown.

Philip's Pioneering Spirit

Philip the evangelist exemplifies the missionary courage that characterized the early Church. Originally chosen as one of the seven deacons to serve tables in Jerusalem, Philip didn't let administrative responsibilities limit his evangelistic vision. When persecution scattered the believers, Philip went to Samaria, a region Jews typically avoided due to cultural and religious prejudices.

His ministry in Samaria required extraordinary courage. Samaritans and Jews had centuries of animosity between them. Jewish teachers avoided Samaritan territories, and Samaritans were hostile to Jewish religious leaders. Yet Philip crossed these cultural boundaries because his encounter with Christ had shattered his ethnic prejudices.

The results were remarkable: "The multitudes with one accord heeded the things spoken by Philip, hearing and seeing the miracles which he did. For unclean spirits, crying with a loud voice, came out of many who were possessed; and many who were paralyzed, and lame were healed. And there was great joy in that city" (Acts 8:6-8).

Philip's Samaritan ministry became a prototype for cross-cultural evangelism. He demonstrated that the Gospel could transcend ethnic barriers, that supernatural power accompanied bold proclamation, and that joy was the natural result of authentic spiritual breakthrough.

The Ethiopian Eunuch and Expanding Horizons

Philip's encounter with the Ethiopian eunuch reveals another dimension of early Church missionary courage, sensitivity to divine guidance in cross-cultural ministry. When an angel instructed Philip to leave his successful Samaritan revival and travel to a desert road, he obeyed without question.

This obedience led to one of the most significant conversions in early Christian history. The Ethiopian eunuch was not just an individual convert but a bridge to an entire continent. As a court official returning to Africa, he carried the Gospel to regions that wouldn't see organized missionary work for centuries.

Philip's willingness to abandon a successful ministry for uncertain divine guidance demonstrates the kind of flexible courage required for effective cross-cultural missions. Missionary courage must be willing to change strategies, locations, and methods in response to divine direction rather than clinging to human plans or comfortable successes.

Barnabas and the Art of Encouragement

While Paul receives most of the attention for missionary courage, Barnabas played an equally crucial role in the early Church's expansion.

His name means "son of encouragement," and his ministry demonstrated that missionary courage includes the willingness to support and develop other missionaries.

Barnabas showed remarkable courage in accepting Paul when other believers were still suspicious of his conversion. He risked his own reputation to advocate for this former persecutor, recognizing that God's grace could transform even the Church's greatest enemy into its most effective advocate.

His partnership with Paul on the first missionary journey required enormous courage. They were venturing into territories where the Gospel had never been preached, where local religions were deeply entrenched, and where opposition was certain. Yet Barnabas was willing to leave the comfort and security of the Antioch church to pioneer new works in foreign lands.

Perhaps most significantly, Barnabas demonstrated the courage to part ways with Paul when they disagreed about taking John Mark on their second journey. Rather than allowing conflict to end their missionary work, Barnabas took John Mark and went to Cyprus, while Paul chose Silas for his second journey. This "disagreement" actually doubled their missionary impact and demonstrated that courage sometimes requires difficult decisions about partnerships and strategies.

Priscilla and Aquila: Tentmaking Missionaries

The missionary courage of Priscilla and Aquila reveals another model for cross-cultural ministry. As tentmakers who traveled for business, they used their professional mobility to carry the Gospel to new locations. They demonstrated that missionary courage doesn't require a full-time religious vocation but can be exercised through secular professions.

Their willingness to risk their lives for Paul's ministry is mentioned in Romans 16:3-4: "Greet Priscilla and Aquila, my fellow workers in Christ Jesus, who risked their own necks for my life, to whom not only I give thanks, but also all the churches of the Gentiles." This couple understood that effective missionary work sometimes requires literal life-and-death courage.

Their ministry to Apollos in Acts 18 reveals another dimension of missionary courage, the willingness to invest in developing other leaders. Rather than competing with Apollos or feeling threatened by his eloquence, they took him aside and "explained to him the way of God more accurately." This courage to develop potential rivals for the sake of Gospel expansion demonstrates the selfless heart required for sustainable missionary work.

Thomas: The Ultimate Border Crosser

While Paul and others focused on the Roman Empire, Apostle Thomas demonstrated perhaps the most dramatic missionary courage by journeying to Southern India in the AD 50s. This former doubter, forever remembered for questioning Christ's resurrection, became the embodiment of faith-driven courage when he left the familiar Middle Eastern world for the completely unknown culture of the Indian subcontinent.

Thomas landed on the Malabar Coast in what is now Kerala, facing challenges that made Paul's missionary journeys seem comfortable by comparison. He encountered people who had never heard of Judaism, let alone Christianity. He dealt with completely different religious systems, Hinduism and Buddhism, that required entirely new approaches to Gospel presentation.

Yet Thomas didn't just visit India, he embraced it. He learned local languages, understood cultural nuances, and preached Christ in ways that resonated with Hindu and Buddhist worldviews while remaining uncompromisingly Christian. His ministry along the Kerala coastal areas produced thousands of converts and established churches that still exist today, nearly two thousand years later.

But Thomas's border-crossing faith couldn't be contained even within India's vast boundaries. He traveled to neighboring lands, establishing churches and training leaders until his martyrdom in AD 72, when he was pierced with a spear while praying, dying as he had lived, on his knees before the God who had transformed his doubt into world-changing faith.

The churches Thomas established became known as "St. Thomas

Christians" and maintained their distinct identity through centuries of foreign invasions, political upheavals, and religious persecution. Their survival testifies to the supernatural foundation laid by one man's extraordinary missionary courage.

The Expanding Circle of Courage

By AD 100, less than seventy years after Christ's crucifixion, the Gospel had spread throughout the Roman Empire and beyond. Christian communities existed in every major city from Britain to India, from Ethiopia to Germany. This expansion occurred without modern transportation, communication, or financial systems. It was accomplished entirely through the missionary courage of believers who refused to let cultural, geographical, or linguistic barriers limit their witness.

This early missionary expansion established patterns that continue to characterize effective cross-cultural ministry:

Cultural Adaptation: Early missionaries learned to present the Gospel in ways that connected with local worldviews while maintaining theological integrity.

Leadership Development: They focused on training local leaders rather than maintaining foreign control of new churches.

Strategic Partnerships: They worked in teams that combined different gifts, backgrounds, and personalities for maximum effectiveness.

Supernatural Dependence: They expected God to confirm their message through signs, wonders, and miraculous provision.

Sacrificial Commitment: They were willing to suffer hardship, persecution, and death rather than compromise their calling.

Flexible Methods: They adapted their strategies to local conditions while maintaining consistency in their message.

The courage of these early missionaries wasn't just personal bravery but corporate commitment to Christ's global mission. They understood that they were part of something larger than individual ministry, they were participants in God's plan to reach every tribe, tongue, and nation with the Gospel.

CHAPTER 3:
Modern Global South Revivals - Courage In Contemporary Context

The Shifting Center of Christianity

One of the most remarkable developments in contemporary Christianity is the explosive growth of the Church in the Global South, Africa, Asia, and Latin America. While Christianity has declined numerically in Europe and North America, it has experienced unprecedented expansion in regions that were largely unreached just a century ago.

This growth has not occurred in comfortable circumstances. The believers driving these movements face poverty, persecution, natural disasters, corrupt governments, and hostile religious environments. Yet their faith continues to spread with a power and passion that echoes the book of Acts. Their missionary courage is demonstrated not just in traveling to distant lands but in faithfully proclaiming Christ in their own dangerous contexts.

The courage of Global South believers reveals that missionary boldness is not limited to cross cultural pioneers but characterizes any Christian who refuses to let difficult circumstances silence their witness. These believers are crossing borders, social, economic, religious, and sometimes geographical, to reach the unreached in their own regions and beyond.

Nigeria: Faith Under Fire

Nigeria presents one of the most dramatic examples of missionary courage in the contemporary world. With over 200 million people representing hundreds of ethnic groups and major Muslim and Christian populations, Nigeria is a microcosm of global religious diversity and conflict.

In northern Nigeria, where Islamic extremist groups like Boko Haram have terrorized Christians for over a decade, pastors continue to plant churches knowing that discovery could mean death. Villages that lose their churches to terrorist attacks rebuild them within months. Believers who flee violence often return to continue their witness despite ongoing danger.

Pastor James Wuye exemplifies this courage. A former Christian militant who lost his hand in religious violence, he experienced a transformation that led him to work for peace between Christians and Muslims. Despite death threats from both extremists and former allies, he continues his ministry of reconciliation, demonstrating that missionary courage sometimes means staying in dangerous places rather than fleeing to safety.

The Redeemed Christian Church of God (RCCG), founded by Nigerian pastor Enoch Adeboye, demonstrates how missionary courage can spread globally. From its humble beginnings, RCCG now operates in over 190 countries with millions of members. Nigerian missionaries have planted churches throughout Africa, Europe, and North America, often serving immigrant communities neglected by traditional denominations.

These Nigerian missionaries don't wait for comfortable circumstances or guaranteed support. They often arrive in foreign countries with minimal resources, working secular jobs while establishing churches. Their courage is sustained by the same faith that enabled the early Church to expand throughout the Roman Empire, the conviction that God's power is greater than any human obstacle.

China: Underground Courage

The house church movement in China represents perhaps the largest demonstration of missionary courage in contemporary Christianity. Despite decades of persecution, imprisonment, and harassment, Chinese believers have built one of the fastest-growing Christian movements in history.

Current estimates suggest there are over 100 million Christians in China, with the vast majority belonging to unregistered house churches that operate outside government control.

These believers meet in homes, offices, and public spaces, knowing that each gathering could result in arrest, fines, or imprisonment.

Pastor Wang Yi of Early Rain Covenant Church in Chengdu exemplifies this courage. Despite repeated warnings from authorities, he continued to preach, teach, and advocate for religious freedom until his arrest in 2018. His final sermon before imprisonment, titled "My Declaration of Faithful Disobedience," revealed the theological foundation for his courage:

"As a pastor of a Christian church, I must faithfully preach the word of God, and fulfill the gospel ministry that the Lord Jesus Christ has entrusted to me. This means that I must continue to preach and must continue to speak on matters of public concern as a preacher of the gospel."

Wang Yi received a nine-year prison sentence for "subverting state power," but his church continues to meet despite ongoing persecution. His courage has inspired believers throughout China and demonstrated that faithful witness is possible even under totalitarian regimes.

The Chinese house church movement has also produced a remarkable missionary vision. Despite facing persecution at home, Chinese believers have launched the "Back to Jerusalem" movement, aiming to evangelize the unreached peoples between China and Jerusalem. This vision has sent Chinese missionaries to some of the world's most dangerous and resistant mission fields, including the Middle East, Central Asia, and North Africa.

India: Ancient Faith, Modern Courage

India, this vast, ancient land where the Apostle Thomas first carried the Gospel in the first century, has never been a quiet mission field. It has been a battlefield of faith, a crucible of conviction, a furnace where the courage of God's people has been tested and proven again and again.

From the 1700s onward, waves of European and American missionaries crossed storm-torn oceans with nothing but a burning call from God. They planted schools, hospitals, and Bible colleges. They confronted oppressive systems, championed social reforms, and ignited sweeping mass movements. Through their sacrificial witness, entire communities, especially Dalit populations long crushed by caste oppression, found dignity, liberation, and a new identity in Christ.

Then the twentieth century dawned, and with it came a spiritual eruption.

The fires of Pentecostalism burst across India in the early 1900s, reshaping the landscape of Indian Christianity. The **Assemblies of God in India** was established in 1918, ushering in a Spirit-filled movement that transcended culture, caste, and language.

Out of this rising tide emerged a young man whose life would become a turning point in Indian church history: **Pastor K. E. Abraham**. Born in 1899 in Kerala, he was among the first in India to fully embrace the Pentecostal awakening. While many watched from a distance, Abraham stepped boldly into the flame.

It was in the quiet village of **Kumbanad**, near **Thiruvalla**, that Abraham began gathering believers in small homes, meetings marked by repentance, tears, worship, and the unmistakable power of the Holy Spirit. These humble gatherings quickly grew into a thriving fellowship. Kumbanad became the unexpected birthplace of a movement that would one day circle the world.

Abraham walked from village to village, often barefoot, often hungry, but always aflame with conviction: **India needed a Spirit-led, Spirit-filled, indigenous Church**. In a time when many Indian churches were still guided by foreign leadership, Abraham championed an authentically Indian Pentecostal identity. He preached with piercing simplicity, fasted often, prayed deeply, healed the sick, confronted darkness, and watched whole families, and sometimes whole villages, turn to Jesus.

By the late 1920s and early 1930s, the revival in Kumbanad had grown so rapidly that it demanded structure and unity. From this need emerged the **Indian Pentecostal Church of God (IPC)**, one of the earliest and now the largest indigenous Pentecostal denominations in India.

Under Abraham's leadership:
- Bible schools trained Indian pastors and evangelists.

- Missionaries were sent from Kerala into Tamil Nadu, Andhra Pradesh, Karnataka, Maharashtra, and eventually into North India.
- House churches sprang up in regions with no previous Christian presence.
- Revival meetings drew thousands hungry for healing, deliverance, and hope.

And what began in Kumbanad did not stay in Kumbanad. By mid-century, IPC congregations had spread across India and into the Middle East, Europe, Africa, Australia, and North America, carried by Indian believers who refused to keep the fire to themselves. Kumbanad's simple prayer huts became a globally recognized center of Pentecostal leadership.

Pastor Abraham authored books, defended Pentecostal doctrine with conviction, and lived a life of prayer and sacrifice that shaped generations of leaders. His imprint remains unmistakable today, in the global IPC network, in countless pastors formed in Kerala, and in the ongoing revival culture that still pulses through Indian Pentecostalism.

Meanwhile, revival was not limited to IPC. The **Church of God movement** spread across the subcontinent. And by the 1990s, a new non-denominational surge exploded across India, marked by rapid church planting, house-church networks, youth revivals, worship movements, and evangelists who refused to bow to cultural pressure. Today, India's Church is one of the most diverse, dynamic, and fastest-growing in the world.

Yet courage remains the price of witness in India. Hindu nationalism has sharpened that cost dramatically.

In many states, believers face anti-conversion laws, police surveillance, mob violence, and social ostracism. Churches are burned. Pastors are beaten. Entire congregations are threatened with starvation or expulsion unless they renounce Christ.

Still, they do not stop.

Brother Yun, the "Heavenly Man," testified that the courage of Indian house-church leaders astonished even him. These believers preach where preaching is illegal, baptize where baptisms are monitored, and plant churches among unreached tribes at the risk of imprisonment or death.

From this soil of sacrifice, India's missions movement continues to rise. Indigenous organizations, such as **Gospel for Asia** (now *Believers Eastern Church*), send thousands of missionaries into regions closed to traditional evangelism. **Dr. K. P. Yohannan**, raised in the same soil where Thomas walked and where Abraham labored, carried the Gospel into the most difficult corners of Asia, raising up an army of frontline workers.

And now, **the seed has become a harvest.**

What began as whispered prayers in tiny village homes has become one of the greatest spiritual expansions of the modern era. India now hosts some of the **largest churches in the world**, monuments not of wealth or architecture, but of relentless faith and supernatural hunger.

Foremost among them is **Calvary Temple Church in Hyderabad**, a Spirit-filled congregation with **over 300,000 members**, one of the largest church fellowships on earth, still growing at a breathtaking pace. What began as a small flock has become a sea of worshipers, a living testament to what God can do when His people refuse to bow to fear.

Across South India, North India, and the megacities of the nation, countless other churches gather tens of thousands each week, evidence that the Gospel is alive, unstoppable, and advancing with force.

Today, the Indian Church stands as a holy paradox:

Persecuted yet multiplying.

Pressed yet unbroken.

Wounded yet unstoppable.

From ancient apostolic beginnings to modern Pentecostal fire, from the dusty roads of Kumbanad to the massive congregations of Hyderabad, India continues to produce some of the most courageous Christian witnesses on earth, men and women who will not bow, will not break, and will not turn back.

Latin America: Pentecostal Fire

The Pentecostal movement in Latin America demonstrates how missionary courage can transform entire regions. Beginning in the early 20th century, Pentecostalism has become the dominant form of Protestantism in Latin America, with adherents now numbering in the hundreds of millions.

This growth has occurred despite political instability, economic hardship, and opposition from established religious institutions. Pentecostal believers in Latin America have shown remarkable courage in proclaiming a Gospel of personal transformation and divine power that challenges both traditional Catholicism and secular materialism.

In countries like Guatemala, El Salvador, and Brazil, Pentecostal churches have grown dramatically among the poor and marginalized. These believers demonstrate missionary courage by sharing their faith in contexts of extreme poverty, violence, and social upheaval.

They plant churches in slums, minister to gang members, and provide hope to people abandoned by other institutions.

The Latin American Missions' movement has also produced remarkable cross-cultural missionaries. Brazilian missionaries now serve throughout Africa, Asia, and the Middle East. Organizations like JOCUM (Youth With A Mission) Brazil send thousands of missionaries worldwide, demonstrating that missionary courage is not limited to Western countries or wealthy churches.

Africa: The New Center of Christianity

Africa has experienced the most dramatic Christian growth of any continent in the 20th and 21st centuries. From approximately 10 million Christians in 1900, Africa now has over 650 million believers, making it the continent with the largest Christian population in the world.

This growth has occurred despite colonialism, civil wars, poverty, disease, and corrupt governments. African Christians have demonstrated extraordinary courage in maintaining their faith through seemingly impossible circumstances and in sharing that faith with others facing similar challenges.

The Democratic Republic of Congo exemplifies both the challenges and the courage of African Christianity. Despite decades of war, foreign intervention, and economic collapse, the Congolese Church continues to grow and send missionaries to neighboring countries. Pastors conduct ministry while dodging armed militias, believers walk hours to attend services, and church planters venture into territories controlled by hostile forces.

South Africa's transformation from apartheid to democracy was significantly influenced by Christian leaders who demonstrated moral courage in opposing racism and advocating for justice. Leaders like Desmond Tutu and Allan Boesak risked their careers and lives to speak prophetically against oppression, demonstrating that missionary courage includes social justice as well as evangelism.

The African mission's movement has produced remarkable indigenous organizations like the Sudan Interior Mission (now SIM) and numerous African Initiated Churches (AICs) that combine traditional African culture with biblical Christianity. These movements demonstrate how missionary courage can create new forms of Christian expression that are both culturally relevant and biblically faithful.

Characteristics of Global South Missionary Courage

Despite their diverse contexts, these Global South movements share several characteristics that reflect authentic missionary courage:

Contextual Relevance: They present Christianity in ways that address local needs, concerns, and worldviews while maintaining biblical integrity.

Supernatural Expectation: They expect God to work miracles, heal the sick, and demonstrate His power in ways that confirm the Gospel message.

Indigenous Leadership: They develop local leaders rather than depending on foreign missionaries or financial support.

Sacrificial Commitment: They are willing to suffer for their faith and continue ministry despite persecution, poverty, or danger.

Holistic Ministry: They address physical, social, and economic needs as well as spiritual concerns, demonstrating the comprehensive nature of God's love.

Missionary Vision: They send their own missionaries to other regions and cultures, understanding that the Great Commission applies to all believers, not just Western churches.

Cultural Confidence: They are proud of their heritage and seek to express Christianity in authentically local ways rather than merely copying Western models.

CHAPTER 4:
Reflection: Where Is God Calling You?

The testimonies of Paul's journeys, the early Church's expansion, and the Global South's contemporary revivals reveal a consistent pattern: God uses ordinary people with extraordinary courage to cross borders and transform lives. These believers were not spiritual supermen born with unusual bravery, they were normal people who encountered an abnormal God and were forever changed by that encounter.

Their courage came not from natural boldness but from supernatural conviction. They believed that the Gospel was true, that Jesus was alive, that eternity was real, and that people without Christ were lost. These beliefs created a sense of urgency and importance that enabled them to overcome fear, opposition, and hardship.

But their courage was also sustained by the community. Paul traveled with partners, the early Church supported one another through persecution, and Global South believers found strength in corporate worship and shared suffering. Missionary courage is not a solo act but a community commitment to advance God's kingdom regardless of personal cost.

As you consider these examples of missionary courage, the crucial question is not whether you admire their dedication but whether you will follow their example. God is calling you to cross borders, perhaps not geographical ones, but certainly barriers that keep you from fully participating in His global mission.

Where is God calling you to step beyond your comfort zones?

Your borders might be:

- **Cultural**: People from different ethnic, economic, or social backgrounds in your own community

- **Generational**: Young people or older adults who seem impossible to reach
- **Professional**: Coworkers, clients, or colleagues who need to hear your testimony
- **Geographic**: Neighborhoods, cities, or regions where the Gospel is not well known.
- **Religious**: People from other faith backgrounds who have never heard an authentic Gospel presentation
- **Social**: Marginalized people who have been overlooked by traditional churches

The same courage that drove Paul across the Roman Empire, that sustained Thomas in India, that empowered the early Church through persecution, and that fuels Global South believers through hardship is available to you today. It comes not from human bravery but from divine encounter, from meeting Jesus in such a real and powerful way that keeping Him to yourself becomes impossible.

Your missionary courage may begin with a conversation with a neighbor, a relationship with someone different from you, or a commitment to serve in a ministry that stretches your comfort zone. It might grow into short-term missions' involvement, support for cross-cultural missionaries, or even a call to leave your familiar environment for full-time missionary service.

But it will certainly involve crossing some border that fear, prejudice, or comfort has kept you from crossing. The same Spirit who compelled Paul to preach to Gentiles, who sent Philip to Samaria, who sustained Thomas in India, and who empowers believers in Nigeria, China, India, and throughout the Global South is living within you, waiting to give you the courage necessary to advance God's kingdom in your generation.

The borders are waiting. The harvest is ready. The Spirit is willing. The question that remains is whether you will let your faith cross the borders or let the borders contain your faith.

Your answer will determine not only the scope of your own spiritual adventure but also the eternal destiny of those who are waiting on the other side of whatever borders God is calling you to cross.

The courage is available. The call is clear. The choice is yours.

What borders is God asking you to cross? on the other side of whatever borders God is calling you to cross. The choice is yours. The faith is available. The borders are calling.

What will you choose?

5. REVIVAL AND RENEWAL

There are moments in history when heaven breaks through the ordinary routines of earth with such power that entire generations are forever changed. These are not gentle improvements or gradual reforms, but explosive interventions of divine presence that shatter spiritual complacency, transform hardened hearts, and redirect the course of human civilization. These moments have a name, revival, and they represent God's periodic invasions of human history to awaken His people and reclaim His rightful place at the center of their lives.

Revival is not a church program or evangelistic campaign. It cannot be manufactured by human effort or scheduled according to human convenience. It is the sovereign work of God among His people, a time when the Holy Spirit moves with such intensity that the supernatural becomes commonplace, the impossible becomes inevitable, and the spiritually dead come alive in ways that leave no doubt about the reality and power of the living God.

Throughout history, these seasons of divine visitation have followed periods of spiritual decline, moral compromise, and religious formalism. When the Church has drifted from its first love, when believers have settled for routine religion instead of a vibrant relationship, when society has forgotten God and pursued its own wisdom, the stage has been set for revival. Like lightning that builds tension in storm clouds before exploding across the sky, spiritual awakening often emerges from the darkness of widespread apostasy and cultural decay.

But revival is more than a historical phenomenon, it is God's pattern for renewal in every generation. The same conditions that preceded great awakenings in the past exist in our time: moral confusion, spiritual hunger, religious emptiness, and cultural crisis. The same God who sent revival to past generations is ready to send it again to any people who will meet His conditions and cry out for His intervention.

The testimonies of revival throughout church history read like chapters from the book of Acts transported to different times and places. In 18th-century England, George Whitefield preached to crowds of thirty thousand while hardened coal miners wept rivers of repentance. In 19th-century America, Charles Finney's meetings produced such conviction that entire cities were transformed as bars closed, theaters emptied, and courts had no cases to try because crime had virtually disappeared. In 20th-century Wales, young coal miner Evan Roberts saw the Holy Spirit fall with such power that 100,000 people were converted in six months and the moral climate of an entire nation was revolutionized.

These were not isolated incidents but repeated demonstrations of what happens when God's people position themselves for divine intervention. Revival has swept through college campuses, transforming students who became missionaries and reformers. It has invaded urban slums, bringing hope to the hopeless and dignity to the despised. It has penetrated rural communities, turning hardened farmers into passionate evangelists. It has crossed denominational boundaries, uniting believers who had been separated by theological disputes and cultural differences.

Yet revival is not just about dramatic public meetings or emotional religious experiences. At its heart, revival is about renewal, the restoration of an authentic relationship between God and His people. It begins in individual hearts that have grown cold toward God and spreads to families, churches, communities, and nations as the fire of divine love consumes everything that has replaced God at the center of human affection and allegiance.

Personal renewal often precedes corporate revival. Throughout history, great awakenings have begun with individuals who became desperate for more of God in their own lives. These were not necessarily spiritual leaders or religious professionals, but ordinary believers who could no longer tolerate the gap between their spiritual potential and their spiritual reality. They began to seek God with unusual intensity, to pray with unprecedented fervency, and to hunger for His presence with holy desperation.

Their personal renewal created a spiritual atmosphere that invited God's broader intervention.

Like kindling that catches fire and ignites larger logs, their individual flames of renewed devotion became the starting points for movements that transformed entire regions. Jonathan Edwards experienced personal revival before the Great Awakening came to New England. John Wesley felt his heart "strangely warmed" at Aldersgate before the Methodist revival transformed England. Evan Roberts cried out "Bend me, Lord!" for months before the Welsh Revival exploded across Wales.

This pattern continues today. Around the world, individuals are experiencing personal renewal that is creating expectations for corporate revival. In prayer rooms and private closets, believers are crying out for God to visit their generation with the same power that marked previous awakenings. They are studying the history of revival, learning its principles, and positioning themselves for divine visitation.

But revival is not just about recovering past experiences, it is about preparing for future purposes. Every great awakening in history has prepared the Church for challenges and opportunities that lay ahead. The Protestant Reformation prepared Christianity for the age of exploration and global missions. The Great Awakenings in America prepared believers for the challenges of building a new nation and eventually abolishing slavery. The revivals of the 19th and early 20th centuries prepared the Church for the challenges of industrialization, urbanization, and two world wars.

Our generation faces challenges that require supernatural intervention: widespread moral confusion, technological disruption of human relationships, global conflicts that threaten civilization, and spiritual darkness that has settled over much of the developed world. These challenges cannot be met through human wisdom, political solutions, or social programs alone. They require the kind of divine intervention that only comes through genuine spiritual awakening.

The question is not whether God wants to send revival, history proves He does, repeatedly and convincingly. The question is whether we will create the conditions that invite His visitation and sustain His work when it comes.

Revival has conditions, not formulas.

It requires desperate prayer, not casual petition. It demands complete surrender, not partial commitment.

It calls for radical holiness, not comfortable compromise.

Those who have experienced revival testify that it is worth any price required to receive it. The presence of God that comes during seasons of awakening is so sweet, so moving, so life-changing that everything else pales in comparison. Believers who taste revival become permanently spoiled for ordinary religious experience. They carry within them a hunger for God's presence that cannot be satisfied by routine worship, predictable prayers, or comfortable Christianity.

Revival also creates legacy. The believers who experience genuine spiritual awakening become different kinds of Christians, bolder in witness, deeper in love, more effective in ministry, and more committed to advancing God's kingdom. Their children are raised in atmospheres of expectation rather than routine. Their churches become centers of spiritual power rather than social clubs. Their communities are transformed by the overflow of divine life working through yielded vessels.

This is why every believer should hunger for revival and position themselves to experience renewal. Not because it is emotionally exciting or socially impressive, but because it represents the fullness of what God intends for His people. Revival is not an optional upgrade to normal Christian experience, it is the restoration of authentic Christianity that makes ordinary religion look pale and powerless by comparison.

The stories you are about to read are not ancient history or impossible dreams. They are testimonies to the unchanging character of a God who delights to reveal Himself to hungry hearts and transform desperate people. They are invitations to believe that the same Spirit who moved in past revivals is ready to move again in any heart, any church, any community that will meet His conditions and cry out for His visitation.

Your heart can experience personal revival. Your family can know seasons of spiritual renewal. Your church can become a center of divine awakening. Your community can be transformed by the power of God working through believers who refuse to settle for anything less than the fullness of His presence.

The fire of revival is always burning in the heart of God, waiting for fuel that will allow it to spread. That fuel is found in hearts that are hungry, lives that are surrendered, and prayers that are desperate. The question is not whether revival will come again, it will. The question is whether you will be part of it when it does.

The choice is yours. The fire is waiting. The conditions are available. Revival and renewal are closer than you think, perhaps just one surrendered heart away.

Will that heart be yours?

CHAPTER 1:
Azusa Street And Charismatic Renewal - From A Humble Warehouse To Global Awakening

The Fire Falls on Azusa Street

An Unlikely Beginning

In 1906, a dilapidated warehouse on Azusa Street in downtown Los Angeles became the epicenter of a spiritual earthquake that would reshape Christianity worldwide. The building was nothing impressive, a former Methodist church turned storage facility, with rough wooden floors, makeshift seating, and walls that hadn't seen fresh paint in years. But within these humble walls, something extraordinary was about to happen that would ignite the largest and fastest-growing movement in Christian history.

The man God chose to lead this revival was equally unlikely. William J. Seymour was a one-eyed African American preacher, son of former slaves, who had been invited to Los Angeles to pastor a small Holiness church. When he arrived and began preaching about the baptism of the Holy Spirit with the evidence of speaking in tongues, the church board locked him out after just one service. They found his message too radical, too dangerous, too different from their comfortable religious routine.

But God's timing is never defeated by human rejection. Seymour began holding prayer meetings in the home of Richard and Ruth Asberry on North Bonnie Brae Street. What started as a small gathering of hungry believers quickly grew beyond the capacity of any home. On April 9, 1906, after days of intense prayer and fasting, the Holy Spirit fell with such power that people began speaking in tongues, weeping, laughing, and experiencing divine healings.

The supernatural presence was so overwhelming that neighbors gathered on the street to witness what was happening inside.

Edward Lee, one of the first to receive the baptism of the Holy Spirit at Bonnie Brae, later described that first outpouring: "The power of God came down like the rain. The Spirit fell on several people at once. They began speaking in tongues and magnifying God. We were all amazed and wondered what this could mean. Some were afraid, but we knew it was God."

The Move to Azusa Street

Within days, the crowds had grown too large for the Asberry home. The little band of believers found the abandoned warehouse at 312 Azusa Street and transformed it into what would become the most famous address in Pentecostal history. They installed rough wooden benches, created a simple pulpit from two wooden crates and a plank, and prepared for what they hoped would be a short-term solution to their space problem.

None of them imagined that this humble building would host continuous revival services for over three years, attract visitors from around the world, and launch a movement that would eventually include over 600 million believers globally. The Azusa Street Mission, as it became known, operated with a simplicity that contrasted sharply with the elaborate religious ceremonies of established churches.

There was no formal liturgy, no scheduled program, no professional choir, and no celebrity speakers. Services began around 10 AM and continued until late at night, seven days a week. People came and went freely, joining in worship, prayer, and testimony as the Spirit led them. The atmosphere was both reverent and spontaneous, orderly yet unpredictable, multicultural yet unified around their common experience of God's presence.

Frank Bartleman, a journalist and participant in the revival, wrote: "The color line was washed away in the blood. A white minister from the South would have a black man lay hands on him to receive the baptism with the Holy Spirit. The Holy Spirit was given leadership, and He alone had the right of way."

The Supernatural Becomes Normal

What made Azusa Street extraordinary was not emotional excitement but supernatural manifestation. People spoke in languages they had never learned, and visitors from other countries recognized their native tongues as being spoken by Americans who had never traveled abroad. Divine healings were commonplace, the blind received sight, the lame walked, and people with chronic illnesses were instantly restored to health.

These weren't staged performances or psychological manipulation. Medical doctors documented healings they could not explain. Skeptics came to expose what they assumed was fraud and left as believers. Newspaper reporters arrived to write sensational stories about religious fanaticism and found themselves kneeling at the altar seeking God.

A. C. Valdez Sr., who attended services as a teenager, later recalled: "I have been in many revivals since that time, but I have never seen the glory of God as I witnessed it at Azusa Street. When we walked within two or three blocks of the building, we could feel the presence of God. People were lying on the ground all around the building, under the conviction of the Holy Spirit."

The revival was characterized by several distinctive features:

Racial Integration: In an era of strict racial segregation, Azusa Street brought together people of all ethnicities in genuine spiritual unity. African Americans, whites, Hispanics, Asians, and Native Americans worshipped side by side, received ministry from one another, and experienced God's presence without regard to racial barriers.

Gender Equality: Women participated fully in ministry, preaching, praying for the sick, and leading services. This was progressive in 1906, when most churches restricted women's roles to singing and children's ministry.

Cross-Denominational Participation: Baptists, Methodists, Presbyterians, Catholics, and people from dozens of other backgrounds came together, discovering that their hunger for God transcended denominational boundaries.

Supernatural Manifestations: Speaking in tongues, divine healing, prophecy, and other spiritual gifts operated regularly, creating an atmosphere where the miraculous was expected rather than exceptional.

The Message Spreads

From Azusa Street, the Pentecostal message spread with remarkable speed. Visitors from other states and countries attended the revival, received the baptism of the Holy Spirit, and returned to their homelands to start similar movements. Within five years, Pentecostal churches had been established on every continent.

Charles Parham, who had taught Seymour about Spirit baptism, initially supported the revival but later distanced himself due to its racial integration. This highlighted one of Azusa Street's most significant contributions, its demonstration that the Gospel transcends racial and social barriers when the Holy Spirit is truly in control.

Lucy Farrow, a former slave who became one of Seymour's key associates, carried the Pentecostal message to Norfolk, Virginia, and other East Coast cities. G. B. Cashwell brought it to the South, where it took root among poor whites and blacks who were hungry for a fresh touch from God. International visitors like Alexander Boddy took the message to England, while Thomas Ball Barratt spread it throughout Scandinavia.

The revival's influence extended beyond Pentecostalism. Traditional denominations began to examine their own spiritual temperature and seek more authentic manifestations of God's power. Missionary societies reported unusual breakthroughs in previously resistant fields. Bible schools and seminaries began to include courses on spiritual gifts and divine healing.

The Opposition and Decline

Not everyone welcomed the Azusa Street revival. Established religious leaders criticized its emotional expressions, questioned its supernatural claims, and condemned its racial integration.

Secular newspapers ridiculed the participants and sensationalized the more unusual aspects of the meetings.

The Los Angeles Times, in typical journalistic fashion of the era, described the revival as "wild scenes" and "weird babble," calling the participants "colored people and a sprinkling of whites" who were engaged in religious fanaticism. Such criticism only served to advertise the revival and draw more curious visitors.

Internal challenges also arose. Some participants began to emphasize the gifts more than the Giver, leading to spiritual pride and divisiveness. Others tried to organize and control what had been spontaneous, causing the Holy Spirit's presence to diminish. Personal conflicts between leaders and doctrinal disagreements gradually fragmented the unity that had characterized the early years.

By 1909, the intensity of the revival had decreased significantly. Seymour continued to pastor the Azusa Street Mission until his death in 1922, but the days of international attention and dramatic supernatural manifestations had ended. However, the impact of those three years of revival would continue to influence Christianity for more than a century.

The Charismatic Renewal

A New Outpouring

Fifty-four years after the Azusa Street revival began to wane, God initiated another wave of spiritual renewal that would eventually touch every major Christian denomination. The Charismatic Renewal, as it came to be known, began in 1960 with the most unlikely candidate imaginable, Dennis Bennett, an Episcopal priest in Van Nuys, California.

Bennett was everything William Seymour was not: white, highly educated, theologically sophisticated, and pastoring an affluent suburban congregation. Yet on April 3, 1960, this respectable Anglican minister announced to his Trinity Episcopal Church congregation that he had received the baptism of the Holy Spirit and spoken in tongues.

The response was immediate and dramatic. Some parishioners rejoiced, others were confused, and many were outraged. By the end of the month, Bennett had resigned his position and moved to St. Luke's Episcopal Church in Seattle, Washington, a small, struggling parish that would become the launching pad for renewal within traditional denominations.

Bennett's experience and testimony opened the door for thousands of mainline Protestants and Catholics to seek and receive the baptism of the Holy Spirit without leaving their denominational affiliations. This was revolutionary, previous Pentecostal movements had typically required believers to join Pentecostal churches to experience spiritual gifts. The Charismatic Renewal demonstrated that the Holy Spirit's power was available within existing church structures.

The Catholic Charismatic Renewal

Perhaps the most surprising development was the spread of charismatic renewal within the Roman Catholic Church. In 1967, a group of Catholic professors and students at Duquesne University in Pittsburgh experienced the baptism of the Holy Spirit while on a weekend retreat. They had been reading about the early church and praying for a deeper spiritual experience when God responded in ways they never expected.

The experience spread to Notre Dame University and the University of Michigan, where Catholic students and faculty began speaking in tongues, experiencing divine healings, and developing a more personal relationship with Jesus Christ. This created a theological crisis, how could good Catholics have experiences that seemed more Protestant than Catholic?

The answer came from church history itself. The students discovered that the spiritual gifts they were experiencing had been present in the early Catholic Church and throughout various renewal movements in Catholic history. They weren't becoming Protestant; they were becoming more fully Catholic by reclaiming their spiritual heritage.

By 1975, over 50,000 Catholics had attended the first National Catholic Charismatic Conference.

Cardinal Leon Joseph Suenens of Belgium became a prominent supporter, providing theological guidance and protecting the movement from opposition within the church hierarchy. Pope Paul VI gave his blessing to the Catholic Charismatic Renewal, and Pope John Paul II later became one of its strongest advocates.

The Catholic Charismatic Renewal brought together practices that had seemed contradictory, traditional Catholic liturgy and spontaneous worship, devotion to Mary, and emphasis on personal relationship with Jesus, papal authority, and spiritual democracy. This integration demonstrated that the Holy Spirit could work within established religious structures while bringing new life and power to ancient traditions.

Denominational Transformation

The Charismatic Renewal spread through virtually every Protestant denomination with remarkable speed and similar patterns. Lutheran charismatics discovered that Martin Luther himself had believed in spiritual gifts. Methodist charismatics found connections to their Wesleyan heritage of personal holiness and divine empowerment. Presbyterian charismatics learned about the work of the Holy Spirit in Reformed theology.

Rather than destroying denominational distinctives, the renewal often strengthened them by providing spiritual power to support theological convictions. Lutheran charismatics became more committed to grace, Methodist charismatics emphasized sanctification, and Presbyterian charismatics focused on God's sovereignty in spiritual gifts.

The renewal also created new forms of Christian expression. Calvary Chapel, founded by Chuck Smith in Costa Mesa, California, combined charismatic worship with strong biblical teaching to reach the hippie generation of the 1960s and 1970s. The Vineyard movement, led by John Wimber, emphasized "power evangelism", using spiritual gifts as tools for reaching non-Christians.

These new movements attracted people who had been turned off by traditional church services but were hungry for authentic spiritual experience. They created more casual atmospheres, contemporary music styles, and practical teaching that addressed real-life issues while maintaining belief in miraculous intervention.

Television and Global Expansion

The Charismatic Renewal coincided with the rise of Christian television, which accelerated its spread beyond anything previous revival movements had experienced. Oral Roberts, who had been a Pentecostal evangelist, brought divine healing into middle-class American living rooms through his television programs. Pat Robertson created the 700 Club, which combined charismatic teaching with news and entertainment.

These television ministries reached millions of viewers who would never have attended Pentecostal churches but were open to experiencing God's power in their own denominational contexts. They provided teaching, testimony, and encouragement for believers who were isolated in non-charismatic churches or communities.

The global expansion of the Charismatic Renewal was even more remarkable than its denominational spread. By the 1980s, charismatic movements existed in virtually every country where Christianity was present. The renewal is adapted to different cultural contexts while maintaining core emphases on spiritual gifts, personal relationship with Jesus, and expectation of supernatural intervention.

In Latin America, the renewal contributed to explosive Protestant growth that challenged Catholic dominance. In Africa, it provided the theological framework for indigenous expressions of Christianity that included divine healing and spiritual warfare. In Asia, it offered supernatural power that could compete with traditional religions' claims of miraculous abilities.

The Third Wave

By the 1980s, a "Third Wave" of renewal was emerging among evangelicals who had been skeptical of both classical Pentecostalism and the Charismatic Renewal. Led by professors like Peter Wagner at Fuller Seminary and John Wimber of the Vineyard movement, this phase emphasized spiritual gifts for evangelism and church growth rather than personal spiritual experience.

The Third Wave introduced concepts like "power evangelism" and "spiritual warfare" to mainstream evangelicalism.

It encouraged believers to expect supernatural confirmation of the Gospel message through healings, prophecies, and miraculous provision. This approach attracted evangelicals who wanted to experience God's power but were uncomfortable with some charismatic practices.

Churches in this movement typically maintained more structured worship services while being open to spiritual gifts operating during ministry times. They emphasized training believers to use spiritual gifts rather than depending on specially gifted leaders. This democratization of spiritual power created thousands of churches where ordinary members regularly prayed for healing, received prophetic insights, and expected God to work miraculously.

CHAPTER 2:
Everyday Revival In Modern Life

Beyond the Sanctuary

One of the most significant developments in contemporary renewal is its movement beyond church buildings into the ordinary spaces of daily life. Unlike previous revivals that were primarily associated with special meetings and designated holy places, modern renewal is increasingly characterized by believers experiencing God's presence and power in their homes, workplaces, and communities.

This shift represents a return to the New Testament pattern where the early Church operated as a seven-day-a-week lifestyle rather than a once-a-week religious gathering. Modern believers are discovering that the same Holy Spirit who falls in church services is equally present in business meetings, family dinners, neighborhood conversations, and workplace challenges.

Revival in the Home

Perhaps nowhere is everyday revival more evident than in Christian families who have discovered that their homes can be centers of spiritual power. These families have moved beyond saying grace before meals and bedtime prayers to creating atmospheres where God's presence is expected, and His intervention is normal.

The Martinez family in Phoenix, Arizona, represents thousands of similar families worldwide. After both parents experienced personal renewal at their church, they began to invite the Holy Spirit into every aspect of their family life. Their home became a place where prayer was spontaneous, worship was natural, and supernatural experiences were common.

"We started praying together as a family every morning before work and school," explains Maria Martinez. "Soon, our children were having dreams and visions from God. Our neighbors began asking us to pray for them because they noticed something different about our family. Our home became a place where people knew they could encounter God."

Their teenage daughter began receiving prophetic insights about her classmates' needs and was able to minister to friends who were struggling with family problems. Their young son started praying for sick people and seeing them healed. Even their non-Christian neighbors began requesting prayer during times of crisis.

This pattern is being repeated in homes around the world where families have decided that revival is not just something that happens at church, but something that transforms the basic unit. of society, the family. These families report stronger marriages, more obedient children, greater financial provision, and increased influence in their communities.

Workplace Transformation

Christian business leaders are discovering that the same spiritual principles that bring renewal to churches can transform workplace environments. They are creating companies where prayer is normal, integrity is standard, and divine guidance influences business decisions.

Tom Johnson, CEO of a construction company in Dallas, Texas, began each workday with voluntary prayer meetings for his employees. Initially, only a few participated, but as workers began experiencing answers to prayer and increased job satisfaction, attendance grew. The company's safety record improved dramatically, employee turnover decreased, and profitability increased despite its commitment to ethical business practices.

"We pray about everything, safety issues, difficult clients, financial challenges, even personnel decisions," Johnson explains. "Our employees know that this is a place where God's presence is welcome, and His guidance is sought. It has created a work environment unlike anything I've experienced in thirty years of business."

Similar transformations are occurring in schools where Christian teachers and administrators create atmospheres of prayer and faith. Healthcare facilities where staff members pray for patients are reporting unusual rates of recovery and family satisfaction. Government offices where Christians serve are experiencing reduced conflict and increased effectiveness.

Community Renewal

Entire communities are experiencing renewal as individual believers begin to live out their faith in public spaces and civic involvement. Rather than keeping their Christianity confined to private belief or church attendance, these believers are bringing the reality of God's power into community problem-solving, neighborhood relationships, and social challenges.

In Stockton, California, a group of pastors began meeting weekly to pray for their city, which was facing economic collapse, high crime rates, and social division. As they continued to intercede, they began to see individual believers step forward to address specific community needs. Christians started neighborhood prayer walks, organized food distribution programs, and created after-school tutoring programs.

Within five years, the city's crime rate had dropped significantly, new businesses had begun to thrive, and community relationships had improved noticeably. While not every positive change could be directly attributed to spiritual renewal, the correlation was strong enough that even secular leaders acknowledged the positive influence of faith-motivated community involvement.

Characteristics of Everyday Revival

These examples of everyday revival share several common characteristics that distinguish them from traditional religious activity:

Integration: Faith is integrated into daily life rather than compartmentalized into religious activities. Prayer, worship, and spiritual gifts operate in ordinary settings alongside regular responsibilities.

Spontaneity: While these believers maintain disciplines of prayer and Bible study, they are also open to spontaneous spiritual experiences throughout their day. They expect God to speak, guide, and intervene in unexpected ways.

Community Impact: Their faith creates a positive influence in their spheres of relationships. Coworkers, neighbors, and family members notice something different and are drawn to inquire about their faith.

Supernatural Expectation: They expect God to work miraculously in ordinary situations. They pray for divine healing, supernatural provision, and spiritual breakthrough with confidence that God will respond.

Servant Leadership: They use whatever influence they have, in families, workplaces, or communities, to serve others and create environments where people can encounter God's love and power.

Overcoming Obstacles

Believers who pursue everyday revival face several common obstacles that require wisdom and persistence to overcome:

Religious Traditions: Some churches and Christian communities are uncomfortable with renewal that operates outside traditional religious structures. Believers may face criticism for being "too charismatic" or "too emotional" in their faith expression.

Secular Resistance: Workplace and community environments may be resistant to open expressions of faith. Believers must learn to be wise as serpents and gentle as doves, finding appropriate ways to demonstrate their faith without violating workplace policies or alienating non-Christian colleagues.

Personal Inconsistency: Living a supernatural lifestyle requires consistent spiritual disciplines and character development. It's easy to become excited about spiritual experiences while neglecting the fruit of the Spirit that makes those experiences credible to others.

Spiritual Warfare: As believers begin to see God work more powerfully in their daily lives, they often encounter increased spiritual opposition.

They must learn to recognize and resist spiritual attacks while maintaining love and forgiveness toward people who oppose their faith.

The Ripple Effect

When individuals experience everyday revival, it creates ripple effects that extend far beyond their immediate circumstances. Their transformed lives influence others who may never attend their churches but observe their daily conduct. Their prayers and service create positive changes in their communities that benefit both believers and non-believers.

Perhaps most importantly, everyday revival demonstrates that Christianity is not just a religion about getting to heaven someday but a relationship with the living God that transforms present reality. This authentic demonstration of faith is often more convincing to skeptics than elaborate apologetic arguments or evangelistic programs.

CHAPTER 3:
What Revival Could Look Like In Your Life

Personal Assessment

Before exploring what revival could look like in your specific circumstances, it's important to honestly assess your current spiritual condition. Revival, by definition, is the restoration of life to something that has become dormant or dead. This requires recognizing areas where your spiritual life needs renewal.

Ask yourself these diagnostic questions:

Spiritual Appetite: Do you hunger for God's Word and presence, or do you read the Bible and pray primarily from duty? When did you last feel genuine excitement about spending time with God?

Supernatural Expectation: Do you regularly expect God to work miraculously in your daily life, or have you settled for natural explanations for everything that happens to you?

Kingdom Impact: Are people being positively influenced toward Christ through your daily life, or could most people interact with you regularly without knowing you're a Christian?

Joy and Peace: Do you experience the joy and peace that Jesus promised His followers, or are you troubled by the same anxieties and frustrations that characterize non-believers?

Spiritual Gifts: Are you regularly using spiritual gifts to bless others, or are you uncertain about whether God has gifted you for ministry?

Honest answers to these questions will reveal where revival is needed most urgently in your life.

Revival in Your Daily Routine

Personal revival often begins with inviting God into the ordinary routines of daily life. Instead of trying to add more religious activities to an already busy schedule, consider how you can invite God's presence into activities you're already doing.

Morning Transformation: Rather than checking your phone or turning on the news immediately upon waking, create a few minutes of conscious connection with God. This doesn't require a lengthy prayer time, it might be as simple as saying, "Good morning, Holy Spirit. I invite You to guide my day and work through me to bless others."

Commute Communion: Transform your drive to work into a mobile prayer meeting. Pray for the people you'll encounter, ask for wisdom about challenges you'll face, and worship God through music or spontaneous praise. Some believers report that their car has become their favorite place to meet with God.

Workplace Witness: Look for opportunities to demonstrate Christ's character through your work ethic, relationships, and responses to stress. Offer to pray for coworkers who are facing challenges. Ask God for supernatural wisdom about job-related decisions. Be alert to divine appointments, unexpected opportunities to minister to colleagues.

Family Faith: If you have a family, begin incorporating prayer into family activities beyond formal devotional times. Pray together about family decisions, celebrate answered prayers, and teach children to expect God to guide and provide for your family.

Evening Evaluation: End each day by processing your experiences with God. Thank Him for His faithfulness, confess any failures or sins, and ask for His blessing on tomorrow's activities.

Revival in Your Relationships

One of the most obvious areas where revival manifests is in transformed relationships. When God's love fills your heart, it naturally overflows to others in ways that can revolutionize your personal connections.

Marriage Renewal: If you're married, revival can transform your relationship from merely functional to genuinely joyful. Begin praying together daily, even if it's initially awkward. Ask God to show you how to love your spouse more effectively. Expect God to provide wisdom for resolving conflicts and grace for overcoming differences.

Parenting with Power: Parents experiencing revival discover supernatural wisdom for training their children and supernatural love for difficult seasons. They begin to see their parenting as a ministry rather than just a responsibility, praying for their children as much as providing for them.

Friendship Evangelism: Revival naturally creates opportunities to share faith with friends who notice positive changes in your life. Rather than feeling pressured to preach to everyone, you begin to attract questions about the source of your peace, joy, and strength.

Difficult Relationships: Perhaps most significantly, revival provides divine grace to love people who have been difficult to love, difficult coworkers, challenging family members, or neighbors who have been sources of frustration.

Revival in Your Community

Personal revival that remains completely private is incomplete. Authentic renewal creates the desire and ability to influence your community positively for Christ's sake.

Neighborhood Impact: Begin praying regularly for your neighbors by name and looking for practical ways to demonstrate Christ's love. This might mean offering help during emergencies, organizing community events, or simply being friendlier and more available.

Service Opportunities: Look for existing community needs where you can volunteer your time and talents. Food banks, homeless shelters, school programs, and community organizations provide opportunities to serve others while demonstrating your faith through actions.

Business Influence: If you own a business or have workplace influence, consider how you can operate according to kingdom principles, treating employees fairly, serving customers excellently, and conducting business with integrity that stands out in your industry.

Civic Engagement: Revival often motivates believers to become more involved in local government, school boards, and community organizations where their values can influence public policy and social conditions.

Revival in Your Spiritual Life

The most fundamental aspect of personal revival is the renewal of your relationship with God Himself. This involves both restoring neglected spiritual disciplines and developing new dimensions of spiritual experience.

Prayer Transformation: Move beyond routine prayers to expectant conversation with God throughout your day. Learn to listen for His voice through Scripture, circumstances, and inner impressions. Develop confidence in bringing every concern to Him and expecting His guidance.

Bible Engagement: Rather than just reading the Bible for information, ask the Holy Spirit to make it come alive as personal communication from God. Read expectantly, looking for specific guidance for your current situations and relationships.

Worship Lifestyle: Cultivate awareness of God's presence throughout your day, finding reasons to praise Him for His creation, provision, and faithfulness. Let worship music and spontaneous thanksgiving become natural expressions of your relationship with Him.

Spiritual Gifts: Ask God to show you how He has gifted you for ministry and begin stepping out in faith to use those gifts. This might mean praying for sick people, encouraging discouraged individuals, or sharing insights God gives you for others' benefit.

Fasting and Focus: Consider incorporating fasting into your spiritual disciplines, not as a religious duty but as a way to express your hunger for more of God and create focused time for prayer and spiritual seeking.

What to Expect

If you seriously pursue revival in your personal life, you can expect several things to happen:

Increased Spiritual Sensitivity: You'll become more aware of God's presence and more responsive to His guidance. You'll also become more discerning about spiritual influences and atmospheres around you.

Greater Joy and Peace: Despite circumstances remaining the same, you'll experience supernatural joy and peace that comes from renewed confidence in God's love and faithfulness.

Enhanced Relationships: Your relationships will improve as God's love flows through you more freely. Even difficult people may respond differently to the grace and patience that revival produces.

Supernatural Provision: You'll begin to notice God's provision in ways you previously overlooked, unexpected opportunities, timely resources, and solutions to problems that exceed natural explanation.

Increased Opposition: As you become more effective for God's kingdom, you may experience increased spiritual opposition. This is actually confirmation that your spiritual influence is growing and threatening Satan's territory.

Expanded Vision: Your concern for others will grow beyond your immediate circle to include people and causes you never previously considered. You may develop a burden for unreached peoples, social justice issues, or community transformation.

Starting Your Revival Journey

Personal revival doesn't require dramatic experiences or a complete life overhaul. It begins with simple steps of faith and consistent spiritual discipline:

1. **Make the Decision**: Decide that you will no longer settle for spiritual mediocrity. Ask God to reveal areas of your life that need renewal and commit to cooperating with His work of transformation.

2. **Begin Small**: Start with manageable changes, a few extra

minutes of prayer, one act of service weekly, or regular Bible reading with an expectant heart.

3. **Find Community**: Connect with others who share your hunger for revival.

   This might be a small group, a prayer partner, or a mentor who can encourage your spiritual growth.

4. **Expect God to Move**: Approach each day with anticipation that God will work through you and speak to you in ways that demonstrate His reality and love.

5. **Stay Flexible**: Be willing to adjust your plans and priorities as God redirects your attention to opportunities and relationships that further His kingdom purposes.

Revival in your life is not just possible, it's God's intention for every believer. The same Spirit who fell at Azusa Street and continues to renew Christians around the world is living within you, ready to transform your ordinary life into an extraordinary demonstration of His power and love.

Your revival begins with your next prayer, your next act of faith, your next decision to trust God more completely than you have before. The fire is ready to fall. The Spirit is waiting to move.

The only question is whether you're ready to be transformed from routine religion to authentic spiritual life.

CHAPTER 4:
Reflection: Your Revival Begins Now

The stories of Azusa Street and the Charismatic Renewal prove that God continues to pour out His Spirit on ordinary people who hunger for extraordinary encounters with Him. From William Seymour's humble warehouse to Dennis Bennett's Episcopal pulpit, from Catholic universities to Protestant denominations, the Holy Spirit has consistently demonstrated that authentic revival transcends human barriers and transforms every life it touches.

But these historical accounts are not just inspiring stories from the past, they are invitations to experience your own personal renewal. The same Spirit who fell on Azusa Street is available to fall fresh on your life. The same power that transformed denominations can transform your daily routine. The same love that broke racial barriers can break through whatever obstacles are limiting your spiritual influence.

Your revival doesn't require a special building, a famous preacher, or dramatic circumstances. It requires only a hungry heart, a surrendered life, and expectant faith. Whether in your family room or workplace, neighborhood or community, God is ready to demonstrate His reality through believers who refuse to settle for ordinary when extraordinary is available.

The fire is still falling. The Spirit is still moving. Your revival is waiting. What will you choose?

III

Living Spirit-Filled Today

*When we surrender the wheel,
we finally arrive at who we were meant to become.*

BEYOND KNOWING:
The Call to Become

Knowledge without application is merely an academic exercise. Inspiration without implementation becomes spiritual entertainment. The testimonies of Pentecost power, the accounts of century-long prayer movements, the stories of missionary courage, and the records of revival fires, all of these historical treasures become meaningless unless they translate into transformed living today.

We stand at a crucial crossroads. Behind us lie two thousand years of documented evidence that God moves effectively among His people. We've traced the unbroken chain from that first upper room in Jerusalem through Moravian prayer closets, missionary journeys to unreached peoples, and revival fires that transformed entire nations. We've seen ordinary believers become extraordinary vessels of divine power, watched comfortable Christians abandon their security for dangerous obedience, and witnessed the supernatural become normal in communities that dared to believe God for the impossible.

But now comes the moment of truth. Now comes the question that separates curious observers from committed participants, interested readers from transformed disciples, those who admire spiritual giants from those who join their ranks.

This is where the rubber meets the road. This is where ancient promises become present reality. This is where the same Spirit who fell on the disciples, empowered the Moravians, sent missionaries to the ends of the earth, and ignited revivals throughout history proves that He is still alive, still active, and still available to ordinary believers who dare to live extraordinarily.

The tragedy of much Christian education is that it produces believers who know about God's power without experiencing it, who can quote Scripture about spiritual gifts without operating in them, who understand theology about the Holy Spirit without being filled with Him. We become experts on spiritual history while remaining novices in spiritual living. We develop impressive vocabularies about supernatural Christianity while maintaining thoroughly natural lifestyles.

But God never intended for His people to be professional observers of His activity. He didn't design the Church to be a museum displaying past miracles but a workshop producing present ones. The same Spirit who raised Jesus from the dead doesn't just want to be studied, He wants to be released. The power that shook Jerusalem, sustained martyrs, and sparked revivals doesn't just want to be admired, it wants to be applied.

Part III is not about admiring spiritual giants from a safe distance. It's about joining their ranks. It's not about studying supernatural Christianity as a historical phenomenon. It's about experiencing it as a daily lifestyle. It's not about adding more information to your theological database. It's about allowing divine transformation to revolutionize your practical reality.

The believers whose testimonies have filled these pages were not born into a different spiritual category than you. They breathed the same air, faced similar challenges, and wrestled with the same human limitations that you confront daily. The difference was not their natural capacity but their supernatural encounter. They met God in ways that ruined them for ordinary living and spoiled them for small dreams.

That same encounter is available to you today. The same Spirit who fell on Pentecost morning is hovering over your life right now. The same fire that transformed fishermen into apostles is ready to transform your routine existence into extraordinary ministry. The same power that enabled first-century believers to turn the world upside down is waiting to work through twenty-first-century believers who will pay the price of surrender necessary to receive it.

Your moment has arrived. You've read the testimonies, studied the principles, and traced the historical patterns. You've seen what God has done through believers who positioned themselves to receive His fullness. Now the question is whether you will create similar conditions in your own life, whether you will open your heart to the same transforming encounters, whether you will step out in the same faith-filled obedience that marked those who have gone before you.

This is not about becoming someone else or copying another person's spiritual experience. This is about becoming fully yourself, the person God created you to be, filled with His Spirit, empowered for His purposes, and released into His calling on your life. It's about discovering that the ordinary life you've been living is actually the launching pad for an extraordinary adventure that begins the moment you say yes to everything God wants to do in and through you.

The principles you're about to explore are not theoretical concepts but practical realities tested by believers in every generation, every culture, and every circumstance. They work because they're based on God's unchanging character and his consistent desire to fill willing vessels with His presence and power. They're available because Jesus paid the price to make them your inheritance. They're possible because the same Spirit who empowered biblical saints' lives is within you today.

But they require more than mental assent. They demand heart surrender. They call for faith-filled action. They invite you to move beyond the safety of spiritual spectatorship into the adventure of supernatural living.

The fire that has burned through twenty centuries of church history is ready to burn in your heart, your home, your workplace, and your community today. The power that transforms cowards into champions, doubters into defenders, and followers into leaders is available to transform whatever areas of your life need divine intervention. The love that compelled missionaries to cross every border is ready to compel you to cross whatever boundaries separate you from God's fullest purposes for your existence.

The question is no longer whether God moved powerfully in biblical times or church history, the evidence is overwhelming. The question is whether you will create space in your life for Him to move powerfully right now. Will you position yourself to receive what He's always been ready to give? Will you step out of the spectator stands and onto the playing field of Spirit-filled living? Will you trade the security of knowing about God's power for the adventure of experiencing it personally?

Your moment has come. Your Pentecost is waiting. Your Spirit-filled life begins now.

The historical accounts you've read were not written to impress you with what God did in the past but to inspire you to believe for what He wants to do in the present. The testimonies of past believers were not recorded to make you feel inferior but to make you expectant.

The same Spirit, the same power, the same love, the same calling, all are yours today. The only question that remains is what you will do with the extraordinary inheritance that has been placed within your reach.

Your transformation from routine to alive is not just possible, it's inevitable once you decide to cooperate fully with what God wants to do in your life. The pages ahead will show you how.

Your Spirit-filled adventure begins with the next page you turn, the next prayer you pray, the next step of faith you take.

The fire is falling. Will you let it consume you?

6. RECOGNIZING THE SPIRIT'S VOICE

Learning to Hear God in the Noise of Modern Life

In a world that never stops talking, the greatest challenge facing believers today may not be finding time to speak to God but learning to recognize when God is speaking to us. We live in an age of constant noise, notifications buzzing, voices chattering, media streaming, and our own thoughts racing at breakneck speed. Yet somewhere in the midst of this cacophony, the gentle voice of the Holy Spirit continues to whisper, guide, warn, encourage, and direct those who have ears to hear.

The ability to recognize God's voice is not a mystical gift reserved for spiritual elites or ancient prophets. It is the birthright of every believer, promised by Jesus Himself when He said, "My sheep hear My voice, and I know them, and they follow Me" (John 10:27). The question is not whether God is speaking, He is. The question is whether we have learned to distinguish His voice from all the other voices competing for our attention.

This is perhaps the most practical skill any Christian can develop. The ability to hear God's guidance in daily decisions, to sense His warnings before danger, to receive His comfort in times of pain, and to know His direction at crucial crossroads can literally transform every aspect of your life. Yet most believers stumble through their days making decisions based solely on human wisdom, missing divine guidance that could save them from mistakes, spare them unnecessary pain, and lead them into opportunities they never could have imagined.

Learning to recognize the Spirit's voice is like developing any relationship, it requires time, attention, and practice.

But the rewards are incomparable. When you can distinguish God's voice from your own thoughts, from Satan's deceptions, and from the world's confusion, you gain access to wisdom that transcends human understanding and guidance that never leads astray.

CHAPTER 1:
The Nature Of God's Voice

How God Speaks Today

Unlike the dramatic manifestations we read about in Scripture, burning bushes, audible voices from heaven, and angelic visitations, God typically speaks to believers today in ways that require spiritual sensitivity to recognize. His voice is usually not louder than our thoughts but different in character, tone, and content.

The Holy Spirit speaks most commonly through what we might call "gentle impressions", thoughts, ideas, or convictions that seem to arise from within us but carry a weight, peace, or authority that distinguishes them from our natural thinking. These impressions often come during prayer, while reading Scripture, or in quiet moments when our minds are receptive to divine input.

Sarah Chen, a nurse in Seattle, learned to recognize these impressions during her night shifts. "I began to notice that sometimes I would have strong urges to check on certain patients more frequently than my normal routine required. At first, I dismissed these as random thoughts. But when I started paying attention, I discovered that these patients almost always needed immediate attention, they were having complications, experiencing pain, or simply needed someone to talk to during a difficult night. I realized God was using these impressions to make me a better nurse and to position me to minister to people at their most vulnerable moments."

God's voice is characterized by several consistent qualities that distinguish it from other influences:

Alignment with Scripture: God will never speak to you in ways that contradict His written Word. His voice through impressions, circumstances, or other means will always be consistent with biblical truth and character.

Peace and Love: Even when God's message involves correction or difficult truth, it carries an underlying tone of love and ultimately produces peace in your spirit, even if it initially creates conviction about sin or needed change.

Fruit-Bearing Direction: God's guidance leads toward spiritual fruit, love, joy, peace, patience, kindness, goodness, faithfulness, gentleness, and self-control. It may involve sacrifice or difficulty, but it always moves you toward greater spiritual maturity and kingdom effectiveness.

Persistent Relevance: God's voice often returns repeatedly to the same themes or directions until you respond, while passing thoughts or emotions tend to fade quickly if ignored.

The Difference Between God's Voice and Other Voices

Learning to hear God requires learning to distinguish His voice from three other primary sources of internal communication: your own thoughts, Satan's deceptions, and the world's influence.

Your Own Voice tends to be self-focused, concerned primarily with your comfort, convenience, and natural desires. It seeks the easiest path, avoids sacrifice, and prioritizes immediate gratification over long-term spiritual growth. Your own voice is often anxious, worried, or frustrated when things don't go according to your plans.

Satan's Voice is characterized by condemnation without hope, discouragement that leads to despair, and suggestions that lead away from God and toward sin. Satan's voice often sounds religious but produces fear, guilt, and spiritual paralysis rather than conviction that leads to repentance and change.

The World's Voice echoes the values and priorities of secular culture, materialism, self-promotion, moral relativism, and the pursuit of success defined by wealth, status, and power. It sounds reasonable and practical, but lacks eternal perspective and spiritual wisdom.

God's Voice, by contrast, is characterized by love, truth, hope, and direction toward spiritual growth and kingdom purposes. Even though it involves difficult obedience, it ultimately produces joy, peace, and spiritual fruitfulness.

David Kim, a businessman in Chicago, learned these distinctions through practical experience: "I used to make business decisions based entirely on profit potential and personal advancement. But as I began to seek God's guidance, I noticed that His voice often led me toward choices that seemed less advantageous in the short term but produced greater satisfaction and better long-term results. When I followed my own voice, I often succeeded financially but felt empty spiritually. When I followed what I sensed was God's direction, I sometimes made less money but experienced deeper fulfillment and saw my business become a platform for ministry to employees and clients."

CHAPTER 2:
Discernment Patterns - How God Confirms His Voice

Divine Promptings: The Spirit's Gentle Push

One of the most common ways God speaks is through gentle promptings, sudden urges to pray for someone, call a friend, take a different route home, or speak an encouraging word to a stranger. These promptings often seem random or inconvenient, which is why they're easy to dismiss as imagination or wishful thinking.

However, believers who learn to recognize and respond to divine promptings discover that they become conduits for God's love and power in ways that constantly amaze them. The key is learning to distinguish between passing thoughts and genuine spiritual promptings.

Divine promptings typically share several characteristics:

Unexpectedness: They arise suddenly, often interrupting your current train of thought or activity with something you weren't previously considering.

Persistence: If ignored, they tend to return repeatedly until you either respond or clearly sense the opportunity has passed.

Other-Centeredness: They usually involve blessing, helping, or ministering to someone else rather than serving your own interests.

Urgency Without Anxiety: They carry a sense of importance or timing without the anxious pressure that characterizes human worry or manipulation.

Maria Rodriguez, a teacher in Phoenix, shares her experience: "I was driving to work one morning when I had a strong urge to stop and buy coffee for my principal, who had been dealing with a difficult parent situation all week. It seemed silly, I was already running late and didn't have extra money to spend. But the prompting was so persistent that I finally stopped. When I gave her the coffee, she started crying and said she had been praying that morning for just some small sign that God cared about her stress. That simple act of obedience opened the door for me to pray with her and share my faith in a way that transformed our working relationship."

Supernatural Wisdom: Beyond Human Understanding

Another way God speaks is through supernatural wisdom, insights, solutions, or understanding that exceed your natural knowledge or experience. This might involve knowing how to handle a relationship conflict you've never faced before, understanding a complex situation with clarity that surprises you, or receiving creative solutions to problems that have stumped others.

Supernatural wisdom often comes during prayer, Bible reading, or quiet reflection, but it can also arrive in the midst of conversations, meetings, or crisis situations when you desperately need divine guidance.

The distinguishing characteristics of supernatural wisdom include:

Clarity in Complexity: God's wisdom often brings simple solutions to complicated problems, helping you see through confusion to the heart of issues.

Long-term Perspective: Divine wisdom considers consequences and outcomes that human thinking might overlook, leading to decisions that prove wise over time, even if they seem difficult initially.

Beneficial for Others: God's wisdom typically benefits not only you but also others involved in the situation, reflecting His heart for all people rather than just your personal interests.

Humility and Dependence: Receiving supernatural wisdom typically increases your awareness of your need for God rather than making you feel spiritually superior or self-sufficient.

James Wright, a counselor in Atlanta, describes his experience: "I was working with a teenage client who had been completely unresponsive to every counseling approach I had tried. During one session, I silently prayed for wisdom, and suddenly I had an insight about a traumatic event in his childhood that we had never discussed. When I gently brought up this topic, he broke down and shared experiences that became the breakthrough point in his healing. I had no natural way of knowing about those experiences, it was pure revelation from God that enabled me to help this young man find freedom."

Divine Peace: The Umpire of the Heart

Perhaps one of the most reliable ways to confirm God's guidance is through the presence or absence of divine peace. Colossians 3:15 instructs believers to "let the peace of God rule in your hearts," with the word "rule" meaning to act as an umpire or final authority in making decisions.

When you're walking in God's will, even if the path is difficult or uncertain, you experience an underlying peace that transcends your circumstances. Conversely, when you're moving away from God's direction, you typically experience unrest, anxiety, or a sense that something isn't right, even if the decision seems logical or beneficial.

This peace is different from mere absence of conflict or stress. It's a positive assurance that you're aligned with God's purposes, even when everything around you are chaotic or challenging. It's the peace Jesus promised when He said, "Peace I leave with you, My peace I give to you; not as the world gives do I give to you" (John 14:27).

Learning to recognize and follow this divine peace requires:

Stillness: Taking time to quiet your heart and mind so you can sense the Spirit's peace rather than being overwhelmed by emotional reactions or external pressures.

Patience: Waiting for peace to confirm direction rather than rushing ahead based on purely logical analysis or emotional impulses.

Obedience: Following peaceful direction even when it conflicts with your natural preferences or seems to involve sacrifice or difficulty.

Experience: Learning through practice to distinguish between divine peace and mere emotional calm or absence of immediate stress.

Rebecca Johnson, a mother of three in Dallas, learned to rely on divine peace for family decisions:

"My husband and I were considering a job opportunity that would require relocating our family across the country. On paper, it looked perfect, better salary, advancement opportunities, and a nice community. But every time we prayed about it, I felt increasingly unsettled in my spirit. My husband felt the same unrest. Even though we couldn't identify any logical reason to decline the opportunity, we decided to follow that lack of peace and stay where we were. Six months later, the company that had offered the position went through major layoffs, and we realized God had protected us from a difficult situation we couldn't have foreseen."

Scripture Illumination: When God's Word Comes Alive

One of the most reliable ways God speaks is through His written Word, but not just through regular Bible study. Sometimes specific verses will seem to leap off the page with particular relevance to your current situation, or passages you've read dozens of times will suddenly carry new meaning that speaks directly to decisions you're facing.

This is different from proof-texting, finding Bible verses that seem to support decisions you've already made. Scripture illumination involves the Holy Spirit using God's Word to provide specific guidance, comfort, or direction that you genuinely need.

Characteristics of genuine Scripture illumination include:

Timing: The passage becomes meaningful at the precise moment you need that particular guidance or encouragement.

Relevance: The verse or passage speaks directly to your specific situation in ways that feel personally directed rather than generally applicable.

Multiple Confirmations: The same theme or message may appear in different parts of Scripture during your devotional reading, sermons you hear, or conversations with other believers.

Alignment: The guidance you receive through Scripture illumination aligns with other forms of divine guidance you're receiving through prayer, circumstances, and wise counsel.

Character Development: The illuminated passage typically calls you toward greater spiritual maturity, sacrificial love, or kingdom purposes rather than merely personal benefit.

Michael Thompson, a college student in Colorado, experienced Scripture illumination during a difficult decision about his major: "I was torn between pursuing engineering, which would lead to financial security, and social work, which aligned more with my heart for helping people but offered much lower income potential. During my morning devotions, I read Matthew 6:33, 'Seek first the kingdom of God and His righteousness, and all these things shall be added to you.' I had read that verse many times, but that morning it seemed to glow on the page. Over the next week, the same message came up in three different sermons and two conversations with Christian mentors. I switched to social work, and God has provided for all my needs while giving me incredible fulfillment in my career."

Divine Confirmation: God's Multiple Witnesses

God often speaks through multiple sources simultaneously to confirm important decisions or directions. This might involve receiving the same guidance through prayer, Scripture, wise counsel, and circumstances, or experiencing several different divine promptings that all point in the same direction.

This pattern of multiple confirmations reflects God's understanding of our human tendency to doubt and our need for assurance when making significant decisions. It also protects us from making major life changes based on single impressions that might be influenced by our own desires or emotional states.

The principle of multiple confirmations has biblical precedent. God gave Gideon multiple signs to confirm his calling (Judges 6:36-40), and Paul received confirmation of his ministry direction through prophecy, circumstances, and inner conviction (Acts 16:6-10).

Types of divine confirmation include:

Counselor Confirmation: Wise, spiritually mature believers independently give you similar advice or express similar concerns about a decision you're considering.

Circumstantial Confirmation: External events line up in ways that either open doors you're sensing God wants you to walk through or close doors you're being warned against entering.

Repeated Messages: The same themes, verses, or guidance appear repeatedly through different sources over a period of time.

Peace and Opposition: You experience supernatural peace about decisions that align with God's will and unrest or obstacles concerning directions that aren't His best for you.

Spiritual Fruit: Following the guidance produces spiritual fruit in your life and a positive impact on others, confirming that the direction was indeed from God.

CHAPTER 3:
Practical Ways To Listen In Prayer

Creating Space for Divine Conversation

Most believers treat prayer like a monologue, talking to God without creating space for Him to respond. Learning to hear God's voice requires transforming prayer from one-way communication to genuine conversation where you speak and then listen for His response.

This requires intentional changes in how you approach prayer:

Slow Down: Instead of rushing through prayer lists or trying to cover multiple topics quickly, focus on one or two issues and give God time to respond to each concern.

Ask Specific Questions: Rather than making general requests for guidance, ask God specific questions about decisions you're facing, people you're concerned about, or directions you're considering.

Create Silence: After asking questions or expressing concerns, spend time in deliberate silence, waiting expectantly for God to respond through impressions, Scripture verses that come to mind, or gentle peace about particular directions.

Write Down Impressions: Keep a journal during prayer times to record thoughts, impressions, or insights that seem to come from beyond your natural thinking. This helps you remember the guidance you receive and track patterns in how God speaks to you.

Expect Response: Approach prayer with confident expectation that God wants to communicate with you, not as a religious duty but as a conversation with someone who loves you and desires to guide you.

Lisa Park, a businesswoman in Portland, transformed her prayer life by implementing these practices: "I used to spend fifteen minutes each morning rapidly going through my prayer list, asking God to bless various people and situations without really expecting Him to say anything back to me. When I learned to slow down and actually listen, everything changed. I started asking God specific questions about business decisions, relationships, and ministry opportunities, then waiting quietly for His response. The insights and guidance I began receiving revolutionized both my personal life and my business. I realized I had been trying to make decisions with only half the information available to me because I wasn't accessing God's wisdom."

Listening with Your Spirit, Not Just Your Mind

One of the biggest obstacles to hearing God's voice is trying to receive spiritual communication through purely mental processes. God is spirit, and He communicates spirit to spirit. Learning to listen with your spirit rather than just your mind requires developing spiritual sensitivity that goes beyond intellectual analysis.

This involves:

Heart Awareness: Paying attention to what you're sensing in your heart or spirit, not just what you're thinking in your mind. God often speaks through gentle impressions in your spirit that your mind might initially dismiss as imagination.

Emotional Discernment: Learning to distinguish between your emotional reactions and spiritual impressions. God's voice often carries different emotional qualities, peace, love, hope, conviction, than your natural emotional responses to situations.

Intuitive Insights: Being open to understanding or knowledge that comes through intuition rather than logical reasoning. God can give you insights about people, situations, or decisions that exceed what you could figure out through analysis.

Spiritual Sensitivities: Becoming aware of spiritual atmospheres, sensing when God's presence is particularly near, or recognizing when spiritual warfare is affecting your environment or relationships.

Faith-Based Receiving: Being willing to act on impressions that seem to come from God, even when you can't logically prove they're from Him, learning through experience to recognize the consistent characteristics of His voice.

Pastor Mark Roberts teaches his congregation to develop spiritual listening: "I encourage people to start by asking God simple questions during prayer and then waiting to see what impressions come to mind. Questions like 'Who should I encourage today?' or 'What do you want to teach me from this Scripture passage?' or 'How can I be a better spouse/parent/employee?' Then I tell them to pay attention to the first thoughts that come to mind that are loving, wise, and aligned with Scripture. Most people are amazed at how specific and helpful these impressions become as they practice listening with their spirits rather than just their minds."

Developing Spiritual Disciplines That Enhance Listening

Certain spiritual disciplines create conditions that make it easier to hear God's voice clearly. These practices quiet the noise in your heart and mind while increasing your sensitivity to divine communication.

Contemplative Bible Reading: Instead of reading Scripture primarily for information, read smaller passages slowly and meditatively, asking God what He wants to show you personally through each verse or phrase.

Worship-Based Prayer: Beginning prayer times with worship and thanksgiving creates a spiritual atmosphere that makes it easier to transition from focus on earthly concerns to receptivity to heavenly guidance.

Fasting from Distractions: Periodically fasting from television, social media, or other noise sources creates mental quiet that makes it easier to recognize God's gentle voice among the competing influences in your mind.

Regular Solitude: Scheduling regular times alone with God, away from responsibilities and relationships, provides opportunity for deeper spiritual listening without external interruptions.

Journaling Prayers: Writing out your prayers and God's responses creates a record of your spiritual conversations and helps you track patterns in how God communicates with you personally.

Walking Prayer: Combining prayer with gentle physical activity like walking often creates relaxed alertness that enhances spiritual sensitivity and makes it easier to receive divine impressions.

Scripture Memorization: Filling your mind with God's Word provides the Holy Spirit with biblical content to bring to your remembrance when you need guidance or encouragement.

Jennifer Martinez, a teacher and mother in Phoenix, developed a routine that enhanced her ability to hear God: "I wake up thirty minutes earlier than necessary and spend that time in worship, Scripture reading, and listening to prayer before my day begins. I also take a fifteen-minute prayer walk during my lunch break and spend ten minutes journaling prayers before bed. These consistent times of focused listening have made me much more sensitive to God's voice throughout the day. I now recognize His promptings to pray for people, His warnings about potential problems, and His guidance about decisions much more readily than when I only prayed sporadically."

CHAPTER 4:
Recognizing God's Voice In Daily Choices

Financial Decisions: Divine Wisdom for Material Matters

One area where learning to hear God's voice proves especially practical is in financial decisions. Whether you're considering major purchases, job changes, investment opportunities, or simply managing a household budget, divine guidance can save you from costly mistakes and lead you toward financial decisions that serve kingdom purposes.

God's voice regarding money typically emphasizes:

Stewardship Perspective: Reminding you that everything you have belongs to God and that financial decisions should be made with accountability to Him rather than just personal preference.

Kingdom Priorities: Guiding you to consider how financial choices affect your ability to give generously, serve others, and advance God's kingdom rather than just increasing your personal comfort or security.

Long-term Wisdom: Providing insight about consequences and outcomes that purely financial analysis might miss, helping you avoid decisions that look profitable short-term but prove unwise long-term.

Faith-Building Opportunities: Sometimes leading you to make financial decisions that require trust in God's provision rather than relying solely on your ability to manage every variable.

Generous Spirit: Prompting you toward generosity even when it doesn't make natural financial sense, often resulting in spiritual and material blessings that exceed what you sacrificed.

Tom and Susan Wilson learned to seek God's guidance for financial decisions after several costly mistakes early in their marriage:

"We bought a house that stretched our budget because it seemed like a good investment, but we never prayed about it. Within two years, Tom's company downsized, and we couldn't make the payments. After losing the house, we committed to seeking God's guidance for all major financial decisions. When we were ready to buy again, we found a much more modest home that didn't seem appealing initially, but when we prayed about it, we both felt strong peace. We bought it, and it became the perfect place to raise our children and host ministry activities. We learned that God's financial guidance often prioritizes His purposes over our preferences."

Relationship Decisions: Love Through Divine Lens

Perhaps no area of life requires divine wisdom more than relationships, whether choosing a spouse, making decisions about friendships, handling family conflicts, or navigating workplace relationships. Human emotions, natural attractions, and social pressures can cloud judgment in ways that lead to painful relational mistakes.

God's voice regarding relationships typically emphasizes:

Character Over Attraction: Directing attention toward a person's spiritual maturity, integrity, and heart character rather than just physical attraction, social status, or emotional chemistry.

Iron Sharpening Iron: Guiding you toward relationships that challenge you toward spiritual growth rather than just providing comfort or entertainment.

Kingdom Purposes: Leading you to invest in relationships that advance God's kingdom and encourage spiritual development rather than just meeting personal emotional needs.

Forgiveness and Reconciliation: Prompting you to pursue forgiveness and restoration in damaged relationships when appropriate, even when it requires sacrifice or vulnerability.

Wise Boundaries: Providing wisdom about when to invest deeply in relationships and when to maintain healthy boundaries with people who might be harmful to your spiritual or emotional well-being.

Rachel Thompson credits divine guidance for her marriage and several key friendships: "I was attracted to men who were charming but spiritually immature, and I kept ending up in relationships that were emotionally exhausting. When I started seeking God's guidance about dating, He led me to focus on character qualities rather than just chemistry. When I met my husband, I wasn't immediately attracted to him, but I felt peace about getting to know him better. As our friendship developed, I realized God had guided me to someone whose heart was truly aligned with His purposes. Our marriage has been a source of spiritual growth and ministry opportunity rather than just personal fulfillment."

Career Guidance: Finding Your Calling

Many believers struggle with questions about career direction, job changes, or discovering their calling. God's guidance in this area often involves long-term vision that goes beyond immediate financial considerations to embrace eternal purposes.

Divine guidance regarding a career typically includes:

Spiritual Gifting Alignment: Leading you toward work that utilizes the gifts and abilities God has given you for kingdom purposes rather than just personal success.

Ministry Opportunities: Opening doors to positions where you can influence others for Christ, serve human needs, and demonstrate Christian character in secular environments.

Character Development: Sometimes guiding you through challenging work situations that develop patience, faith, and other spiritual qualities rather than just advancing your career goals.

Provision and Purpose: Balancing practical needs for financial support with opportunities to serve God's purposes through your professional skills and relationships.

Season Awareness: Helping you recognize when it's time to stay in current situations for continued learning and when it's time to move toward new opportunities and responsibilities.

David Chen felt called to leave a lucrative law practice to become a high school teacher:

"For years, I made excellent money as a corporate lawyer, but I felt increasingly empty about spending my life helping wealthy companies get wealthier. During a men's retreat, God spoke to me clearly about using my analytical skills and communication abilities to influence young people rather than just advancing corporate interests. When I shared this with my wife, she said she had been sensing the same direction. We took a significant pay cut, but I've never been more fulfilled. I'm able to mentor students, coach the debate team, and demonstrate Christian character to teenagers during their most formative years. Several of my former students have told me that my example influenced their decisions to follow Christ."

Daily Decisions: God in the Details

Learning to hear God's voice transforms even small daily decisions into opportunities for divine guidance. This might involve sensing direction about which route to take to work, whom to call during a free moment, how to respond to a difficult email, or what to say to an upset child.

While not every minor decision requires divine consultation, developing sensitivity to God's voice in small matters prepares you to recognize His guidance in major decisions and creates a lifestyle of partnership with the Holy Spirit.

Examples of everyday divine guidance include:

Divine Appointments: Sensing prompts to make phone calls, send emails, or visit people that result in timely encouragement or ministry opportunities you couldn't have planned.

Safety and Protection: Receiving impressions to avoid certain routes, situations, or decisions that later prove to have prevented accidents, conflicts, or other problems.

Ministry Moments: Being prompted to speak encouraging words, offer prayers, or provide practical help at exactly the moments when people most need those expressions of God's love.

Wisdom for Parenting: Receiving insights about how to handle discipline situations, educational decisions, or relationship issues with your children that produce better results than your natural parenting instincts might have achieved.

Workplace Excellence: Getting ideas for solving problems, improving processes, or serving colleagues that enhance your professional effectiveness while demonstrating Christian character.

Common Obstacles to Clear Hearing

Several factors can interfere with your ability to recognize God's voice clearly:

Noise and Busyness: Schedules so packed with activity that you never create quiet space for spiritual listening.

Unconfessed Sin: Guilt or shame about ongoing sin that creates spiritual static and makes it difficult to sense God's presence and guidance.

Prideful Self-Reliance: Trusting your own wisdom and experience more than divine guidance, asking for God's blessing on decisions you've already made rather than seeking His direction before deciding.

Emotional Turbulence: Anxiety, anger, depression, or other strong emotions that overwhelm spiritual sensitivity and make it hard to distinguish God's voice from emotional reactions.

Disobedience to Previous Guidance: Ignoring or delaying obedience to guidance you've already received, which can diminish your sensitivity to future divine communication.

Spiritual Warfare: Recognizing when Satan is actively trying to confuse, discourage, or deceive you, and taking spiritual authority over these attacks through prayer and Scripture.

CHAPTER 5:
Developing Confidence In Divine Communication

Testing and Confirming What You Hear

One of the biggest obstacles to following divine guidance is uncertainty about whether the impressions you're receiving are actually from God. This uncertainty often leads believers to ignore genuine divine communication while waiting for more dramatic confirmation.

Learning to test and confirm God's voice involves several practical steps:

Scripture Alignment: Any impression you believe is from God must align with biblical truth and character. God will never lead you to do anything that contradicts His written Word.

Character Fruit: Divine guidance typically calls you toward greater love, holiness, service, and spiritual maturity rather than selfishness, compromise, or spiritual laziness.

Multiple Confirmations: Important decisions often receive confirmation through several sources, prayer, Scripture, wise counsel, circumstances, and inner peace, all pointing in the same direction.

Time and Peace: If you're unsure about guidance you think you're receiving, wait on God for additional confirmation. Genuine divine guidance typically increases in clarity over time, while false impressions tend to fade.

Wise Counsel: Share what you believe God is saying with mature believers who know you well and can help you discern whether the guidance aligns with Scripture and God's character.

Start Small: If you're uncertain about your ability to hear God's voice, start by asking for guidance about small decisions where mistakes won't have major consequences, then gradually develop confidence in larger matters.

Pastor Sarah Williams teaches her congregation a simple framework for testing divine guidance: "I encourage people to ask four questions about any impression they think might be from God: Does this align with Scripture? Does this produce peace in my spirit? Does this call me toward love and service? Would mature Christians who know me well affirm this direction? If the answer to all four questions is yes, they can move forward with confidence. If any answer is no or unclear, they should wait for more clarity."

Growing in Spiritual Sensitivity

Like any relationship skill, recognizing God's voice improves with practice and attention. Believers who develop strong sensitivity to divine communication typically cultivate specific habits that enhance their spiritual hearing:

Regular Solitude: Consistently spending time alone with God in prayer, worship, and Scripture reading develops familiarity with His voice and character.

Immediate Obedience: Responding quickly to clear divine promptings builds confidence and increases sensitivity to future guidance.

Spiritual Community: Participating in relationships with other believers who also seek to hear God's voice provides accountability, encouragement, and confirmation.

Worship Lifestyle: Maintaining awareness of God's presence throughout daily activities creates a spiritual atmosphere that makes divine communication more natural and recognizable.

Scripture Saturation: Regular Bible study and memorization provide the Holy Spirit with biblical content to bring to your remembrance when you need guidance.

Journal Keeping: Recording spiritual insights, answered prayers, and divine guidance creates a track record that builds faith and helps you recognize patterns in how God speaks to you personally.

Expectant Faith: Approaching each day with anticipation that God will guide, speak, and work through you creates spiritual alertness that makes you more responsive to divine communication.

The Transformation of Guided Living

Believers who learn to recognize and follow God's voice consistently report profound changes in every area of their lives:

Reduced Anxiety: Knowing that God is actively guiding your decisions reduces worry about making mistakes or facing uncertain futures.

Increased Effectiveness: Divine guidance often leads to strategies, relationships, and opportunities that produce better results than purely human planning.

Deeper Intimacy with God: Regular spiritual communication transforms your relationship with God from formal religion to an intimate partnership.

Greater Purpose: Following divine guidance connects your daily activities to eternal purposes, making even ordinary tasks feel meaningful and significant.

Supernatural Provision: God often provides resources, opportunities, and solutions in response to faithful obedience to His guidance.

Ministry Fruitfulness: Learning to hear God's voice enhances your ability to minister to others effectively, knowing when to speak, what to say, and how to serve.

Spiritual Authority: Confidence in God's guidance increases your boldness in prayer, evangelism, and spiritual warfare.

Michael and Patricia Johnson describe the transformation that occurred when they learned to seek divine guidance consistently: "Before we learned to listen for God's voice, we made decisions based primarily on logic, emotions, and financial considerations. We weren't bad people, but our lives felt ordinary and sometimes purposeless. When we began seeking God's guidance for everything from career decisions to daily schedules, our lives became an adventure. We've seen miraculous provision, divine appointments that led to ministry opportunities, and protection from dangers we didn't even know we were facing. We still use wisdom and common sense, but now we have access to supernatural wisdom that transcends human understanding. Our marriage is stronger, our ministry is more effective, and our children are growing up expecting God to guide and provide in ways we never experienced as young believers."

Your Voice-Hearing Journey Begins Now

Learning to recognize the Spirit's voice is not a destination but a journey, a lifelong adventure of developing intimacy with the God who loves you and desires to guide every aspect of your life. Like any relationship, this communication deepens over time through consistent interaction, mutual trust, and shared experiences.

The voice that spoke the universe into existence, that called Abraham from his homeland, that guided Moses through the wilderness, that directed Jesus through His earthly ministry, and that empowered the early Church to turn the world upside down is the same voice that wants to guide you through your daily decisions, relationships, and calling.

You don't need special qualifications or spiritual gifts to hear God's voice, you need only a relationship with Jesus Christ and a heart that's open to divine communication. The Holy Spirit who lives within every believer is ready to speak, guide, comfort, and direct any Christian who creates space to listen and develops sensitivity to recognize His communication.

Your voice-hearing journey begins with your next conversation with God. Instead of doing all the talking, ask Him a specific question and then wait expectantly for His response. Pay attention to impressions, insights, or peace that seem to come from beyond your natural thinking. Test these impressions against Scripture, seek wise counsel, and step out in faith to obey what you believe God is saying.

The more you practice listening, the more clearly you'll hear. The more quickly you obey, the more confident you'll become. The more you depend on divine guidance, the more supernatural your life will become.

God is speaking. The question is: Are you listening?

Your adventure in divine communication starts now. Open your heart, quiet your mind, and prepare to hear the voice of the One who knows you better than you know yourself and loves you more than you can imagine.

The conversation of a lifetime is about to begin.

7. EMPOWERED FOR HEALING AND WHOLENESS

Becoming God's Instrument of Restoration in a Broken World

In a world shattered by pain, brokenness, and despair, God has chosen to make ordinary believers His agents of extraordinary healing. This is not just about dramatic miraculous interventions or professional ministry, this is about the pioneering reality that every Spirit-filled Christian carries within them the power to bring healing, wholeness, and restoration to the hurting people they encounter every day.

When Jesus walked the earth, healing was not an occasional miracle but a constant expression of His character. He healed the sick, mended the brokenhearted, set captives free, and restored what sin had destroyed. Before ascending to heaven, He made an astounding declaration: "Most assuredly, I say to you, he who believes in Me, the works that I do he will do also; and greater works than these he will do, because I go to My Father" (John 14:12).

This promise was not given to apostles, pastors, or professional healers alone, it was spoken to anyone who believes in Jesus. That includes you. The same Spirit who empowered Jesus to heal the sick, comfort the mourning, and restore the broken is living within you right now, waiting to flow through your prayers, your words, your presence, and your touch to bring healing to a world desperate for wholeness.

Yet most believers live far below this inheritance. We've relegated healing to medical professionals, emotional restoration to trained counselors, and relational reconciliation to relationship experts.

We've forgotten that God's original design was for His people to be conduits of His healing power, ambassadors of His restoring love, and instruments of His wholeness in every sphere of human brokenness.

The time has come to reclaim this calling. The time has come to discover that you are not just saved to go to heaven someday, you are empowered to bring heaven to earth today through simple acts of faith-filled ministry that can transform lives, heal hearts, and restore what has been broken or lost.

CHAPTER 1:
Understanding God's Heart For Wholeness

The Comprehensive Nature of God's Healing

When we think of healing, we often limit our understanding to physical ailments, cancer disappearing, bones mending, sight being restored. While God certainly heals bodies in miraculous ways, His heart for healing encompasses the totality of human brokenness. He desires to restore not just our physical health but our emotional well-being, our damaged relationships, our wounded spirits, and our fractured sense of identity and purpose.

The Hebrew word "shalom," often translated as peace, actually means wholeness, completeness, and restoration in every area of life. This is what God offers through Jesus Christ, not just forgiveness of sins or healing of diseases, but complete restoration of everything that sin has damaged or destroyed.

Consider the areas where people around you need healing:

Physical Healing: Bodies ravaged by disease, chronic pain, disabilities, and the effects of aging, stress, and unhealthy living. God's power can heal instantly or gradually, sometimes through supernatural intervention and sometimes through wisdom about natural remedies and medical care.

Emotional Healing: Hearts broken by trauma, abuse, rejection, loss, and disappointment. Minds tormented by anxiety, depression, fear, and mental anguish. God's healing can restore joy, peace, and emotional stability to people who have been emotionally devastated.

Relational Healing: Marriages destroyed by betrayal, families fractured by conflict, friendships ended by misunderstanding, and communities divided by prejudice or competition. God specializes in reconciliation and can restore relationships that seem permanently damaged.

Spiritual Healing: Souls separated from God by sin, guilt, shame, and spiritual confusion. Hearts that have grown cold toward God, faith that has been damaged by religious hurt or life circumstances, and spiritual gifts that have been suppressed or misdirected.

Identity Healing: People who don't know who they are, what they're worth, or what their purpose is in life. God can heal identity wounds and reveal to people their true value and calling as His beloved children.

Sarah Martinez, a teacher in Phoenix, discovered this comprehensive understanding of healing when she began praying for her students: "I started by praying for their physical needs, illnesses, injuries, and chronic conditions. But as I spent more time with them, I realized their greatest needs were emotional and relational. I began praying for healing from family trauma, peer rejection, academic anxiety, and identity confusion. I was amazed at how God worked through simple prayers and words of encouragement to bring transformation that went far beyond what any educational program could accomplish."

Jesus' Model of Holistic Ministry

Jesus' earthly ministry provides the perfect model for comprehensive healing ministry. He never separated physical healing from emotional restoration or spiritual salvation from relational reconciliation. His healing ministry addressed the whole person, body, soul, spirit, and relationships.

When Jesus healed the paralytic lowered through the roof (Mark 2:1-12), He began by forgiving the man's sins, addressing his spiritual need before healing his physical condition. When He encountered the woman caught in adultery (John 8:1-11), He offered both forgiveness and practical guidance for changed living. When He healed the demoniac of Gadara (Mark 5:1-20), He restored not only his mental health but also his social relationships and sense of purpose.

This integrated approach to healing recognizes that human beings are complex creatures whose physical, emotional, spiritual, and social dimensions are interconnected. Healing in one area often facilitates healing in others, while brokenness in one dimension can affect all the others.

Modern believers who embrace Jesus' model of holistic ministry discover that God wants to use them to bring restoration in multiple dimensions of people's lives simultaneously. They learn to pray not just for specific symptoms but for the underlying causes and contributing factors that may be maintaining someone's brokenness.

The Authority You Already Possess

One of the greatest obstacles to believers operating in healing ministry is the misconception that healing power is reserved for specially gifted individuals or professional ministers. This belief causes ordinary Christians to refer hurting people to "qualified" experts while remaining passive observers of others' pain.

But Jesus gave healing authority to all His followers, not just the twelve apostles. Luke 10:1-9 records that Jesus sent out seventy ordinary disciples with specific instructions to heal the sick and proclaim the kingdom of God. These weren't trained theologians or experienced ministers, they were regular believers who received authority to do the works of Jesus.

This same authority has been passed down to every believer through the Holy Spirit. When you became a Christian, you didn't just receive forgiveness for your sins, you received the Spirit of the One who healed the sick, raised the dead, and restored broken lives. This power is not dormant within you, it's actively waiting to be released through your faith-filled prayers and ministry.

The authority to heal comes through several biblical realities:

Union with Christ: Because you are "in Christ," His authority becomes your authority, His power becomes available through you, and His compassion becomes the motivation for your ministry to others.

The Indwelling Holy Spirit: The same Spirit who empowered Jesus' healing ministry lives within you, ready to work through your prayers, words, and actions to bring restoration to others.

The Great Commission: Jesus' command to "heal the sick" (Matthew 10:8) was not given only to the original disciples but to all who would follow Him throughout history.

Spiritual Gifts: The gifts of healing mentioned in 1 Corinthians 12:9 are distributed among believers according to the Spirit's will, meaning that every believer has potential for some dimension of healing ministry.

Kingdom Citizenship: As citizens of God's kingdom, you have authority to enforce kingdom principles, including healing, wholeness, and restoration, in earthly situations where Satan's kingdom has brought destruction.

David Kim, a businessman in Seattle, discovered this authority when he began praying for coworkers: "I always thought healing was something that happened in church through pastors or special healing ministries. Then I started praying for colleagues who shared their struggles with me, health issues, family problems, work stress. I was amazed at how often people experienced breakthroughs after I prayed for them. I realized that God's healing power isn't limited to church buildings or professional ministers, it's available anywhere believers are willing to step out in faith and pray for others."

CHAPTER 2:
Physical Healing Through Ordinary Believers

Starting with Simple Faith

Many believers hesitate to pray for physical healing because they fear nothing will happen, which might embarrass them or disappoint the person requesting prayer. This fear keeps countless Christians from stepping into the healing ministry that Jesus commanded all believers to practice.

The key to beginning is understanding that you're not responsible for producing healing, you're only responsible for offering it in faith. God is the healer, the Holy Spirit provides the power, and Jesus has already paid the price for healing through His death and resurrection. Your role is to be a willing vessel through which God's healing power can flow.

Start with simple situations where you can gain confidence:

Family Members: Pray for headaches, minor injuries, colds, or other common ailments among your family members. Children are often especially responsive to healing prayer because they haven't yet been conditioned to doubt God's willingness to heal.

Close Friends: Offer to pray for friends who mention health concerns, chronic conditions, or upcoming medical procedures. Most people are honored when someone offers to pray for their healing, even if they're not particularly religious.

Church Community: Participate in prayer teams or healing services at your church, learning from more experienced believers while gaining practical experience in healing ministry.

For Yourself: Don't neglect to pray for your own physical needs.

God wants you to experience His healing power personally, which builds faith for ministering healing to others.

Maria Rodriguez, a mother of three in Dallas, began her healing ministry with her children's minor injuries: "When my kids would get hurt playing, I started praying immediately instead of just applying bandages and giving pain medication. I was amazed at how often their pain would disappear immediately or their healing would accelerate dramatically. My children began asking for prayer first whenever they got hurt because they learned to expect God to heal. This built my confidence to offer healing prayer to other families, and I've seen God work miraculously through simple prayers."

Practical Methods for Healing Prayer

Healing prayer doesn't require elaborate rituals or special techniques, but certain biblical principles can enhance the effectiveness of your ministry:

Laying on of Hands: Jesus and the early disciples frequently laid hands on people while praying for healing (Mark 16:18, Acts 28:8). Physical contact creates a point of connection that can facilitate the flow of healing power and demonstrates God's personal care for the individual.

Speaking to the Condition: Jesus often spoke directly to diseases, infirmities, and symptoms rather than just asking God to heal (Mark 4:39, Luke 4:39). Speaking with authority to sickness demonstrates faith that God's kingdom is more powerful than any physical condition.

Praying in Jesus' Name: Using Jesus' name in healing prayer is not a magical formula but an acknowledgment that healing comes through His authority and the victory He accomplished through His death and resurrection.

Commanding vs. Requesting: While both approaches have biblical precedent, commanding healing in Jesus' name often demonstrates greater faith than merely requesting God to consider healing someone.

Persistent Prayer: Some conditions require persistent prayer rather than single prayer sessions.

Jesus told parables about persistent prayer (Luke 11:5-13, 18:1-8), and some healing may come gradually through continued intercession.

Expectant Faith: Approaching healing prayer with confident expectation that God wants to heal creates a spiritual atmosphere that facilitates miraculous intervention.

Pastor Michael Thompson teaches practical healing prayer in his church: "I encourage people to keep healing prayer simple and faith-filled. Place your hands on the person's shoulders or the affected area, speak directly to the condition in Jesus' name, command healing, and restoration, and then thank God for what He's doing even before you see physical evidence. Most people are surprised at how often they see immediate improvement or complete healing when they pray with confident authority rather than tentative requests."

When Physical Healing Doesn't Come Immediately

One of the greatest challenges in healing ministry is maintaining faith and continuing to offer prayer when people aren't healed immediately or dramatically. This experience can create doubt about God's willingness to heal or your ability to minister effectively.

Several factors can help you maintain perspective and continue in healing ministry despite disappointments:

God's Timing: Some healing comes instantly, some comes gradually, and some comes through medical intervention rather than supernatural miracle. God's timing is perfect even when it doesn't match our expectations.

Hidden Healing: Sometimes God heals internal conditions, prevents more serious illness, or accelerates natural healing processes in ways that aren't immediately obvious but become evident over time.

Emotional and Spiritual Healing: Even when physical symptoms remain, God often brings emotional peace, spiritual strength, or relational healing that helps people cope with their physical challenges in supernatural ways.

Multiple Sessions: Some conditions require repeated prayer sessions rather than single encounters.

Persistent intercession demonstrates faith and love while creating opportunities for God to work progressively.

Learning Process: Every healing prayer session teaches you something about faith, spiritual authority, or God's character, even when dramatic physical healing doesn't occur immediately.

Seeds of Faith: Your willingness to pray for healing plants seeds of faith in people's hearts that may bear fruit later through increased spiritual hunger or openness to God's work in their lives.

Jennifer Park, a nurse in Portland, learned to maintain hope despite mixed results in healing prayer: "When I first started praying for patients, I expected everyone to be healed immediately and dramatically. When that didn't happen consistently, I became discouraged and almost stopped praying altogether. But I began to notice that even when people weren't healed physically, they often experienced peace, hope, or spiritual breakthroughs that were equally significant. I learned to celebrate every manifestation of God's goodness rather than measuring success only by physical healing."

CHAPTER 3:
Emotional And Relational Restoration

Healing the Hidden Wounds

While physical ailments are visible and obvious, emotional, and relational wounds often cause deeper, more lasting damage to people's lives. These hidden injuries, rejection, betrayal, abuse, trauma, loss, and disappointment, can destroy someone's capacity for joy, peace, love, and purpose even when their body is perfectly healthy.

God's heart for healing extends especially to these broken places in human experience. The prophet Isaiah described Jesus' mission as being sent to "heal the brokenhearted, to proclaim liberty to the captives, and the opening of the prison to those who are bound" (Isaiah 61:1). This emotional and spiritual restoration is as much a part of Christian healing ministry as physical miracles.

Believers who learn to minister emotional healing discover that God often works through them in ways that professional counselors and therapists cannot accomplish. While psychology and counseling have important roles, there are dimensions of emotional healing that require spiritual intervention, forgiveness of deep wounds, release from spiritual bondage, restoration of identity, and healing of soul-level trauma.

Common areas where people need emotional healing include:

Childhood Trauma: Abuse, neglect, abandonment, or exposure to violence that created deep wounds and unhealthy patterns of thinking and relating.

Rejection and Betrayal: Experiences of being rejected by parents, spouses, friends, or communities that have damaged their sense of worth and ability to trust others.

Grief and Loss: Death of loved ones, divorce, miscarriage, job loss, or other significant losses that have created unresolved sorrow and depression.

Identity Confusion: Messages from family, culture, or personal experiences that have distorted their understanding of their value, purpose, and identity as God's beloved children.

Fear and Anxiety: Traumatic experiences or chronic stress that have created patterns of fear, worry, and anxiety that interfere with their ability to live in peace and freedom.

Shame and Guilt: Past sins, failures, or traumatic experiences that have created deep shame and guilt that keep them from experiencing God's love and forgiveness fully.

Becoming a Safe Place for Broken Hearts

Before you can minister emotional healing effectively, you must become the kind of person that wounded people feel safe approaching. This requires developing character qualities and communication skills that create environments where people feel valued, understood, and loved.

Essential qualities for emotional healing ministry include:

Non-judgmental Love: Accepting people where they are without condemning their past choices, current struggles, or emotional reactions. This doesn't mean approving of sin, but it means loving people unconditionally while trusting God to bring conviction and change.

Confidentiality: Maintaining strict confidentiality about personal information people share with you, never using their struggles as prayer requests or illustrations without explicit permission.

Patient Listening: Taking time to truly hear people's stories, validate their pain, and understand their perspective without rushing to give advice or spiritual platitudes.

Emotional Stability: Maintaining your own emotional health so that you can offer strength and peace to others rather than being overwhelmed by their pain or trauma.

Spiritual Discernment: Learning to recognize when emotional issues have spiritual roots, unforgiveness, spiritual bondage, or identity lies, that require spiritual intervention alongside emotional support.

Hope-filled Perspective: Consistently pointing people toward God's power to heal and restore while acknowledging the reality of their pain and the time that healing may require.

Lisa Johnson, a teacher in Chicago, became known among her colleagues as someone who could help with emotional struggles: "I didn't set out to become a counselor, but I began to notice that people naturally opened up to me about their personal problems. At first, I just listened and offered to pray, but I started to see patterns in how God brought healing to emotional wounds.

People who had been struggling with depression, anxiety, or relationship issues for years began to experience breakthroughs after we prayed together and addressed the spiritual roots of their emotional pain."

Simple Practices for Emotional Healing

Emotional healing ministry doesn't require professional training or complex techniques, but certain biblical approaches can facilitate God's healing work in damaged hearts:

Prayer for Inner Healing: Asking the Holy Spirit to reveal and heal traumatic memories, emotional wounds, and unhealthy patterns of thinking while inviting Jesus' presence into painful experiences.

Forgiveness Ministry: Helping people identify relationships where forgiveness is needed and guiding them through the process of releasing resentment, bitterness, and desire for revenge.

Identity Declaration: Speaking truth about people's identity as God's beloved children, helping them replace lies they've believed about themselves with biblical truth about their worth and purpose.

Breaking Spiritual Bondage: Recognizing when emotional problems have spiritual roots and using spiritual authority to break generational patterns, curses, or demonic oppression that may be maintaining emotional bondage.

Prophetic Encouragement: Asking God to show you His heart for the person and sharing insights, words of knowledge, or encouragement that He gives you about their situation and His plans for their healing.

Scripture Application: Using specific Bible verses to address emotional wounds, fear, shame, and other issues while helping people personalize God's promises for their situations.

Community Support: Connecting emotionally wounded people with a healthy Christian community where they can experience ongoing love, accountability, and encouragement throughout their healing journey.

Relational Reconciliation Ministry

One of the most prevailing forms of healing ministry involves helping people restore damaged relationships, marriages on the brink of divorce, families fractured by conflict, friendships ended by misunderstandings, and communities divided by prejudice or competition.

God specializes in reconciliation. Paul wrote that "God was in Christ reconciling the world to Himself" and that He has given believers "the ministry of reconciliation" (2 Corinthians 5:18-19). This means that every Christian has both the calling and the authority to help facilitate healing in broken relationships.

Relational healing often requires:

Impartial Listening: Hearing all sides of conflicts without taking sides or making premature judgments about who is right or wrong.

Truth-telling with Love: Helping people recognize their own contributions to relational problems while maintaining love and respect for their dignity and worth.

Forgiveness Facilitation: Guiding people through the process of forgiving others and seeking forgiveness for their own offenses, even when relationships cannot be fully restored.

Communication Skills: Teaching people how to express their needs, feelings, and perspectives in ways that promote understanding rather than defensiveness.

Boundary Setting: Helping people establish healthy boundaries in relationships that have been characterized by manipulation, abuse, or unhealthy dependency.

Spiritual Warfare: Recognizing when relational conflicts have spiritual dimensions and taking authority over spirits of division, unforgiveness, and hatred that may be influencing the situation.

Tom and Susan Martinez learned to minister relational healing after God restored their own marriage: "We went through a very difficult period where we almost divorced, but God intervened and healed our relationship in miraculous ways. After that experience, other couples began asking us for help with their marriage problems. We learned to pray with couples, help them communicate more effectively, and address spiritual issues that were contributing to their conflicts. We've seen dozens of marriages saved and families restored through simple ministry that flows from our own experience of God's healing power."

CHAPTER 4:
Words That Heal And Restore

The Power of Encouragement

In a world filled with criticism, negativity, and discouragement, believers who learn to speak words of life, hope, and encouragement become potent instruments of healing. The book of Proverbs declares that "death and life are in the power of the tongue" (Proverbs 18:21), and Jesus taught that "out of the abundance of the heart the mouth speaks" (Matthew 12:34).

When your heart is filled with God's love and your mind is renewed by His truth, your words naturally become sources of healing and restoration for others. This doesn't require special speaking abilities or profound theological knowledge, it requires a heart that sees people through God's eyes and speaks to them from His perspective.

Words of encouragement can bring healing in several ways:

Identity Affirmation: Helping people see themselves as God sees them, beloved, valuable, gifted, and called for specific purposes, rather than through the lens of past failures, current struggles, or other people's opinions.

Hope Declaration: Reminding people of God's faithfulness, His power to change circumstances, and His good plans for their future, especially when they're going through difficult seasons.

Strength Impartation: Speaking courage, confidence, and spiritual strength to people who feel overwhelmed, defeated, or inadequate for the challenges they're facing.

Vision Casting: Helping people see possibilities they haven't considered, potential they haven't recognized, or purposes they haven't discovered.

Faith Building: Sharing testimonies of God's faithfulness, biblical promises that apply to their situations, or insights about how God might be working in their circumstances.

Love Expression: Simply communicating that they are loved, valued, and not alone in their struggles, whether through words, actions, or presence.

Rachel Thompson, a mother and part-time office worker in Phoenix, discovered the power of encouraging words: "I began to notice how often people around me seemed discouraged or defeated. I started asking God to show me His heart for each person I encountered and to give me words that would encourage them.

I was amazed at how often a simple compliment, word of appreciation, or expression of confidence in someone would completely change their countenance and attitude. I realized that many people are starving for someone to speak positively into their lives."

Practical Ways to Offer Healing Words

Developing a ministry of encouraging words doesn't require formal training or special occasions, it can be integrated into ordinary daily interactions in ways that bring supernatural healing to people's hearts:

Specific Compliments: Instead of generic praise, offer specific observations about people's character, abilities, or positive impact you've noticed in their lives.

Prophetic Insights: Ask God to show you His perspective on people you encounter and share appropriate insights about their potential, calling, or His heart for them.

Scripture Personalization: Share Bible verses that God brings to mind for specific people, personalizing the promises to their situations and needs.

Testimony Sharing: When appropriate, share brief testimonies of how God has worked in similar situations to build faith and hope for their circumstances.

Future-Focused Words: Help people see beyond their current difficulties to the good things God has planned for their future, the growth that will come from current challenges, or the ministry that will flow from their experiences.

Prayer Declarations: Offer to pray with people and speak biblical truths over their lives, their families, and their situations during prayer times.

Written Encouragement: Send cards, emails, or text messages that express appreciation, encouragement, or prayers for people who are going through difficult times.

Healing Through Prophetic Ministry

One of the most powerful ways God brings healing through believers is through prophetic ministry, receiving and sharing insights, words of knowledge, or visions that God gives about people's lives, situations, or His purposes for them.

This is not fortune-telling or psychological manipulation, but genuine spiritual revelation that comes from the Holy Spirit to build up, encourage, and strengthen people in their faith and calling. The apostle Paul wrote that "he who prophesies speaks edification and exhortation and comfort to men" (1 Corinthians 14:3).

Prophetic ministry for healing often includes:

Words of Knowledge: Supernatural information about people's situations, needs, or background that you couldn't know naturally, demonstrating God's intimate awareness of their lives.

Healing Insights: Understanding about root causes of physical, emotional, or spiritual problems that helps direct prayer and ministry more effectively.

Identity Revelations: God's perspective on someone's calling, gifting, or purposes that helps them understand their value and direction in life.

Timing Words: Insights about God's timing for breakthrough, change, or new seasons in people's lives that provide hope and direction for current circumstances.

Warning or Guidance: Occasional words of caution about potential problems or guidance about decisions people are facing, always delivered with love and humility.

Comfort and Hope: Messages of God's love, faithfulness, and good plans that provide comfort during difficult seasons and hope for the future.

Michael Davis, a businessman in Denver, began operating in prophetic ministry after experiencing it himself: "A stranger at church approached me and shared specific details about my business struggles and family situation that he couldn't have known naturally. He then shared encouraging words about God's plans for my future that gave me hope during a very dark time. Everything he shared proved accurate and helpful. This experience opened my heart to seek prophetic insights for others. Now I regularly receive words of knowledge and encouragement that I share with people, and I've seen how these insights bring healing and hope to hurting hearts."

Guidelines for Healing Words Ministry

Because words have such power to heal or wound, believers who engage in encouraging and prophetic ministry need wisdom about how to share healing words appropriately and effectively:

Love as Motivation: Ensure that your words flow from genuine love for people rather than desire to appear spiritual or gain attention for your insights.

Scripture Alignment: Any prophetic or encouraging words should align with biblical truth and character, never contradicting God's written Word.

Appropriate Timing: Learn to discern when people are receptive to encouragement and when they need different types of ministry or support.

Humility in Delivery: Share insights with humility, acknowledging that you may not have complete understanding and inviting people to pray about and test what you've shared.

Confidentiality: Maintain strict confidentiality about personal information God reveals to you, sharing insights only with the individuals concerned unless given explicit permission to share more broadly.

Follow-up Support: When possible, offer ongoing prayer, encouragement, or practical support to people who receive prophetic ministry rather than just delivering words and moving on.

Team Ministry: Work with other mature believers when possible, allowing multiple witnesses to confirm important prophetic words and provide accountability for your ministry.

CHAPTER 5:
Stepping Into Your Healing Calling

Overcoming Fear and Doubt

The greatest obstacle preventing most believers from stepping into healing ministry is fear, fear of failure, fear of embarrassment, fear of disappointment, and fear of getting in over their heads with people's serious problems. These fears are understandable but they're not from God, and they can be overcome through faith and experience.

Common fears about healing ministry include:

"What if nothing happens?" Remember that you're not responsible for producing healing, you're only responsible for offering it in faith. God is sovereign over results, and even when dramatic healing doesn't occur, your prayers and ministry often bring comfort, hope, and spiritual blessing to people.

"What if I pray for someone and they get worse?" This fear assumes that prayer can somehow harm people, which contradicts Scripture and God's character. Prayer offered in faith and love never causes harm, even when it doesn't produce the results we hope for.

"What if people think I'm weird or presumptuous?" Most people are honored when someone offers to pray for their healing or share words of encouragement, even if they're not particularly religious. Your genuine care for their well-being usually overrides any concerns about religious differences.

"What if I hear wrong or share something that's not from God?" This is why humility, Scripture alignment, and mature counsel are important. But don't let fear of making mistakes keep you from stepping out in faith. God uses imperfect vessels, and you'll learn to hear His voice more clearly through practice.

"What if I can't handle the emotional intensity of people's problems?" Start with smaller situations and build your capacity gradually. God won't give you more than you can handle, and He'll provide wisdom and strength for every situation He calls you into.

Jennifer Martinez, a teacher in San Antonio, overcame her fears by starting small: "I was terrified of praying for healing because I didn't want to disappoint people if nothing happened. So, I started by offering to pray for minor things, headaches, stressful days, upcoming tests, or meetings. As I saw God respond to these small prayers, my confidence grew. Eventually, I felt comfortable praying for more serious conditions and sharing prophetic insights. I learned that God honors faith-filled steps, even when they're small and tentative."

Developing Healing Partnerships

While every believer can minister healing individually, developing partnerships with other believers often enhances effectiveness and provides mutual support and accountability. Healing partnerships can take several forms:

Marriage Teams: Couples who minister healing together often find that their different perspectives, gifts, and approaches complement each other effectively.

Prayer Partners: Two or more believers who regularly pray together for healing opportunities and support each other's healing ministry.

Church Teams: Groups within local churches who are trained and deployed for healing ministry during services, hospital visits, or community outreach events.

Workplace Ministry: Christians in the same workplace who support each other in ministering to colleagues and looking for opportunities to pray and encourage.

Neighborhood Outreach: Believers in the same community who coordinate efforts to minister healing and encouragement to neighbors, especially during times of crisis or need.

Online Networks: Connections with other healing-ministry believers through social media, email, or video calls that provide encouragement, prayer support, and shared learning.

Tom and Lisa Johnson began ministering healing as a couple after both experienced personal healing in their own lives: "We discovered that I tend to receive words of knowledge and prophetic insights, while Lisa has unusual faith for physical healing. When we minister together, people often experience both spiritual revelation and physical breakthrough. We've learned that God often works through teams to provide complete ministry that addresses multiple dimensions of people's needs."

Creating Healing Opportunities

Rather than waiting for formal ministry opportunities, believers called to healing ministry can create opportunities through intentional lifestyle choices and community involvement:

Hospital and Care Facility Visits: Volunteering to visit patients in hospitals, nursing homes, or care facilities creates natural opportunities to offer prayer, encouragement, and healing ministry.

Community Service: Participating in food banks, homeless shelters, community events, or disaster relief creates relationships with people who often need physical, emotional, and spiritual healing.

Workplace Ministry: Being known as someone who cares about colleagues creates opportunities for coworkers to request prayer or share personal struggles during difficult times.

Neighborhood Presence: Being available and approachable in your neighborhood through friendly relationships, community involvement, or simply being outside and accessible to neighbors.

Small Group Leadership: Leading or participating in small groups, Bible studies, or support groups creates environments where healing ministry can occur naturally within Christian community.

Social Media Outreach: Using social media platforms to share encouraging content, offer prayer, or connect with people who express needs or struggles online.

Professional Integration: Finding appropriate ways to integrate faith and healing ministry into your professional responsibilities, whether through prayer, encouragement, or acts of service.

Your Healing Legacy

As you step into healing ministry, remember that every person you pray for, encourage, or minister to represents potential for exponential kingdom impact. People who experience God's healing through your ministry often become hungry for more of God, begin their own healing ministries, or influence others toward faith and spiritual growth.

The healing ministry you begin today could create a legacy that extends far beyond what you can see or imagine. Every prayer offered in faith, every word of encouragement spoken in love, and every act of healing service performed in Jesus' name contributes to God's kingdom advancing and people's lives being transformed.

Your healing calling is not optional, it's part of your identity as a believer. You may never see dramatic miraculous healings, but you can participate in God's healing work through simple acts of faith, love, and obedience that bring hope and restoration to people who desperately need to encounter God's goodness through your life.

The world is filled with broken people waiting for someone to offer them healing in Jesus' name. That someone could be you. Your healing ministry begins with your next prayer, your next word of encouragement, your next act of love offered in faith believing that God wants to work through you to bring wholeness to a hurting world.

Step forward in faith. The healing power of Jesus Christ is available through you today.

Your Healing Journey Begins Now

The same Jesus who healed the sick, restored the brokenhearted, and brought wholeness to broken lives two thousand years ago lives within you today through His Spirit.

The power that raised Him from the dead is available to flow through your prayers, your words, your presence, and your faith to bring healing to people who desperately need to experience God's restoring love.

You are not just a believer, you are a healing agent, commissioned by Christ and empowered by His Spirit to continue His ministry of restoration in your generation. This calling is not reserved for pastors or professional ministers, it belongs to every follower of Jesus who is willing to step out in faith and allow God to work through them.

Your healing ministry begins with your next act of faith-filled love. It might be praying for a family member's headache, speaking words of encouragement to a discouraged friend, or simply offering to pray with someone who shares a struggle with you. Start where you are, with what you have, and trust God to use your simple offerings of faith to accomplish His purposes of healing and restoration.

The broken world around you are waiting for believers who will demonstrate God's healing power through practical acts of love. Your community is filled with people who need physical healing, emotional restoration, relational reconciliation, and spiritual wholeness. You have been positioned in their lives not by accident but by divine appointment to be God's instrument of healing in their time of need.

Your healing journey begins now. Step forward in faith. The Spirit of the One who heals all diseases, comforts all sorrows, and restores all brokenness is ready to work through you in ways that will amaze both you and those you minister to.

The healing power of Jesus Christ is alive within you. What will you do with it?

8. COURAGE TO LOVE AND LEAD

Spirit-Led Leadership Beyond the Pulpit

Leadership is not a position, it's a posture. It's not about titles, corner offices, or organizational charts. It's about the courage to step forward when everyone else steps back, to speak truth when others remain silent, to love when love is costly, and to lead when leadership requires sacrifice. God has called every Spirit-filled believer to be a leader, regardless of their formal position or professional title. You may never stand behind a pulpit or sit in a boardroom, but you are called to lead in your sphere of influence, your family, your workplace, your community, your school. The question is not whether you're a leader, but what kind of leader you will choose to be.

In a world desperate for authentic leadership, God is raising up a generation of believers who will lead not through position or power, but through love and service. These are ordinary people, parents, students, employees, volunteers, who have discovered that the greatest leadership comes not from commanding others but from serving them, not from demanding respect but from earning it through character, not from exercising authority but from demonstrating authenticity.

This is Spirit-led leadership, leadership that flows from an intimate relationship with God, that serves others ahead of self, that seeks God's kingdom purposes over personal advancement, and that operates in supernatural wisdom and courage that can only come from above. It's leadership that transforms not just organizations but souls, not just productivity but people, not just circumstances but character.

The world is waiting for leaders like this. Your family needs leadership like this. Your workplace is desperate for leadership like this. Your community is crying out for leadership like this.

The question is: Will you answer the call?

CHAPTER 1:
Understanding Spirit-Led Leadership

Leadership as Calling, Not Career

The greatest leadership crisis of our time is not the absence of leaders but the abundance of people in leadership positions who lack the character, vision, and authentic calling necessary to lead others well. We have confused leadership with management, authority with influence, and position with purpose.

True leadership, the kind that transforms lives and changes the world, begins with divine calling. It starts when God places His heart for others within you, when He gives you vision for what could be rather than acceptance of what is, when He empowers you with courage to step into situations where your influence can make an eternal difference.

This calling is not limited to those in formal leadership positions. Some of the most influential leaders in history held no official titles, mothers who shaped their children's character, teachers who inspired students to greatness, friends who influenced their peers toward righteousness, employees who transformed workplace culture through servant leadership.

Consider the spheres where God has positioned you for leadership influence:

Family Leadership: Whether as parents, siblings, or extended family members, you have opportunities to lead through example, wisdom, and sacrificial love that shapes the trajectory of people's lives for generations.

Workplace Leadership: Regardless of your position on the organizational chart, you can lead through excellence, integrity, and service that influences colleagues, improves culture, and demonstrates kingdom values in secular environments.

Community Leadership: Through involvement in schools, neighborhoods, civic organizations, or volunteer groups, you can provide leadership that addresses practical needs while pointing people toward spiritual solutions.

Peer Leadership: Among your friends, classmates, or social circles, you can lead through wisdom, courage, and authentic faith that influences others toward better choices and deeper spiritual hunger.

Ministry Leadership: Within your church or Christian organizations, you can lead through service, vision, and spiritual maturity that helps advance God's kingdom purposes.

Sarah Chen, a single mother working as a nurse in Seattle, never considered herself a leader until she recognized how God was using her influence: "I thought leadership was for executives and pastors. But I began to see how my coworkers came to me for advice, how my children looked to me for guidance, and how my neighbors trusted my judgment about community issues. I realized that God had positioned me as a leader in multiple spheres, and I needed to step up to that calling with intentionality and courage."

Characteristics of Spirit-Led Leaders

Spirit-led leadership differs fundamentally from worldly leadership in its motivation, methods, and goals. While secular leadership often focuses on personal advancement, profit maximization, and power accumulation, Spirit-led leadership prioritizes service, stewardship, and spiritual transformation.

Servant's Heart: Spirit-led leaders understand that leadership is about serving others rather than being served. They ask not, "How can this benefit me?" but "How can I benefit others through this opportunity?"

Kingdom Vision: They see beyond immediate circumstances to God's eternal purposes, making decisions based on spiritual values rather than just temporal concerns.

Character-Driven: Their leadership flows from who they are rather than what they do, grounded in integrity, humility, and authentic relationship with God.

Others-Focused: They use their influence to develop other leaders, empower team members, and create opportunities for others to succeed rather than hoarding power for themselves.

Wisdom-Seeking: They regularly seek God's guidance for leadership decisions, recognizing their dependence on divine wisdom that exceeds human understanding.

Courage-Demonstrating: They're willing to make difficult decisions, speak uncomfortable truths, and stand for righteousness even when it's costly or unpopular.

Love-Motivated: Their leadership is motivated by genuine love for the people they lead rather than personal ambition or professional obligation.

The Cost and Reward of Leadership

Authentic leadership always comes with a price. It requires sacrifice, vulnerability, and the willingness to accept responsibility for others' well-being and development. Spirit-led leaders must count this cost and decide whether they're willing to pay it for the sake of serving others and advancing God's kingdom.

The costs of leadership include:

Personal Sacrifice: Giving up comfort, convenience, and personal preferences to serve others' needs and advance shared purposes.

Increased Responsibility: Accepting accountability not just for your own choices and results but for the people you influence and the outcomes of your leadership decisions.

Criticism and Opposition: Facing resistance from people who don't share your vision, values, or methods, including criticism that may be unfair or personally painful.

Loneliness and Pressure: Bearing burdens that others don't understand and making decisions that others don't have to live with.

Target for Attack: Becoming a focus for spiritual warfare as Satan attempts to undermine your influence and destroy your effectiveness.

However, the rewards of Spirit-led leadership far outweigh the costs:

Eternal Impact: Influencing people's lives in ways that affect not just their temporal circumstances but their eternal destinies.

Kingdom Advancement: Participating in God's work of transforming communities, organizations, and cultures according to His purposes.

Personal Growth: Developing character, wisdom, and spiritual maturity that comes only through the challenges and responsibilities of leadership.

Multiplication Effect: Training and releasing other leaders who will continue the work long after your direct involvement ends.

Divine Partnership: Experiencing the joy and fulfillment that comes from working closely with God to accomplish His purposes through your leadership.

CHAPTER 2:
Leadership In The Family

Parenting as Ultimate Leadership

No leadership position carries greater eternal significance than parenthood. Parents are called to be the primary spiritual leaders in their children's lives, shaping not just behavior but character, not just success but significance, not just temporal achievement but eternal destiny.

Yet many Christian parents have abdicated this leadership responsibility, delegating spiritual formation to churches, character development to schools, and life guidance to peers or popular culture. They've reduced parenting to providing physical needs and maintaining behavioral compliance rather than embracing their calling as their children's first and most influential spiritual leaders.

Spirit-led parenting requires:

Spiritual Authority: Understanding that God has given parents authority not just over their children's behavior but for their spiritual development, and exercising this authority through love, wisdom, and consistent example.

Vision Casting: Helping children see God's purposes for their lives, their potential for kingdom impact, and their identity as beloved children of God rather than just focusing on immediate behavioral compliance.

Character Formation: Prioritizing the development of spiritual fruit, love, joy, peace, patience, kindness, goodness, faithfulness, gentleness, and self-control, over academic achievement, or social success.

Discipleship Modeling: Demonstrating an authentic relationship with God through your own spiritual disciplines, responses to difficulty, and daily decision-making rather than just teaching religious concepts.

Legacy Thinking: Making parenting decisions based on long-term spiritual outcomes rather than short-term convenience or social pressure.

Maria Rodriguez, a mother of three in Phoenix, transformed her parenting when she embraced it as spiritual leadership: "I used to focus mainly on getting my kids to behave and succeed academically. But I realized that God had called me to be their primary spiritual leader, responsible for shaping their hearts and character. I began praying with them daily, sharing my faith struggles and victories, and helping them see how God was working in their circumstances. The difference in our family culture has been remarkable, deeper relationships, more authentic conversations, and children who are developing their own genuine faith rather than just following religious rules."

Marriage Leadership for Both Partners

In marriage, both spouses are called to leadership, though their roles and expressions may differ. Healthy marriages are characterized by mutual submission, shared vision, and complementary leadership strengths that serve the marriage partnership and advance God's purposes through their union.

Spiritual Leadership: Taking initiative to pray together, discuss spiritual matters, seek God's guidance for family decisions, and create a home environment that honors God and demonstrates His love to children and visitors.

Emotional Leadership: Providing emotional stability, encouragement, and support during difficult seasons while maintaining healthy boundaries and honest communication about feelings and needs.

Practical Leadership: Taking responsibility for various aspects of family life, finances, household management, child-rearing, social relationships, based on gifts, availability, and mutual agreement rather than rigid gender roles.

Vision Leadership: Working together to develop a shared vision for your marriage and family, making decisions that advance those purposes rather than just responding to immediate pressures or circumstances.

Service Leadership: Using your marriage as a platform for serving others, whether through hospitality, mentoring younger couples, or demonstrating healthy relationship patterns to your community.

Tom and Jennifer Martinez learned to share leadership in their marriage after early years of conflict over control and decision-making: "We both wanted to be in charge, which created constant tension and power struggles. Through marriage counseling and prayer, we learned that leadership in marriage isn't about one person being in charge but about both partners using their strengths to serve each other and advance shared purposes. Now we lead together in different areas based on our gifts and passions, and our marriage has become a source of strength rather than stress."

Single Parents and Blended Family Leadership

Single parents and those in blended families face unique leadership challenges that require extra measures of wisdom, courage, and dependence on God's grace. They must often fulfill roles that were designed for two parents while navigating complex relational dynamics and addressing children's emotional needs that may result from family disruption.

Spirit-led leadership in these contexts includes:

Acknowledging Limitations: Recognizing that you cannot be everything your children need and intentionally connecting them with other healthy adult influences, grandparents, mentors, youth pastors, coaches, who can provide additional support and guidance.

Seeking Divine Wisdom: Relying more heavily on prayer, Scripture, and godly counsel for parenting decisions because you don't have a spouse to share the burden and provide different perspectives.

Creating Stability: Establishing consistent routines, clear expectations, and reliable emotional support that help children feel secure despite family disruption or complexity.

Modeling Resilience: Demonstrating how to handle adversity, disappointment, and challenge with faith and grace, showing children that God's strength is available during difficult circumstances.

Building Community: Developing relationships with other families, church members, and friends who can provide practical support and spiritual encouragement for both you and your children.

Forgiveness and Healing: Addressing your own emotional wounds and helping children process their feelings about family changes while pointing everyone toward God's healing and restoration.

Lisa Johnson, a single mother of two teenagers, discovered that her family challenges actually developed stronger leadership abilities: "After my divorce, I felt overwhelmed by the responsibility of raising my children alone. But I learned to depend on God in ways I never had when I was married. I became a better leader because I had to seek divine wisdom for every decision, rely on community support, and demonstrate faith during difficult circumstances. My children have developed unusual spiritual maturity because they've seen God's faithfulness through our family challenges."

CHAPTER 3:
Workplace Leadership Without Titles

Influence Through Excellence

One of the most compelling forms of leadership is the influence that comes through consistent excellence, integrity, and service that demonstrates kingdom values in secular environments. You don't need a management position to be a leader at work, you need character, competence, and commitment that earn respect and create opportunities to influence others positively.

Work Ethic Leadership: Demonstrating diligence, reliability, and quality in your work that sets a standard others want to follow while showing that faith produces excellence rather than mediocrity.

Character Leadership: Maintaining integrity in small matters that builds trust and credibility, giving you influence when larger issues arise or when coworkers need wisdom and guidance.

Service Leadership: Looking for opportunities to help colleagues, solve problems, and contribute to team success without seeking credit or recognition, demonstrating the servant leadership that Jesus modeled.

Wisdom Leadership: Providing insights, solutions, and perspectives that help others succeed while giving God credit for wisdom that exceeds your natural abilities.

Peace Leadership: Maintaining composure during stressful situations, offering hope during discouraging circumstances, and providing stability when others are overwhelmed by workplace pressures.

Relationship Leadership: Building authentic friendships with coworkers that create opportunities for spiritual conversations and ministry during times of personal crisis or need.

David Kim, an accountant in Chicago, discovered his workplace leadership calling when he began focusing on service rather than advancement: "I used to be frustrated because I wasn't getting promoted as quickly as I wanted. But I started focusing on how I could serve my colleagues and contribute to our team's success rather than just advancing my own career. I began staying late to help coworkers meet deadlines, offering to train new employees, and looking for ways to improve our processes. Within a year, I was recognized as an informal leader even though my title hadn't changed. More importantly, several coworkers began asking me about my faith because they noticed something different about my attitude and work ethic."

Creating Positive Culture

Individual believers can have a remarkable influence on workplace culture through consistent demonstration of kingdom values and intentional investment in positive relationships with colleagues. This influence often extends far beyond what formal position or authority could accomplish.

Encouraging Words: Regularly speaking positive, encouraging words that build up colleagues rather than participating in gossip, criticism, or negative conversations that tear down morale.

Conflict Resolution: Serving as a peacemaker when conflicts arise between coworkers, helping people find common ground and solutions that serve everyone's interests.

Celebration of Others: Recognizing and celebrating colleagues' successes, contributions, and positive qualities in ways that boost morale and create a positive team culture.

Problem-Solving: Approaching workplace challenges with faith-filled optimism and creative solutions rather than complaining or giving up when difficulties arise.

Stress Management: Demonstrating supernatural peace and wisdom during high-pressure situations that help calm and guide others through difficult circumstances.

Inclusive Community: Creating workplace friendships that cross departmental, hierarchical, and demographic boundaries, demonstrating the unity that characterizes God's kingdom.

Ethical Leadership in Difficult Situations

Christian employees often face situations where they must choose between personal advantage and ethical behavior, between popular opinion and biblical values, between career advancement and conscience integrity. These moments provide opportunities for powerful leadership that can influence entire organizations.

Honest Reporting: Maintaining truthfulness in reports, presentations, and communications even when honesty might create problems or uncomfortable conversations.

Fair Treatment: Treating all colleagues with respect and dignity, regardless of their position, background, or relationship to your career advancement.

Resource Stewardship: Using company resources responsibly and efficiently, recognizing that faithful stewardship in small matters builds trust for larger responsibilities.

Customer Service: Serving customers with excellence and integrity that reflects God's heart for people rather than just maximizing profits or minimizing effort.

Team Collaboration: Working cooperatively with colleagues even when you disagree with their methods or don't receive credit for shared successes.

Whistle-Blowing Wisdom: Knowing when and how to address unethical practices or policies in ways that serve justice while maintaining appropriate relationships and procedures.

Rachel Thompson, a marketing manager in Denver, faced a situation that tested her ethical leadership: "My company was considering a marketing campaign that I felt was deceptive about our product's capabilities. I had to decide whether to go along with the team or voice my concerns. I prayed about it and decided to speak up, suggesting alternative approaches that were both honest and effective. Initially, some colleagues thought I was being overly cautious, but when our honest approach resulted in better long-term customer relationships and fewer complaints, my influence in the company increased significantly. Several team members later told me they respected my willingness to stand for integrity even when it was unpopular."

CHAPTER 4:
Student Leadership And Academic Influence

Leadership in Learning Environments

Students at every level, elementary, middle school, high school, college, and graduate school, have unique opportunities for leadership that can influence peer culture, support struggling classmates, and demonstrate faith in academic environments that may be hostile to Christian values.

Student leadership requires courage because it often means standing against peer pressure, choosing excellence over popularity, and maintaining Christian values in environments that may mock or oppose faith. Yet students who embrace this calling often have a profound influence on their generation.

Academic Excellence: Pursuing learning with diligence and integrity that demonstrates the connection between faith and intellectual achievement, showing that Christianity enhances rather than hinders academic success.

Peer Encouragement: Supporting classmates who are struggling academically, socially, or emotionally through friendship, tutoring, and practical assistance that demonstrates Christ's love.

Respectful Dissent: Engaging respectfully with teachers and classmates when course content or class discussions conflict with biblical values, learning to articulate faith perspective with wisdom and grace.

Service Initiative: Looking for opportunities to serve school communities through volunteer work, peer mentoring, or leadership in student organizations that address practical needs.

Character Demonstration: Maintaining integrity in academic work, relationships, and extracurricular activities even when others choose shortcuts or compromise.

Spiritual Boldness: Sharing faith appropriately when opportunities arise, whether through classroom discussions, informal conversations, or involvement in Christian student organizations.

Michael Torres, a high school student in San Antonio, discovered his leadership calling through service to struggling classmates: "I noticed that several students in my math class were failing because they didn't understand the concepts. I started offering free tutoring during lunch periods, not just helping with homework but teaching them study strategies and encouraging them to believe in their abilities. Word spread, and soon I was helping students in multiple subjects.

Teachers began referring struggling students to me, and I realized that God was using my academic abilities to serve others and demonstrate His love. Several students I tutored became interested in my faith because they saw that I cared about their success."

Campus Ministry Leadership

Christian students in high school and college campuses have opportunities to provide spiritual leadership through involvement in campus ministry organizations, prayer groups, Bible studies, and evangelistic activities. These leadership roles often prepare students for lifelong ministry while influencing their educational communities for Christ.

Bible Study Leadership: Leading or participating in student Bible studies that create community among Christian students and provide opportunities for spiritual growth and mutual encouragement.

Prayer Initiative: Organizing prayer groups for campus needs, academic challenges, and spiritual breakthroughs that demonstrate faith in God's power to work in educational environments.

Evangelistic Outreach: Participating in campus evangelism through relationship building, service projects, and organized events that share the Gospel with non-Christian students.

Mentorship Roles: Serving as mentors for younger or newer students, helping them navigate academic challenges while providing spiritual guidance and support.

Social Justice: Addressing campus issues like racism, inequality, or moral concerns through a Christian perspective and service that demonstrates God's heart for justice and mercy.

Community Building: Creating an inclusive Christian community that welcomes students from different backgrounds, denominations, and levels of spiritual maturity.

Preparing for Future Leadership

Student years provide crucial preparation for lifelong leadership by developing character, competence, and vision that will influence future career, family, and ministry opportunities. Students who take seriously their current leadership opportunities are better prepared for the greater responsibilities they'll face in adulthood.

Character Development: Using academic and social challenges to develop integrity, perseverance, and wisdom that will serve them throughout life.

Skill Building: Developing communication, organization, and team-building skills through student leadership roles that prepare them for professional and ministry responsibilities.

Vision Formation: Discovering their calling, gifts, and passion for serving God and others through exploration of different leadership opportunities and ministry experiences.

Relationship Investment: Building friendships and mentor relationships with peers, teachers, and adult leaders that provide ongoing support and accountability for future leadership roles.

Global Perspective: Participating in missions' trips, service projects, or international studies that expand their understanding of God's heart for the world and their role in His global purposes.

Jennifer Martinez, now a successful businesswoman and ministry leader, credits her student leadership experiences with shaping her life direction:

"In college, I got involved in campus ministry and discovered that I loved teaching Bible studies and organizing service projects. Those experiences helped me realize that God had called me to leadership, and they gave me practical skills and spiritual confidence that I've used throughout my career. The leadership abilities I developed as a student prepared me for roles I never could have imagined when I was in school."

CHAPTER 5:
Community Leadership And Civic Engagement

Neighborhood Influence

Every believer lives in a community that needs Christian leadership, not necessarily elected officials, or formal organization heads, but individuals who will take initiative to address needs, build relationships, and demonstrate God's love through practical service and wise involvement in community affairs.

Neighborhood leadership often begins with simple acts of service and relationship-building that create opportunities for greater influence and more formal leadership roles. It requires seeing your residence not just as personal space but as a ministry assignment where God has positioned you for specific purposes.

Relational Investment: Getting to know neighbors as individuals with real needs, concerns, and dreams rather than just people who happen to live nearby.

Service Initiative: Looking for opportunities to help with neighborhood needs, organizing block parties, coordinating disaster response, addressing safety concerns, or improving community appearance.

Conflict Resolution: Serving as a peacemaker when neighborhood disputes arise, helping neighbors find solutions that serve everyone's interests.

Resource Sharing: Using your skills, tools, knowledge, or connections to help neighbors with practical needs, home repairs, job searches, childcare, or transportation.

Advocacy Leadership: Representing neighborhood concerns to local government, schools, or other organizations that affect community life.

Hospitality Ministry: Creating welcoming spaces where neighbors can build relationships, celebrate together, and support each other during difficult times.

Tom and Susan Wilson discovered their calling for neighborhood leadership after experiencing community support during a family crisis: "When our youngest son was diagnosed with a serious illness, our neighbors rallied around us with meals, childcare, and emotional support. We realized that we wanted to create that same kind of community for others. We started hosting neighborhood barbecues, organizing a community garden, and coordinating help for neighbors facing challenges. Over time, we became informal leaders in our community, and we've had many opportunities to share our faith and pray with neighbors who trust our judgment and care about our opinions."

Civic Engagement and Public Service

Christian citizens have responsibility to engage in civic life not just as voters but as active participants in local government, school boards, community organizations, and public service that shapes the conditions under which families live, and children are raised.

This engagement requires wisdom to navigate political differences while maintaining Christian witness, courage to speak truth about moral issues, and commitment to serve the common good rather than just narrow partisan interests.

Informed Citizenship: Staying informed about local, state, and national issues that affect community life while maintaining biblical perspective on political and social questions.

Elected Office: Running for school board, city council, county commission, or other positions where Christian perspective and servant leadership can influence public policy.

Board Service: Serving on nonprofit boards, community organizations, or civic committees that address specific needs like poverty, education, healthcare, or economic development.

Volunteer Leadership: Taking leadership roles in community service organizations, charitable groups, or volunteer programs that address practical needs while demonstrating Christian love.

Public Speaking: Accepting opportunities to speak at public meetings, community forums, or civic events about issues where Christian perspective can contribute to community dialogue.

Prayer and Intercession: Regularly praying for community leaders, local challenges, and spiritual breakthrough in your region while encouraging other believers to do the same.

David Chen, an engineer who serves on his city council, explains his motivation for civic engagement: "I realized that if Christians don't participate in local government, we forfeit our opportunity to influence the decisions that affect our communities. I ran for city council not as a partisan politician but as a servant leader who wants to apply biblical principles to public policy. I've been able to advocate for policies that protect families, support small businesses, and create opportunities for community organizations to address social needs. My faith perspective has brought a different voice to our local government discussions."

Crisis Leadership

Communities regularly face crises, natural disasters, economic challenges, social unrest, or health emergencies, that create opportunities for Christian leaders to demonstrate faith, provide practical help, and offer hope during difficult circumstances.

Crisis leadership often reveals who the real leaders are in a community, as titles and positions become less important than character, competence, and willingness to serve others during challenging times.

Emergency Response: Taking initiative during disasters to organize relief efforts, coordinate volunteers, and provide practical assistance to those most affected.

Resource Mobilization: Using connections, skills, and influence to gather resources needed for crisis response, funds, supplies, equipment, or expertise.

Emotional Support: Providing comfort, encouragement, and hope to community members who are struggling with fear, loss, or trauma resulting from crisis situations.

Communication Leadership: Helping coordinate accurate information, dispel rumors, and maintain calm communication during chaotic situations.

Recovery Planning: Participating in long-term planning for community recovery and improvement that addresses not just immediate damage but underlying vulnerabilities.

Spiritual Ministry: Offering prayer, pastoral care, and spiritual guidance to community members who are questioning faith or seeking meaning during difficult circumstances.

Maria Rodriguez led her neighborhood's response to flooding that damaged dozens of homes: "When our community was hit by severe flooding, I felt called to coordinate our recovery efforts. I organized volunteer teams, helped families connect with insurance and FEMA resources, and coordinated donations of supplies and funds. More importantly, I was able to pray with families who were devastated by their losses and share hope about God's faithfulness during difficult times. The crisis gave me leadership credibility that opened doors for ongoing ministry and influence in our community."

CHAPTER 6:
The Courage To Lead When It Costs

Leading Through Opposition

True leadership often requires making decisions that are unpopular, taking stands that are controversial, and pursuing courses of action that generate resistance from people who prefer comfort over change, status quo over spiritual growth, or personal benefit over kingdom purposes.

This kind of leadership requires supernatural courage that comes only through intimate relationship with God and confidence in His calling and support. It means being willing to be misunderstood, criticized, or even attacked for doing what you believe God has called you to do.

Standing for Truth: Speaking biblical truth about moral, ethical, or spiritual issues even when those truths are unpopular or culturally unacceptable.

Confronting Sin: Addressing sin, compromise, or destructive behavior in family, workplace, or community contexts where confrontation might damage relationships or create conflict.

Advocating for Justice: Speaking up for people who are being treated unfairly or oppressed, even when advocacy might cost you popularity or advancement.

Challenging Systems: Questioning organizational practices, cultural norms, or traditional approaches that you believe are harmful or inconsistent with kingdom values.

Protecting Vulnerable: Defending children, elderly, minorities, or others who cannot protect themselves, even when protection requires personal sacrifice.

Refusing Compromise: Maintaining integrity and biblical standards even when compromise would be easier, more profitable, or more socially acceptable.

Pastor Sarah Williams describes the cost of leadership in her church context: "When I became senior pastor, I discovered that our church had developed some unhealthy patterns, gossip, favoritism, and avoidance of difficult conversations. Addressing these issues required confronting influential members who didn't want to change, which created significant conflict and criticism. Some people left the church, and there were times when I questioned whether the pain was worth it. But as we worked through these challenges, our church became healthier, more unified, and more effective in ministry. I learned that sometimes love requires difficult leadership that people don't initially appreciate."

Leading When You Don't Feel Qualified

Many people avoid leadership opportunities because they don't feel qualified, experienced, or equipped for the responsibilities involved. However, God often calls ordinary people to extraordinary leadership roles, providing the wisdom, courage, and abilities they need as they step out in faith and obedience.

The key is recognizing that your qualifications come not from your natural abilities or experience but from God's calling and empowerment. When God calls you to lead, He also commits to equip you for the task.

Dependence on God: Acknowledging your limitations while trusting in God's unlimited wisdom and power to work through your weaknesses.

Learning Orientation: Approaching leadership as a learning opportunity, seeking mentorship, training, and feedback that helps you grow into the role.

Team Building: Recognizing your limitations and surrounding yourself with people whose strengths complement your weaknesses.

Character Focus: Emphasizing character development over competency development, recognizing that integrity and humility are more important than technical skills.

Faith-Filled Risk: Taking steps of faith that require you to depend on God's provision rather than your own abilities or resources.

Growth Mindset: Viewing mistakes and failures as learning opportunities rather than disqualifications from leadership roles.

Michael Thompson, a businessman who reluctantly accepted leadership of his church's building committee, describes his experience: "I had no construction experience and felt completely unqualified to oversee a major building project. But when no one else was willing to take the role, I felt God calling me to step up. I had to learn everything from the ground up, ask lots of questions, and depend heavily on prayer and wise counsel. The project was successful not because of my expertise but because God provided the wisdom and resources we needed. More importantly, the experience taught me that God's calling is more important than my qualifications."

Leading Through Personal Struggles

Leaders are not immune to personal challenges, family crises, health problems, or spiritual struggles. In fact, leadership responsibilities often increase during personal difficulties, requiring supernatural grace to continue serving others while dealing with private pain.

Learning to lead through personal struggles develops character, increases empathy, and demonstrates faith that influences others profoundly. It also teaches dependence on God's strength rather than personal resources.

Vulnerability and Honesty: Sharing appropriate details about personal struggles in ways that build connection with others and demonstrate that leaders are human too.

Seeking Support: Accepting help from others and allowing the community to support you during difficult seasons rather than trying to maintain a facade of having everything together.

Maintaining Priorities: Continuing to fulfill leadership responsibilities while also taking care of personal and family needs, finding balance between service and self-care.

Finding Purpose in Pain: Looking for ways that your struggles can help you understand and serve others who face similar challenges.

Modeling Faith: Demonstrating how to trust God during difficult circumstances rather than just teaching about faith during comfortable seasons.

Growing Through Adversity: Using personal challenges as opportunities for character development and spiritual growth that enhances your leadership effectiveness.

Jennifer Martinez led her company through a major reorganization while dealing with her husband's cancer diagnosis: "I had to make difficult decisions about layoffs and department restructuring while spending evenings at the hospital. There were days when I felt like I couldn't handle both responsibilities. But I found that being honest with my team about my situation actually strengthened my leadership. They saw that I was committed to both my family and my work responsibilities, and they worked harder to support the reorganization because they trusted my character. My husband's recovery became a testimony to my colleagues about God's faithfulness during difficult times."

Your Leadership Moment

Leadership is not a someday calling, it's a today's opportunity. Somewhere in your sphere of influence, people need the kind of leader you can become. Your family needs your spiritual leadership. Your workplace needs your ethical influence. Your community needs your servant heart. Your generation needs your courage.

The world is not lacking for people who want to be in charge, it's desperate for people who are willing to serve. It's not missing people who seek positions, it's hungry for people who pursue purposes. It's not short on people who demand respect, it's starving for people who demonstrate love.

This is your moment to step into the leadership calling that God has placed on your life. You don't need permission from others or perfect qualifications from yourself. You need only the courage to love people enough to lead them toward something better than where they are today.

Your leadership begins with your next act of courage, your next decision to serve rather than be served, your next choice to speak truth in love, your next step of faith into a situation where your influence can make an eternal difference.

The people in your sphere of influence are waiting for someone to lead with love, serve with courage, and point them toward hope. That someone could be you. That someone should be you.

Your leadership moment is now. What will you do with it?

9. REVIVAL IN THE EVERYDAY

When the Sacred Transforms the Ordinary

The most impressive revivals in history have not been confined to church buildings or special religious meetings. They have spilled out into the streets, invaded workplaces, transformed family dinners, and turned ordinary conversations into extraordinary encounters with the living God. These revivals succeeded not because they were spectacular but because they were seamless, faith became as natural as breathing, prayer as common as conversation, and the presence of God as real as the chair you're sitting in.

This is the revival our generation desperately needs, not another church program or religious event, but a supernatural invasion of ordinary life that makes the sacred inseparable from the mundane. It's a revival where the Holy Spirit is as present at your breakfast table as He is in the sanctuary, where divine appointments happen in grocery store aisles, where business meetings become opportunities for intercession, and where family conversations become platforms for spiritual breakthrough.

For too long, we've compartmentalized our faith into religious activities while leaving our daily lives untouched by divine reality. We pray in church but worry about traffic. We worship on Sundays but compete ruthlessly on Mondays. We read Scripture in our devotions but rely on worldly wisdom in our decisions. We've created an artificial separation between the spiritual and the secular that God never intended and that robs us of the abundant life Jesus promised.

The revival of the everyday shatters this false dichotomy. It recognizes that every moment is a sacred moment, every conversation is a potential divine appointment, every meal is an opportunity for communion, and every workplace interaction is a chance to demonstrate kingdom reality.

It's a revival that doesn't require special buildings or professional ministers, it only requires believers who refuse to leave God at church and instead carry His presence into every corner of their ordinary lives.

This is not about being religious in secular settings or forcing spiritual conversations into inappropriate contexts. This is about living so authentically in relationship with God that His presence naturally flows through your personality, your priorities, your responses to stress, your treatment of others, and your approach to life's daily challenges and opportunities.

The world is dying for this kind of authentic Christianity, not more religious activity but genuine spiritual reality that transforms ordinary people into extraordinary demonstrations of God's love, power, and wisdom. Your family needs this revival. Your workplace is desperate for it. Your community is crying out for it. And it can begin today, in your life, in the most ordinary circumstances imaginable.

CHAPTER 1:
The Spirit At The Dinner Table

Transforming Family Meals from Routine to Sacred

The dinner table represents one of the most effective yet underutilized opportunities for revival in the everyday. What could be more ordinary than eating together? Yet when the Spirit of God is intentionally invited into family meals, the dinner table becomes an altar, conversations become ministry opportunities, and shared food becomes communion that nourishes souls as well as bodies.

Most families have reduced mealtime to fuel stops, quick refueling between activities, entertainment consumption while eating, or silent efficiency designed to get through the necessity of eating as quickly as possible. But families experiencing everyday revival have discovered that mealtimes can become the spiritual heartbeat of their homes, creating atmosphere and opportunities for God to work in powerful ways.

Creating Sacred Space: This begins with simple changes that signal that mealtime is special, turning off televisions and putting away devices, lighting candles, or playing worship music softly, taking time to truly see and connect with each person at the table rather than rushing through food consumption.

Prayer That Connects: Moving beyond rote blessing prayers to authentic conversation with God about the day's experiences, challenges, and blessings. Include prayers for specific needs family members are facing, gratitude for God's provision and faithfulness, and requests for His presence and blessing on the evening together.

Storytelling with Purpose: Encouraging family members to share not just what happened during their day but how they saw God working, answered prayers they experienced, or ways they were able to serve or bless others. These stories create expectation for divine activity and help everyone develop eyes to see God's presence in ordinary circumstances.

Scripture and Spiritual Conversation: Naturally weaving biblical truth into dinner conversation, not forced Bible studies but organic discussions about how God's Word applies to current family situations, decisions, or challenges that family members are facing.

Worship and Celebration: Allowing meals to become times of spontaneous worship when someone shares answered prayer, family victories, or evidence of God's goodness. This might include singing simple songs of thanksgiving, expressing gratitude to God aloud, or celebrating His faithfulness in specific ways.

The Martinez family in Phoenix transformed their dinner table after recognizing how rushed and disconnected their mealtimes had become: "We realized that we were gathering around the same table every night but not really connecting with each other or with God. We started by simply turning off the TV during dinner and asking each person to share one thing they were grateful for and one way they wanted prayer. These simple changes revolutionized our family culture. Our children began sharing their struggles and victories more openly, we started praying together about decisions, and our dinner table became a place where everyone knew they would encounter God's presence and our family's love."

Family Devotions That Work

Traditional family devotions often fail because they feel forced, artificial, or disconnected from real life. But when family worship emerges naturally from daily experiences and responds to actual needs, it becomes an able catalyst for everyday revival.

Effective family devotions share several characteristics:

Life-Connected: Rather than following a predetermined curriculum, these devotions address current family situations, challenges, and opportunities using biblical wisdom and spiritual perspective.

Age-Appropriate: Involving every family member at their level of understanding and participation rather than talking over children's heads or boring teenagers with elementary concepts.

Interactive: Encouraging questions, discussion, and participation from everyone rather than just having parents lecture children about spiritual topics.

Prayer-Focused: Spending as much time praying together as talking together, teaching family members to seek God's guidance, provision, and blessing for specific needs and situations.

Practical: Connecting spiritual truths to practical decisions and daily challenges that family members are actually facing, rather than abstract theological concepts.

Spontaneous: Being willing to set aside planned activities when God seems to be working in family members' hearts or when current circumstances create teachable moments.

Sarah Chen, a single mother of two teenagers in Seattle, developed a family devotion approach that worked with her busy schedule and adolescent children: "Traditional family devotions felt artificial and met resistance from my teens. Instead, I started looking for natural opportunities to have spiritual conversations, during car rides, while folding laundry together, or when one of them was struggling with a problem. I would ask questions like 'How do you think God sees this situation?' or 'What do you think the Bible would say about this decision?' These organic conversations became more meaningful than any formal devotion time we'd ever had."

Holiday and Celebration Revival

Holidays and family celebrations provide natural opportunities to create spiritual traditions that embed faith into family culture and create positive associations between spiritual reality and joyful experiences.

Rather than just adding prayer to secular celebrations, families experiencing everyday revival create traditions that make God central to their celebrations while enhancing rather than replacing the joy and fun of special occasions.

Birthday Traditions: Incorporating prayer for the birthday person's coming year, sharing what family members appreciate about their character and contributions, or creating spiritual goals alongside personal goals.

Holiday Customs: Developing family traditions that connect holidays to spiritual themes, Thanksgiving gratitude journals, Christmas service projects, Easter resurrection celebrations that emphasize new life in Christ.

Anniversary Celebrations: Using wedding anniversaries as opportunities to renew commitment to God as well as each other, sharing testimonies of God's faithfulness to the marriage, or blessing the couple through family prayer.

Achievement Recognition: Celebrating academic, athletic, or personal achievements by recognizing God's gifts and provision while encouraging continued faithfulness in using abilities for kingdom purposes.

Crisis Commemoration: Creating traditions that recognize how God brought families through difficult seasons, using these memories to build faith for future challenges.

Spiritual Milestones: Celebrating baptisms, confirmations, spiritual breakthroughs, or ministry commitments with special family traditions that emphasize the eternal significance of spiritual decisions.

Extended Family and Hospitality Ministry

The dinner table's revival influence extends beyond immediate family to include extended family gatherings and hospitality toward neighbors, friends, and strangers. When families make their homes centers of spiritual warmth and acceptance, they create environments where people naturally encounter God's love.

This hospitality ministry requires intentional preparation and prayer, but can become one of the most effective forms of evangelism and discipleship available to ordinary families.

Welcoming Atmosphere: Creating homes where people feel genuinely loved and accepted regardless of their spiritual condition, social status, or personal struggles.

Natural Spiritual Conversation: Learning to weave faith into conversations with non-Christian guests in ways that feel natural and non-threatening rather than forced or manipulative.

Prayer Opportunities: Offering to pray for guests' needs or struggles in ways that demonstrate care and concern rather than spiritual superiority.

Service Expression: Using hospitality as a way to serve people practically, providing meals during difficult times, offering homes for gatherings, or simply creating spaces where people can experience community and acceptance.

Testimony Sharing: Finding appropriate opportunities to share how God has worked in your family's life without making guests feel pressured to respond in particular ways.

Follow-up Friendship: Building ongoing relationships with people you serve rather than just offering one-time hospitality, creating opportunities for continued spiritual influence.

Tom and Jennifer Wilson began hosting neighborhood dinners as a way to build relationships and share their faith naturally: "We started inviting neighbors over for casual dinners with no agenda except getting to know them better. As relationships developed, people began sharing their struggles and asking for prayer. Several neighbors have come to faith through friendships that began around our dinner table. We've discovered that hospitality creates opportunities for spiritual conversations that feel natural and authentic rather than forced or artificial."

CHAPTER 2:
The Sacred Workplace

Carrying God's Presence to Your Job

For most adults, the workplace consumes more waking hours than any other activity except sleep. Yet many believers treat their jobs as spiritual dead zones where faith has little relevance and God's presence is rarely acknowledged or experienced. This compartmentalization robs both believers and their workplaces of the transforming power that comes when God's kingdom intersects with earthly employment.

Workplace revival doesn't require dramatic manifestations or inappropriate religious behavior. It begins when believers recognize their jobs as ministry assignments and their workplaces as mission fields where they have been strategically positioned to demonstrate God's character and advance His kingdom through ordinary work done with extraordinary heart.

Excellence as Witness: Approaching work responsibilities with diligence, integrity, and quality that reflects God's character and demonstrates that faith produces excellence rather than mediocrity. This means being consistently reliable, maintaining high standards, and going beyond minimum requirements in ways that stand out in workplace cultures often characterized by self-interest and minimal effort.

Relationship Building: Investing in genuine friendships with colleagues based on authentic care and interest rather than an evangelistic agenda. These relationships create trust and credibility that open doors for spiritual conversations when appropriate opportunities arise naturally through work interactions or personal crises.

Peace Under Pressure: Maintaining supernatural calm during stressful situations, deadline pressures, or workplace conflicts in ways that demonstrate God's peace and create curiosity about the source of your stability and wisdom.

Servant Leadership: Looking for opportunities to help colleagues succeed, solve problems, and navigate workplace challenges, regardless of your official position or personal benefit from these service activities.

Ethical Integrity: Maintaining biblical standards in business practices, relationship dynamics, and decision-making even when compromise would be easier, more profitable, or more politically advantageous within organizational culture.

Prayer Integration: Finding appropriate ways to pray for colleagues, workplace challenges, and organizational decisions while respecting workplace boundaries and avoiding inappropriate religious pressure.

David Kim, a software engineer in Austin, discovered his workplace calling when he began seeing his job as a ministry: "I used to compartmentalize my faith completely from my work life. But I started asking God how He wanted to use me in my workplace and began looking for opportunities to serve colleagues and demonstrate Christian character through my work. I became known as someone who could be trusted with confidential information, who would help struggling team members, and who maintained peace during high-stress projects. Over time, coworkers began asking me about my faith because they noticed something different about my approach to work and relationships."

Divine Appointments in Ordinary Meetings

Business meetings, lunch conversations, and casual workplace interactions provide countless opportunities for divine appointments, moments when God orchestrates circumstances to position believers where they can minister to colleagues, share wisdom, or demonstrate His love through ordinary work relationships.

Recognizing and responding to these divine appointments requires spiritual sensitivity and willingness to step beyond normal professional boundaries in appropriate ways.

Listening for Needs: Paying attention not just to work-related information but to personal struggles, concerns, and needs that colleagues share in casual conversations or that become evident through their behavior and attitudes.

Offering Prayer: Finding appropriate ways to offer prayer for colleagues' personal or professional challenges, whether through immediate prayer during conversations or committed intercession during private prayer times.

Sharing Wisdom: Contributing biblical perspective to workplace discussions about ethics, relationships, or decision-making without being preachy or judgmental toward those who don't share your values.

Providing Support: Offering practical help during colleagues' personal crises, rides to medical appointments, meals during family emergencies, or simply listening ears during difficult seasons.

Speaking Truth: Finding loving ways to address workplace gossip, unfair treatment, or ethical concerns while maintaining positive relationships and professional appropriateness.

Demonstrating Grace: Responding to workplace conflicts, unfair criticism, or difficult personalities with grace and forgiveness that reflects Christ's character and creates curiosity about your motivational source.

Maria Rodriguez, a marketing manager in Denver, learned to recognize divine appointments during routine business interactions: "I began to pray before meetings and ask God to show me opportunities to minister to colleagues. I was amazed at how often people would share personal struggles or ask for advice about non-work issues. I learned to listen for these opportunities and offer appropriate prayer, encouragement, or practical help. Several colleagues have said that conversations with me during difficult times helped them reconsider their spiritual beliefs or seek God during crisis situations."

Transforming Break Room Culture

Workplace break rooms, lunch areas, and informal gathering spaces often become centers for gossip, complaining, or negative conversation that drains energy and creates a toxic workplace atmosphere. Believers who intentionally bring different energy to these spaces can gradually transform workplace culture in ways that benefit everyone.

Positive Conversation: Consistently contributing encouragement, appreciation, and constructive perspectives to workplace conversations rather than participating in criticism, gossip, or complaining.

Conflict Resolution: Serving as peacemakers when workplace tensions arise, helping colleagues find common ground and solutions rather than taking sides or escalating conflicts.

Celebration of Others: Recognizing and celebrating colleagues' successes, personal milestones, and positive contributions in ways that build morale and create a positive workplace atmosphere.

Encouragement During Difficulty: Offering hope and support when colleagues are struggling with work challenges or personal problems, providing perspective that helps people persevere through difficult circumstances.

Inclusive Community: Creating welcoming environments where all colleagues feel valued and included regardless of their background, position, or personality characteristics.

Stress Relief: Bringing humor, joy, and light-heartedness to workplace environments in ways that reduce stress and create a more enjoyable work experience for everyone.

Workplace Prayer and Spiritual Influence

While maintaining appropriate boundaries and respecting workplace policies about religious expression, believers can find many opportunities to pray for their workplaces and exercise spiritual influence in their professional environments.

Individual Intercession: Regularly praying for colleagues, workplace challenges, and organizational decisions during personal prayer times, asking God to work through circumstances and relationships to accomplish His purposes.

Crisis Response: Offering prayer during workplace emergencies, personal crises, or difficult seasons when colleagues are more open to spiritual support and encouragement.

Decision-Making: Seeking God's wisdom for work-related decisions and sharing insights appropriately when colleagues request advice or perspective on challenging situations.

Spiritual Warfare: Recognizing when workplace conflicts or problems have spiritual dimensions and praying against negative spiritual influences while promoting a spiritual atmosphere that welcomes God's presence.

Evangelistic Opportunities: Being alert to natural opportunities to share faith when colleagues express spiritual hunger, ask religious questions, or face situations where the Gospel message might bring hope and comfort.

Community Building: Creating opportunities for believing colleagues to support and encourage each other through informal fellowship, prayer partnerships, or service projects that benefit the workplace or broader community.

Jennifer Park, a nurse manager in Portland, organized prayer support among Christian staff members: "We had several believing nurses and support staff who felt called to pray for our hospital unit but didn't know how to coordinate our efforts appropriately. We started meeting once a week during lunch breaks to pray for patients, families, and staff members who were facing difficult situations. We also began praying together before particularly challenging shifts. The spiritual atmosphere in our unit improved dramatically, and we began seeing more frequent healings and positive outcomes that we attributed to increased prayer coverage."

CHAPTER 3:
Conversations That Transform

The Art of Natural Spiritual Conversation

One of the greatest barriers to everyday revival is believers' fear or awkwardness about introducing spiritual topics into ordinary conversations. Many Christians oscillate between two extremes, either avoiding spiritual conversation entirely or forcing religious content into inappropriate contexts in ways that feel artificial and make others uncomfortable.

The key to transforming ordinary conversations into spiritual encounters is learning to speak naturally about faith as an integrated part of life rather than as a separate religious category. When your relationship with God is authentic and central to your identity, spiritual topics arise naturally in conversations without feeling forced or manipulative.

Listening for Spiritual Hunger: Paying attention to comments people make that reveal spiritual questions, needs, or interests, expressions of discouragement, wonder about life's meaning, gratitude for blessings, or concern about moral issues.

Sharing Personal Experience: Contributing your perspective to conversations in ways that naturally include your faith without being preachy, "I've been praying about that situation," "God has really been teaching me," or "I'm grateful for how God has provided."

Asking Good Questions: Using questions that help people think about spiritual dimensions of their experiences, "How do you think God sees that situation?" or "What do you think gives life meaning during difficult times?"

Offering Prayer: Finding appropriate ways to offer prayer for people's needs or concerns expressed during normal conversations, whether immediate prayer or committed intercession.

Sharing Hope: A Contributing perspective that offers hope during difficult conversations without minimizing people's pain or offering simplistic solutions to complex problems.

Creating Safety: Establishing conversational environments where people feel free to express doubts, questions, or spiritual struggles without fear of judgment or religious pressure.

Sarah Martinez, a teacher in San Antonio, learned to have spiritual conversations naturally with colleagues: "I used to either avoid spiritual topics completely or try to force them into conversations where they didn't fit. I learned to simply be myself, someone who prays, reads the Bible, and includes God in my daily life. When colleagues asked about my peace during stressful times or my perspective on difficult situations, I could naturally share how my faith influenced my responses. These authentic conversations led to deeper relationships and multiple opportunities to share the Gospel."

Turning Complaints into Prayer Opportunities

Daily conversations often include complaints about circumstances, frustrations with people, or worries about future events. These common human expressions provide natural opportunities to introduce prayer and spiritual perspective without seeming artificial or manipulative.

Transforming Worry: When people express anxiety about future events, offer to pray with them about their concerns while also sharing biblical perspectives about God's faithfulness and provision.

Addressing Frustration: When colleagues complain about difficult people or situations, suggest prayer as a practical response while offering to intercede for wisdom and improved relationships.

Responding to Discouragement: When people express discouragement about personal or professional setbacks, offer hope through prayer and sharing testimonies of how God has worked through similar situations.

Handling Conflict: When people share relationship conflicts, suggest prayer for wisdom, reconciliation, and God's intervention while offering practical biblical principles for conflict resolution.

Processing Grief: When people are dealing with loss or disappointment, offer prayer for comfort and healing while sharing appropriate hope about God's comfort and eternal perspective.

Celebrating Blessings: When people share good news or positive developments, suggest thanking God together for His goodness and provision, helping people recognize divine blessing in ordinary circumstances.

Michael Thompson, a businessman in Chicago, learned to redirect common complaints toward spiritual solutions: "Instead of just commiserating with colleagues who complained about problems, I started asking if I could pray about their situations. Most people were honored by the offer, even those who weren't particularly religious. This simple practice opened many doors for deeper spiritual conversations and demonstrated practical care that strengthened my workplace relationships while creating opportunities for ministry."

Social Media as Mission Field

Social media platforms provide unprecedented opportunities for everyday revival through digital conversations that can influence hundreds or thousands of people simultaneously. However, these platforms also present unique challenges requiring wisdom about how to share faith authentically without becoming preachy or contributing to online negativity.

Encouraging Content: Sharing posts that encourage, inspire, and point people toward hope without being exclusively religious in nature, creating an online presence that reflects God's heart for people.

Prayer Requests and Testimonies: Appropriately sharing personal prayer requests and testimonies of answered prayer in ways that invite others to participate or celebrate God's goodness without oversharing private information.

Thoughtful Responses: Contributing constructive, grace-filled responses to controversial topics or negative conversations rather than avoiding difficult issues or participating in online arguments.

Direct Message Ministry: Using private messaging to offer prayer, encouragement, or support to friends who share struggles or challenges through their social media posts.

Community Building: Creating online groups or participating in digital communities that provide spiritual support, encouragement, and accountability for believers while welcoming non-Christians who might benefit from positive influence.

Evangelistic Opportunities: Being alert to natural opportunities to share Gospel hope when people express spiritual questions, existential concerns, or life crises through their social media presence.

Lisa Johnson, a mother and part-time office worker in Dallas, developed an effective social media ministry: "I started being more intentional about sharing my faith naturally through social media without being preachy or political. I would post brief prayers during difficult times, share testimonies of God's provision, and offer encouragement during challenging seasons. Several people contacted me privately to ask for prayer or share their own struggles. My Facebook page became a source of hope and encouragement for friends who were going through difficult times, and several have begun attending church or seeking spiritual guidance as a result of our online interactions."

Evangelistic Conversations That Feel Natural

The goal of spiritual conversation is not to pressure people into religious decisions but to create opportunities for them to encounter God's love and truth in ways that feel authentic and respectful. Effective evangelism flows naturally from genuine relationships and addresses real needs rather than following prescribed formulas or scripts.

Building Relationships First: Investing time and attention in getting to know people as individuals with real needs, interests, and concerns rather than seeing them primarily as evangelistic targets.

Addressing Felt Needs: Connecting Gospel truth to problems, questions, or concerns that people are actually experiencing rather than presenting abstract theological concepts that don't address their current reality.

Sharing Personal Testimony: Contributing your story of how God has worked in your life during appropriate conversations rather than presenting evangelistic arguments or trying to convince people through logic alone.

Demonstrating Love: Showing genuine care for people's well-being through practical service, emotional support, and consistent friendship that reflects God's love before talking about God's love.

Respecting Free Will: Presenting Gospel truth clearly while respecting people's freedom to respond positively or negatively without applying pressure, manipulation, or guilt to influence their decisions.

Following Up with Support: Offering ongoing friendship and spiritual support to people who express interest in faith, rather than just leading them to pray a prayer and then disappearing from their lives.

David Chen, an engineer in Seattle, developed natural evangelistic conversations through workplace relationships: "I stopped trying to present the Gospel to every coworker I met and instead focused on building genuine friendships based on mutual respect and shared interests. As these relationships developed, people began asking me about my peace during stressful situations, my perspective on moral issues, and my source of hope during difficult times. These questions created natural opportunities to share my faith story and explain how Jesus had changed my life. Several colleagues have come to faith through these authentic relationships rather than through any evangelistic program or presentation."

CHAPTER 4:
Supernatural Ordinary Moments

Finding God in Routine Activities

One of the most profound aspects of everyday revival is discovering God's presence in the most mundane activities of daily life. Washing dishes, commuting to work, grocery shopping, doing laundry, these routine tasks become opportunities for communion with God when believers learn to practice His presence throughout ordinary activities.

This is not about constantly thinking religious thoughts or turning every activity into formal prayer, but about developing awareness that God is present in every moment and interested in every aspect of your life. It's learning to include Him naturally in your thoughts, decisions, and responses throughout the day.

Commute Communion: Transforming travel time into prayer time, worship time, or spiritual learning time rather than just enduring transportation as a necessary inconvenience.

Household Worship: Finding ways to pray, sing, or commune with God while doing household chores, turning necessary domestic work into opportunities for spiritual refreshment.

Shopping with Purpose: Praying for people you encounter in stores, asking God to guide purchases, and looking for opportunities to bless clerks, fellow shoppers, or service workers with kindness and encouragement.

Exercise as Spiritual Discipline: Using physical activity as time for prayer, gratitude, or meditation on Scripture while caring for the body God has given you as His temple.

Meal Preparation as Service: Approaching cooking and meal preparation as acts of service to God and others, praying for those who will eat the food and thanking God for His provision.

Rest as Spiritual Practice: Learning to rest well as an act of trust in God's sovereignty rather than feeling guilty about non-productive time or filling every moment with activity.

Maria Rodriguez discovered God's presence during routine activities after feeling disconnected from Him despite regular church attendance: "I felt like I only connected with God during formal prayer times or church services, which made my faith feel compartmentalized from real life. I started talking to God throughout my day, while folding laundry, driving carpool, or preparing meals. I was amazed at how this simple practice transformed my sense of His presence and made every ordinary activity feel meaningful. My daily routine became a continuous conversation with God rather than just the mechanics of getting things done."

Divine Appointments in Unexpected Places

When believers live with expectant awareness of God's presence, ordinary errands and routine activities become opportunities for divine appointments, unexpected encounters with people who need exactly what God wants to provide through you at that moment.

These divine appointments rarely announce themselves in advance. They appear as interruptions to your schedule, unexpected delays, or "coincidental" encounters that become opportunities for ministry when you recognize them as God-orchestrated opportunities.

Grocery Store Encounters: Meeting people in checkout lines, parking lots, or aisles who need encouragement, prayer, or practical help that you're uniquely positioned to provide.

Medical Appointment Ministry: Using waiting rooms, hospital visits, or medical procedures as opportunities to minister to other patients, family members, or healthcare workers who are dealing with stress, fear, or discouragement.

Transportation Opportunities: Encountering fellow passengers, service workers, or stranded motorists who need assistance, encouragement, or simply human kindness that demonstrates God's care.

Service Industry Connections: Building relationships with people who provide regular services, postal workers, restaurant servers, maintenance staff, who rarely receive personal attention but often carry heavy personal burdens.

Neighborhood Encounters: Being available for spontaneous conversations with neighbors who are outside, walking dogs, or dealing with yard work, creating opportunities for relationship building and ministry.

Crisis Response: Being prepared to offer help, prayer, or comfort during unexpected emergencies, accidents, or difficult situations that arise in public spaces.

Jennifer Martinez learned to recognize divine appointments during routine activities: "I started praying before leaving home each day that God would make me sensitive to opportunities to serve others during errands and appointments. I was amazed at how often I encountered people who needed exactly what I could offer, a listening ear, a word of encouragement, practical help, or prayer. I realized that God had been orchestrating these encounters all along, but I had been too busy or self-focused to recognize them as ministry opportunities."

Workplace Miracles in Ordinary Jobs

God desires to work miraculously through believers in their ordinary jobs, not necessarily through dramatic supernatural manifestations but through supernatural wisdom, provision, protection, and influence that advance His kingdom while meeting practical needs.

These workplace miracles often go unrecognized because they occur through natural processes enhanced by supernatural intervention, projects succeeding against odds, relationships improving unexpectedly, resources appearing when needed, or wisdom emerging for complex problems.

Problem-Solving Breakthrough: Receiving divine insight for work challenges that human analysis couldn't resolve, leading to solutions that benefit entire organizations.

Relationship Restoration: Experiencing supernatural grace to forgive difficult colleagues or seeing hostile workplace relationships transformed through patient love and consistent character.

Resource Provision: Discovering that necessary resources, funding, or support become available through unexpected sources when you've committed projects to prayer.

Protection and Safety: Being protected from workplace accidents, office politics, or career-threatening situations through divine intervention that may appear coincidental but exceeds statistical probability.

Influence Expansion: Finding that your workplace influence grows beyond your position or experience level because people recognize wisdom, integrity, and character that exceed normal professional qualifications.

Career Advancement: Experiencing career opportunities and advancement that align with your calling rather than just your ambition, opening doors for greater kingdom influence.

Tom Wilson, a construction supervisor in Phoenix, began seeing miracles in his ordinary work: "I started praying about work projects, asking God for wisdom about safety issues and solutions to construction problems. I noticed that projects I prayed about consistently went more smoothly than expected, fewer accidents, better cooperation among workers, creative solutions to difficult challenges. My reputation for successful projects grew, and I realized that God was enhancing my natural abilities with supernatural wisdom. This gave me credibility to share my faith with workers and contractors who respected the results they saw in projects I managed."

Family Miracles in Everyday Life

Families experiencing everyday revival regularly witness God's miraculous provision, protection, guidance, and intervention in ways that strengthen faith and create testimonies of His faithfulness for future generations.

These family miracles often occur through ordinary means, timely phone calls, unexpected resources, health improvements, relational breakthroughs, or educational opportunities, but their timing and circumstances reveal divine orchestration.

Financial Provision: Experiencing God's supply for family needs through unexpected sources, creative solutions, or resources that appear exactly when needed without compromising family values or relationships.

Health and Healing: Seeing family members recover from illnesses, overcome chronic conditions, or avoid serious health problems through divine intervention combined with medical care and prayer.

Educational Success: Watching children succeed academically or overcome learning challenges through supernatural wisdom and favor that goes beyond natural ability or tutoring support.

Relational Restoration: Experiencing a breakthrough in family conflicts, restoration of damaged relationships, or improved communication that creates harmony previously thought impossible.

Protection and Safety: Being protected from accidents, dangerous situations, or harmful influences through divine intervention that keeps family members safe during risky circumstances.

Spiritual Growth: Witnessing family members' hearts open to God, experiencing breakthroughs in prayer lives, or seeing spiritual gifts develop in ways that strengthen faith and ministry effectiveness.

Sarah Chen, a single mother in Seattle, began documenting family miracles to strengthen her children's faith: "I started keeping a journal of answered prayers and evidence of God's provision in our family life. Over time, we accumulated so many testimonies of His faithfulness, timely financial provision, protection from accidents, healing from illnesses, and breakthroughs in relationships, that my children developed unshakeable confidence in God's care for our family. These recorded miracles became family treasures that we share during difficult times to remind ourselves of God's consistent faithfulness."

CHAPTER 5:
Creating Revival Culture

Home Atmospheres That Welcome God

Homes experiencing everyday revival are characterized by spiritual atmospheres that make God's presence natural and expected rather than forced or artificial. These atmospheres develop through intentional choices about environment, conversations, priorities, and responses to both blessings and challenges.

Creating revival culture at home doesn't require elaborate religious displays or constant spiritual activity, but it does require families that prioritize spiritual reality over material accumulation, eternal values over temporal success, and kingdom purposes over personal comfort.

Physical Environment: Making choices about home decor, entertainment, and atmosphere that reflect spiritual values, Scripture displays, worship music, books that encourage faith, and spaces dedicated to prayer or family worship.

Conversational Culture: Establishing family communication patterns that include spiritual topics naturally, sharing answered prayers, discussing how God is working in family members' lives, and processing life experiences from a spiritual perspective.

Priority Alignment: Making family schedule and resource decisions that demonstrate God's importance, prioritizing church attendance, family devotions, service opportunities, and relationships with other believers over competing activities.

Conflict Resolution: Addressing family disputes through biblical principles of forgiveness, reconciliation, and mutual submission rather than through power struggles, manipulation, or unresolved resentment.

Celebration Practices: Creating family traditions that recognize God's goodness, thanksgiving for answered prayers, celebration of spiritual milestones, and acknowledgment of His provision during both ordinary and special occasions.

Hospitality Ministry: Using the home as a place where others can experience God's love through genuine welcome, practical service, and spiritual encouragement that demonstrates kingdom values to visitors.

The Johnson family in Dallas intentionally created a revival atmosphere in their home: "We realized that our house felt more like a hotel where family members came and went rather than a place where we encountered God together. We started playing worship music during dinner preparation, displaying Bible verses in common areas, and having brief prayer times before family members left for work or school. We also began hosting neighbors for meals and small group meetings. These simple changes created an atmosphere where spiritual conversations happened naturally, and everyone expected to encounter God in our home."

Community Transformation Through Individual Revival

When individuals and families experience authentic everyday revival, their transformation naturally influences broader community culture through workplace relationships, neighborhood connections, school involvement, and civic participation that demonstrates kingdom values in public contexts.

This community influence happens not through organized programs or evangelistic campaigns but through consistent demonstration of character, wisdom, and love that makes people curious about the source of transformed lives.

Workplace Culture: Individual believers experiencing revival bring different energy to work environments, integrity in business practices, servant leadership, conflict resolution skills, and genuine care for colleagues' welfare that improves organizational culture.

Neighborhood Relationships: Families walking in revival become known for hospitality, helpfulness during crises, and positive influence that makes their streets more friendly, safe, and caring places to live.

School Involvement: Parents experiencing revival contribute differently to educational communities, volunteering motivated by service rather than status, advocating for policies that benefit all children, and building relationships with educators based on partnership rather than conflict.

Civic Participation: Citizens influenced by revival engage in local government, community organizations, and public issues from perspectives that prioritize community welfare over partisan politics or personal advantage.

Economic Influence: Business owners and employees experiencing revival conduct commerce according to kingdom principles, fair wages, honest advertising, excellent service, and concern for community impact that influences local business culture.

Cultural Leadership: Individuals empowered by revival contribute to community arts, media, education, and entertainment in ways that promote values and content that strengthen rather than undermine family and community life.

Michael Thompson, a businessman in Chicago, saw his personal revival influence his entire business community: "When I began seeking God's guidance for business decisions and treating employees and customers according to biblical principles, other business owners began asking about my motivation and methods. I started a monthly breakfast meeting for local entrepreneurs where we discussed business challenges from a Christian perspective. This group has influenced business practices throughout our community and created accountability for ethical behavior that has improved the reputation of our entire business district."

Multigenerational Revival Legacy

One of the most influential aspects of everyday revival is its potential to create a spiritual legacy that influences not just current family members but future generations who inherit cultures of faith, expectation for God's activity, and natural integration of spiritual reality into ordinary life.

Families experiencing authentic revival don't just change their own spiritual experience, they establish patterns, traditions, and atmospheres that shape their children's understanding of normal Christianity and create expectation for continued divine activity in future generations.

Modeling Authentic Faith: Demonstrating to children what it looks like to depend on God for daily decisions, seek His guidance for practical problems, and experience His provision during both easy and difficult circumstances.

Creating Spiritual Traditions: Establishing family customs that embed spiritual reality into ordinary life, blessing traditions, prayer practices, celebration customs, and service activities that become natural parts of family culture.

Teaching Through Experience: Helping children recognize God's activity in their own lives rather than just learning about Him through abstract concepts, creating personal testimonies and spiritual memories that build lifelong faith.

Developing Spiritual Gifts: Encouraging and training children to recognize and develop their spiritual gifts through age-appropriate ministry opportunities that build confidence in God's ability to work through them.

Building Kingdom Perspective: Teaching children to see their talents, opportunities, and resources as tools for serving God's purposes rather than just personal advancement or family success.

Preparing for Leadership: Intentionally developing character, wisdom, and spiritual maturity in children that prepares them to influence their own generation for Christ rather than just maintaining their parents' faith.

The Martinez family has seen three generations influenced by their commitment to everyday revival: "When my husband and I began experiencing God's presence in our daily lives, our children naturally absorbed this reality as normal Christianity. They grew up expecting God to answer prayers, provide for needs, and guide decisions. Now our adult children are raising their own families with the same spiritual integration, and our grandchildren are developing faith that exceeds what we experienced at their age.

The revival that began in our living room is now influencing a third generation."

Overcoming Obstacles to Everyday Revival

Despite its appeal and biblical foundation, everyday revival faces several obstacles that prevent many believers from experiencing consistent spiritual integration in ordinary life. Understanding and addressing these obstacles is crucial for maintaining revival culture over time.

Busyness and Distraction: Modern life's pace and complexity can crowd out spiritual awareness and make it difficult to maintain consciousness of God's presence during daily activities. This requires intentional choices about schedule priorities and technology boundaries.

Religious Compartmentalization: Cultural conditioning that separates spiritual and secular activities can make it feel artificial or inappropriate to include God in ordinary conversations and decisions. Overcoming this requires persistent practice and community support.

Fear of Others' Reactions: Concern about how family members, colleagues, or friends will respond to increased spiritual integration can limit authentic faith expression. This fear often proves unfounded when spiritual reality is shared naturally rather than being forced.

Inconsistency and Failure: Everyone experiences seasons of spiritual dryness, failed attempts at spiritual discipline, or lapses in faith integration that can create discouragement. Success in everyday revival requires grace for failure and commitment to restart rather than perfectionist expectations.

Spiritual Warfare: Increased spiritual activity often triggers spiritual opposition that manifests through increased conflict, discouragement, or circumstances that make spiritual integration more difficult. Recognition and resistance to spiritual attacks is essential for maintaining revival culture.

Lack of Community Support: Individual or family attempts at everyday revival can feel isolated without a broader community of believers who share similar commitments and can provide encouragement, accountability, and practical support.

Lisa Johnson learned to overcome obstacles that initially hindered her family's revival experience: "We started strong but faced several challenges that made us want to give up, schedule pressures that crowded out prayer times, teenagers who resisted spiritual conversations, and workplace situations that made faith integration difficult. We learned that everyday revival is more like marathon running than sprinting, it requires pacing, persistence, and grace for imperfect progress. The key was not giving up during difficult seasons but adjusting our approach and continuing to seek God's presence in whatever ways were possible during each season of family life."

CHAPTER 6:
The Ripple Effect Of Ordinary Faithfulness

Small Acts, Eternal Impact

The most prevailing aspect of everyday revival is often invisible, the cumulative effect of thousands of small acts of faithfulness that create spiritual momentum, influence lives in ways you may never know, and contribute to kingdom advancement through ordinary obedience rather than dramatic ministry.

Every prayer whispered during routine activities, every word of encouragement spoken to discouraged colleagues, every act of service performed without recognition, and every decision made according to kingdom principles rather than personal advantage create ripple effects that extend far beyond immediate circumstances.

Modeling for Children: Every spiritual conversation a child overhears, every prayer they witness during ordinary difficulties, and every demonstration of faith during family challenges shape their understanding of authentic Christianity and create spiritual memories that influence their adult faith.

Influencing Coworkers: Every demonstration of integrity during business dealings, every peaceful response to workplace stress, and every offer of prayer for colleagues' needs plants seeds of spiritual curiosity that may bear fruit years later through circumstances you never know about.

Impacting Community: Every act of neighborly kindness, every contribution to community welfare, and every demonstration of kingdom value in civic involvement influences community culture in ways that benefit people you may never meet.

Affecting Extended Networks: Every social media post that encourages rather than complains, every conversation that offers hope rather than despair, and every demonstration of joy despite difficult circumstances influences extended networks of relationships in ways that multiply your spiritual impact.

Creating Legacy: Every spiritual tradition established, every prayer commitment maintained, and every act of faithfulness performed creates a legacy that influences future generations through patterns, memories, and spiritual atmospheres that outlast your lifetime.

Contributing to Revival: Every believer who experiences authentic everyday revival contributes to a broader spiritual awakening that influences regions, nations, and generations through individual faithfulness that combines with other believers' revival to create movements that transform cultures.

Sarah Chen, now in her seventies, reflects on the cumulative impact of decades of everyday faithfulness: "When I started seeking God's presence in ordinary activities forty years ago, I never imagined the long-term impact. My children developed a strong faith that carried them through life challenges. My grandchildren have grown up expecting God to work in their lives. Former coworkers still contact me for prayer about important decisions. Neighbors who aren't Christians still ask for spiritual advice during crises. I realized that every small act of faithfulness created influence I never saw but that God used to advance His kingdom in ways I'm still discovering."

Creating Movements Through Ordinary Lives

History's greatest spiritual movements have typically begun not with famous leaders or dramatic events but with ordinary believers who experienced authentic revival in their personal lives and naturally influenced their spheres of relationship through consistent demonstration of transformed living.

The Wesley brothers' Methodist movement began in small group meetings where ordinary believers shared their struggles and victories. The Moravian missionary movement emerged from a community prayer meeting where regular church members committed to intercession.

The modern Pentecostal movement started in humble settings where working-class believers experienced supernatural encounters with God.

Contemporary everyday revival has the potential to create similar movements as ordinary believers discover that authentic spiritual integration attracts people who are hungry for reality beyond religious formalism and cultural materialism.

Family Revival Centers: Homes that become known as places where God's presence is real, and people experience spiritual breakthrough through family hospitality and authentic Christian community.

Workplace Transformation: Businesses, schools, hospitals, and organizations that experience culture change through employees who bring kingdom values and spiritual wisdom to their professional responsibilities.

Neighborhood Networks: Communities where multiple families experience everyday revival create informal networks of mutual support, spiritual encouragement, and practical service that influence entire geographic areas.

Church Renewal: Local churches that catch vision for everyday revival often experience renewal as members discover that Christianity is meant to be lived seven days a week rather than confined to Sunday services and church programs.

Regional Influence: Areas with high concentrations of believers experiencing everyday revival often develop reputations for integrity in business, excellence in education, care for the needy, and quality of community life that attract others seeking similar environments.

Cultural Impact: Movements of everyday revival can influence broader cultural trends toward family stability, community involvement, ethical business practices, and social responsibility that benefit entire societies.

Tom and Jennifer Martinez have seen their personal revival contribute to broader community transformation: "What began as our family seeking God's presence in ordinary life gradually influenced other families in our church and neighborhood. Now we have networks of families who pray together, serve together, and support each other through life challenges.

Our children have friends whose families share similar values. Our business community has groups that meet for prayer and accountability. We've seen our small beginning contribute to a broader revival that has influenced our entire region."

The Eternal Perspective of Ordinary Faithfulness

The ultimate significance of everyday revival lies not in temporary improvements to earthly circumstances but in the eternal impact that extends beyond this life into eternity. Every person is influenced toward faith, every believer encouraged toward spiritual growth, and every demonstration of God's reality contributes to eternal purposes that will be fully revealed only in heaven.

This eternal perspective provides motivation to persist in faithful living even when results aren't immediately visible, circumstances remain difficult, or efforts seem unappreciated by those around you.

Treasure in Heaven: Jesus taught that acts of faithfulness performed for kingdom purposes, rather than earthly recognition, become treasures stored in heaven where they produce eternal rewards and significance.

Eternal Relationships: People influenced toward faith through your everyday revival become eternal relationships that will continue beyond earthly life, making every evangelistic conversation and demonstration of God's love investments in the eternal community.

Generational Impact: Spiritual legacy created through faithful living influences children, grandchildren, and future generations in ways that extend your impact centuries beyond your lifetime through people you may never meet.

Kingdom Advancement: Every act of everyday faithfulness contributes to the advancement of God's kingdom on earth, participating in His eternal plan to redeem creation and establish His rule over all earthly systems and relationships.

Divine Partnership: Everyday revival makes you a partner with God in His work of transformation, redemption, and restoration that began with creation and will culminate with Christ's return and the establishment of new heavens and new earth.

Eternal Satisfaction: The deep satisfaction that comes from authentic spiritual living provides a foretaste of eternal joy that awaits those who faithfully serve God's purposes rather than pursuing temporal pleasure or achievement.

David Kim, reflecting on twenty years of everyday revival, shares his eternal perspective: "The temporal benefits of living with spiritual integration, better relationships, greater peace, more meaningful work, are wonderful, but they pale in comparison to the eternal significance of this lifestyle. I've seen people come to faith through ordinary conversations. I've watched children develop unshakeable spiritual foundations. I've participated in God's work of transformation in ways I never could have imagined. The knowledge that my ordinary faithfulness contributes to God's eternal purposes gives meaning to every routine activity and makes every day feel like a sacred adventure."

The revival our world desperately needs will not begin in conference centers or church buildings, it will begin in your kitchen, your workplace, your neighborhood, and your daily conversations. It will start when ordinary believers like you decide that compartmentalized Christianity is no longer acceptable and that every moment of life can become an opportunity to experience and express the reality of God's presence and power.

You don't need special qualifications, dramatic spiritual experiences, or perfect circumstances to begin living in everyday revival. You need only the decision to include God naturally in your ordinary activities, to see your daily responsibilities as ministry opportunities, and to carry your faith authentically into every conversation and relationship.

The Spirit of God who fell on Pentecost, who sustained the Moravians through century-long prayer, who empowered missionaries to cross every border, and who ignited revivals throughout church history is living within you right now. He's not waiting for special occasions or religious settings to work through your life, He's ready to transform your ordinary moments into extraordinary encounters with divine reality.

Your family is waiting for someone to bring spiritual reality into routine activities and ordinary conversations.

Your workplace needs someone who will demonstrate kingdom values through excellent work and authentic relationships. Your community is desperate for neighbors who will serve, encourage, and demonstrate hope during difficult circumstances.

That someone can be you. That someone should be you.

Your everyday revival begins with your next conversation, your next meal, your next routine activity, approached with awareness that God is present and interested in every detail of your life. It continues as you learn to pray during commutes, worship while doing chores, serve colleagues during workplace challenges, and include a spiritual perspective in family discussions.

The world is tired of religious performance that has no power to transform real life. It's hungry for authentic spirituality that makes ordinary people extraordinary examples of God's love, wisdom, and grace. It's desperate for believers who don't just talk about faith but live it naturally in every circumstance and relationship.

This is your invitation to stop compartmentalizing your faith and start integrating it into every aspect of your existence. This is your call to become a catalyst for the kind of revival that transforms communities, influences cultures, and creates lasting change through ordinary believers living supernatural lives.

The revival that begins in your ordinary moments can create ripple effects that influence your family, transform your workplace, strengthen your community, and contribute to a spiritual awakening that extends far beyond what you can see or imagine.

Your everyday revival starts now, with your next breath, your next thought, your next opportunity to include God in the ordinary activities of ordinary life. The Spirit is ready. The opportunity is available.

The only question is: Will you begin?

The sacred is waiting to transform your ordinary.

What will you choose?

IV

Your Pentecost Journey

Every generation faces the same question:
Will you let the echo die to silence, or
will you be the voice that carries it forward?

Observation Ends and Transformation Begins

The time for observation is over. The season of preparation is complete. You have traced the footsteps of those who have gone before, from that first upper room in Jerusalem to the prayer closets of Moravian believers, from missionary journeys that crossed impossible borders to revival fires that transformed entire nations. You have witnessed the testimonies, studied the principles, and examined the patterns. You have seen what God has done through ordinary people who positioned themselves for extraordinary encounters with His Spirit.

Now comes your moment of decision. Now comes your invitation to step from the spectator stand onto the field of supernatural living. Now comes your opportunity to discover that the same Spirit who fell on Pentecost, the same fire that sustained the Moravians, the same power that empowered missionaries and ignited revivals, is not just a historical fact, it is a present reality, available to transform your life in ways that will amaze you.

This is your Pentecost journey, not a program to complete or a formula to follow, but a personal adventure with the living God who wants to fill you, empower you, and work through you in ways that exceed your wildest imagination. It's a journey from routine religion to authentic relationship, from spiritual mediocrity to supernatural living, from comfortable Christianity to costly discipleship that changes everything it touches.

But journeys require more than good intentions and inspiring stories. They require practical steps, personal commitment, and persistent faith that moves beyond initial enthusiasm to lifelong transformation. They demand that you move from knowing about God's power to experiencing it, from admiring spiritual giants to becoming one, from reading testimonies to creating them.

Part IV is your roadmap for this journey. It's not just about understanding what God can do, it's about positioning yourself to receive what He wants to give you. It's not just about being inspired by others' experiences, it's about having your own encounters that create testimonies your children's children will treasure. It's not just about adding spiritual activities to your life, it's about allowing spiritual reality to transform every aspect of your existence.

Your Pentecost journey will be uniquely yours. God doesn't work through cookie-cutter formulas or identical experiences. He meets each person where they are, works through their personality and circumstances, and creates encounters that fit their calling and capacity. But while the details may differ, the pattern remains consistent: desperate hearts seeking more of God, surrendered lives opening to His fullness, expectant faith creating space for His work, and obedient actions releasing His power.

Some of you will experience dramatic encounters that mark clear before-and-after moments in your spiritual journey. Others will discover a gradual transformation that unfolds over months or years as you consistently position yourself for God's work in your life. Some will see miraculous signs and wonders that leave no doubt about divine intervention. Others will experience supernatural peace, wisdom, and fruitfulness that quietly revolutionizes every relationship and responsibility.

All of these are authentic expressions of God's Spirit working in human lives. The goal is not to achieve specific manifestations or copy others' experiences, it's to receive everything God wants to give you and become everything He created you to be. It's to live so fully in His presence and power that your ordinary life becomes an extraordinary testimony to His reality.

But be warned: this journey will cost you everything and give you everything. It will cost you your independence and give you a divine partnership. It will cost you your comfort zones and give you supernatural adventures. It will cost you your small dreams and give you a kingdom vision. It will cost you your old life and give you an abundant life that exceeds anything you could have imagined.

The choice is yours. The invitation is extended. The Spirit is waiting.

Your Pentecost journey can begin with your next prayer, your next step of faith, your next decision to trust God more completely than you ever have before.

The question that has faced every generation since that first Pentecost remains unchanged: Will you settle for reading about what God has done in others' lives, or will you position yourself to experience what He wants to do in yours?

Your journey begins now.

Are you ready?

10. THE ECHO CONTINUES

Pentecost as Inheritance, Not History

The sound that shattered the morning calm in Jerusalem two thousand years ago was not a one-time event, it was the inaugural note of a symphony that continues to this day. The rushing mighty wind that filled that upper room was not a historical curiosity, it was the first breath of a divine hurricane that has been sweeping across the earth ever since. The tongues of fire that rested on those first disciples were not ancient relics, they were the lighting of torches that have been passed from generation to generation, hand to hand, heart to heart, until they reach you today.

You are not reading about someone else's spiritual inheritance. You are discovering your own. You are not studying ancient history. You are exploring the present possibility. The echo of that first Pentecost has been reverberating through two millennia of church history, growing stronger rather than weaker, more widespread rather than more limited, more accessible rather than more exclusive.

Every revival that has shaken nations, every missionary who has crossed impossible borders, every believer who has lived in supernatural power, and every ordinary person who has become an extraordinary demonstration of God's reality has been an echo of that first Pentecost morning. They have been living proof that what happened in Jerusalem was not a unique historical moment but the establishment of a new normal, a pattern of divine-human partnership that would characterize every generation of believers until Christ's return.

The echo continues in you. The fire still burns within you. The power that transformed fishermen into apostles, cowards into martyrs, and doubters into world-changers is not dormant within you, it is actively waiting to be released through your faith, your surrender, your obedience, and your bold expectation that God wants to work as mightily through your life as He has through every Spirit-filled believer throughout history.

But echoes can fade if they are not amplified. Fires can diminish if they are not fed. Inheritance can be forfeited if it is not claimed. The question that confronts you today is not whether this inheritance is available, twenty centuries of testimony prove that it is. The question is whether you will receive it, steward it, and pass it on to the next generation with the same power and passion that brought it to you.

CHAPTER 1:
Understanding Your Inheritance

What Pentecost Made Available to You

When the Holy Spirit fell on that first group of disciples, He was not just empowering a small band of followers for a specific mission. He was establishing a new covenant reality that would be available to every person who believes in Jesus Christ throughout all of history. What happened on Pentecost was the down payment of an inheritance that belongs to every member of God's family.

Your inheritance includes everything that was demonstrated on that first Pentecost and has been manifested throughout church history in the lives of believers who have walked in the fullness of God's Spirit.

Divine Empowerment: The same power that enabled the disciples to speak in languages they had never learned, to heal the sick with authority, and to proclaim the Gospel with supernatural boldness is your inheritance. This is not power for the spiritually elite but for every believer who will position themselves to receive it.

Supernatural Wisdom: The wisdom that enabled untrained fishermen to confound religious scholars that gave Stephen the ability to speak with such authority that his opponents could not resist, and that provided Paul with insights that became the theological foundation of Christianity is available to you for every decision and challenge you face.

Miraculous Provision: The provision that sustained the early church through persecution that supplied resources for global missionary expansion, and that has met the needs of believers throughout history who have trusted God completely is part of your spiritual inheritance.

Kingdom Authority: The authority that enabled the disciples to cast out demons, establish churches in hostile territories, and transform entire communities through the Gospel is not reserved for apostolic ministry but is available to every believer who understands their position in Christ and exercises faith accordingly.

Prophetic Insight: The ability to hear God's voice, receive divine guidance, and speak His word into situations and people's lives is not limited to Old Testament prophets or New Testament apostles but is part of the normal Christian life that becomes your inheritance through the Holy Spirit's presence within you.

Evangelistic Fruitfulness: The fruitfulness that enabled the early church to multiply from 120 believers to thousands within weeks, and ultimately to penetrate every known civilization within three centuries, is available to believers today who carry the same Spirit and proclaim the same Gospel with the same faith and boldness.

Sarah Martinez, a teacher in Phoenix, discovered her spiritual inheritance when she stopped seeing Pentecost as ancient history: "I grew up hearing about the disciples and their amazing experiences, but I thought those things were for them in their time. When I realized that the same Spirit who filled them lives in me, everything changed. I began expecting God to work through me in supernatural ways. I started praying for my students' needs and seeing remarkable answers. I began sharing my faith with colleagues and watching people respond in ways I never experienced before. I realized that what I had been admiring as their experience was actually my inheritance."

Why Many Believers Don't Live in Their Inheritance

Despite the clear biblical teaching that the Holy Spirit's power is available to every believer, and despite two thousand years of church history demonstrating this reality, many Christians live far below their spiritual inheritance. Understanding why this happens is crucial to ensuring that you don't forfeit what God has made available to you.

Ignorance of What's Available: Many believers have never been taught about their spiritual inheritance. They know about salvation from sin and eternal life in heaven, but they're unaware that God has also provided power for victorious living, gifts for effective ministry, and resources for supernatural impact in their current circumstances.

Theological Barriers: Some have been taught that the supernatural gifts and experiences recorded in the New Testament were only for the apostolic age and are no longer available today. This teaching, while well-intentioned, effectively closes believers off from major portions of their spiritual inheritance.

Fear of the Supernatural: Others have been exposed to counterfeit or manipulative expressions of spiritual power and have concluded that it's safer to avoid supernatural experiences altogether rather than risk deception or embarrassment.

Satisfaction with Mediocrity: Some believers have become comfortable with a level of Christianity that provides forgiveness and eternal security but doesn't demand much change or growth in their current lives. They prefer predictable, manageable faith to the adventure and challenge of supernatural living.

Lack of Desperation: Many Christians in comfortable circumstances don't feel desperate enough for God's power to pay the price of surrender, discipline, and faith required to walk in their full inheritance. They have enough natural resources and abilities to manage their lives without supernatural intervention.

Religious Tradition: Church traditions that emphasize form over power, doctrine over experience, and respectability over authenticity can create cultures where spiritual inheritance is acknowledged intellectually but never experienced practically.

Personal Unworthiness: Some believers feel too flawed, too ordinary, or too inexperienced to receive the kind of spiritual empowerment they read about in Scripture. They assume that such experiences are for people who are more spiritual, more mature, or more qualified than they are.

Michael Thompson, a businessman in Chicago, identified what had kept him from his spiritual inheritance: "I thought I was a good Christian because I attended church regularly and tried to live morally. But I realized I had been settling for salvation insurance instead of an abundant life. I was more concerned about avoiding hell than experiencing heaven's power on earth. When I understood that God wanted to fill me with the same Spirit that empowered the disciples, I had to confront my comfort with spiritual mediocrity and my fear of what total surrender to God might require."

Claiming Your Inheritance

Understanding your spiritual inheritance is only the first step. Like any inheritance, it must be claimed, received, and activated through specific steps of faith and obedience. The inheritance exists whether you claim it or not, but you won't benefit from it until you take possession of what belongs to you.

Acknowledge Your Need: The first step in claiming your inheritance is honest recognition that you need more than you currently have. This requires moving beyond satisfaction with current spiritual experience to holy dissatisfaction that drives you to seek everything God has made available.

Study Your Rights: Spend time in Scripture discovering what God has promised to provide for believers. Study the lives of the disciples before and after Pentecost. Read about the experiences of believers throughout church history who have walked in spiritual power. Let these testimonies create faith and expectation for your own experience.

Identify Barriers: Honestly examine your life for attitudes, beliefs, habits, or commitments that might be preventing you from receiving God's fullness. This might include unconfessed sin, unforgiveness toward others, pride, fear, or simply busyness that crowds out spiritual priorities.

Create Space: Make room in your life for God to work by establishing spiritual disciplines, setting aside time for prayer, seeking, and arranging your priorities to accommodate whatever God might want to do in your circumstances.

Ask in Faith: Based on God's clear promises, ask Him to fill you with His Spirit and empower you for the life and ministry He has called you to. This isn't begging for something He's reluctant to give but claiming what He's eager to provide.

Expect Response: Approach God with confident expectation that He will respond to your faith-filled request. Create an atmosphere of anticipation rather than doubt, believing that He wants to give you your inheritance more than you want to receive it.

Step Out in Obedience: When God begins to move in your life, respond with immediate obedience even when you don't fully understand what's happening or feel completely prepared for what He's asking you to do.

Jennifer Park, a nurse in Portland, describes her process of claiming her spiritual inheritance: "I realized I had been living like a spiritual pauper when God had made me a spiritual heir. I started studying every passage in the New Testament about the Holy Spirit's work in believers' lives. I identified several areas where I had been settling for less than God's best, my prayer life, my faith for healing, my boldness in sharing the Gospel. I began asking God specifically to fill me with His Spirit and empower me for the ministry He had given me. Within weeks, I was experiencing answers to prayer, supernatural wisdom for patient care, and opportunities to minister healing and encouragement that I had never had before."

CHAPTER 2:
Becoming A Modern-Day Witness

The Pattern of Pentecost Witnesses

The disciples who were transformed on Pentecost provide a pattern for what God wants to do in every believer who receives the fullness of His Spirit. Their transformation from fearful followers to fearless witnesses, from confused disciples to confident leaders, from powerless believers to powerful ministers demonstrates the potential that exists in every Christian who positions themselves for similar encounters with God's Spirit.

Understanding this pattern helps you know what to expect as you step into your own role as a Spirit-filled witness in your generation.

Before Pentecost: The disciples had been with Jesus for three years, had seen His miracles, heard His teachings, and witnessed His resurrection. They believed in Him and were committed to following Him, but they were still operating primarily in human strength and wisdom. They argued about greatness, failed in ministry attempts, and abandoned Jesus during His crucifixion. They were believers, but they were not yet empowered.

At Pentecost, Everything changed when the Holy Spirit filled them. The same people who had been fearful became bold, those who had been confused received clarity, and those who had been powerless were empowered for supernatural ministry. The transformation was immediate, obvious, and permanent.

After Pentecost: Their ministry became supernaturally effective in ways that human training or natural ability could never have produced. They healed the sick, cast out demons, performed miracles, and proclaimed the Gospel with such power that thousands were converted, and entire communities were transformed.

This same pattern is available to every believer today. You may have been following Christ for years, attending church regularly, and trying to live a Christian life, but if you haven't been filled with the Holy Spirit's power, you're living in the "before Pentecost" phase of Christian experience. God wants to bring you into your own Pentecost transformation that will revolutionize both your relationship with Him and your effectiveness in ministry.

David Kim, an accountant in Seattle, experienced this transformation pattern: "I had been a Christian for fifteen years, served as a deacon, and taught Sunday school, but I knew something was missing. When I learned about the Holy Spirit's empowerment for ministry, I realized I had been trying to serve God in my own strength. I sought God for baptism in the Holy Spirit, and the change was remarkable. My prayers became more effective, my teaching was more anointed, and people began coming to me for spiritual counsel. I went from serving out of duty to ministering out of divine empowerment."

Characteristics of Spirit-Filled Witnesses

Modern believers who walk in their Pentecost inheritance demonstrate consistent characteristics that mark them as authentic Spirit-filled witnesses. These characteristics develop naturally as the Holy Spirit works through surrendered lives, creating transformation that influences every area of their existence.

Supernatural Boldness: Like Peter, who went from denying Jesus before a servant girl to preaching fearlessly before hostile religious leaders, Spirit-filled believers develop the courage to share their faith, stand for righteousness, and obey God regardless of opposition or cost.

Divine Wisdom: They receive insights and understanding that exceed their natural education or experience, enabling them to provide counsel, make decisions, and solve problems through supernatural wisdom rather than just human intelligence.

Miraculous Power: They regularly see God work through their prayers and ministry in ways that can only be explained by supernatural intervention, healings, provision, protection, and breakthroughs that exceed natural possibility.

Evangelistic Fruitfulness: People are drawn to Christ through their witness in ways that exceed what their personality, presentation skills, or ministry training could accomplish naturally. The Spirit working through them creates conviction and conversion that only God can produce.

Spiritual Discernment: They develop the ability to discern spiritual atmospheres, recognize truth and deception, and understand situations from God's perspective rather than being limited to surface appearances.

Sacrificial Love: They demonstrate supernatural love that enables them to serve difficult people, forgive deep hurts, and lay down their lives for others' spiritual and physical welfare.

Kingdom Perspective: They make decisions based on eternal values rather than temporal concerns, prioritizing God's purposes over personal comfort or advancement.

Worship Lifestyle: Their lives become expressions of worship as they recognize God's presence and respond to His goodness in ordinary circumstances as well as extraordinary experiences.

Your Unique Witness Assignment

While every Spirit-filled believer shares common characteristics, each person has a unique assignment from God that matches their personality, circumstances, calling, and the specific needs of their generation. Understanding your particular witness assignment helps you focus your spiritual development and ministry efforts in directions that maximize your kingdom impact.

Geographic Assignment: God has positioned you in specific locations, neighborhoods, cities, regions, where your influence can advance His kingdom purposes. Your witness assignment includes the people and circumstances in your geographic sphere of influence.

Relational Assignment: The family members, coworkers, friends, and acquaintances in your life are not accidental connections but divine assignments. God has positioned you in these relationships because He wants to use you to demonstrate His love and truth to these specific people.

Professional Assignment: Your career, job, or volunteer responsibilities provide platforms for witnesses that are unique to your skills, position, and opportunities. Spirit-filled believers see their work as ministry assignments rather than just income sources.

Generational Assignment: You have been called to influence your generation in ways that address the specific challenges, opportunities, and spiritual needs of your time period. What your generation needs from Spirit-filled witnesses may differ from what previous generations required.

Cultural Assignment: The cultural background, language, and social connections that characterize your life position you to reach people who might not be reached by believers from different cultural contexts.

Gifting Assignment: The spiritual gifts, natural talents, and developed skills that God has given you create opportunities for ministry and witness that are unique to your particular combination of abilities.

Maria Rodriguez, a teacher in San Antonio, discovered her unique witness assignment: "I realized that God had strategically positioned me as a bilingual educator in a predominantly Hispanic community where many families were struggling with cultural transitions and economic challenges. My witness assignment wasn't just to be a good teacher but to demonstrate God's love to students and families who needed to see authentic faith lived out in someone who understood their cultural experience. This perspective transformed how I approached my job and helped me recognize ministry opportunities I had been missing."

Overcoming Modern Witness Challenges

Contemporary believers face unique challenges in fulfilling their witness assignments that require wisdom, courage, and dependence on the Holy Spirit's guidance and power.

Understanding these challenges and learning biblical responses helps Spirit-filled believers maintain effective witness in difficult cultural environments.

Secular Hostility: Many workplaces, schools, and social environments are hostile to Christian faith and values, making witness challenging and sometimes risky. Spirit-filled believers must learn to demonstrate Christ's character and share His truth in ways that are both bold and wise.

Cultural/Religious Relativism: The prevailing cultural belief that all religious views are equally valid makes exclusive Christian truth claims seem intolerant or narrow-minded to many people. Witnesses must learn to communicate the absolute truth with love and humility.

Information Overload: People are bombarded with so much information and so many competing messages that cutting through the noise to communicate the Gospel effectively requires supernatural insight and divine appointments.

Spiritual Confusion: New Age beliefs, eastern religions, and pseudo-Christian cults create spiritual confusion that makes clear Gospel presentation more challenging than in previous generations, when basic biblical concepts were more widely understood.

Moral Compromise: The normalization of behaviors and values that contradict biblical standards creates tension for believers who want to maintain witness relationships while not compromising their convictions.

Technology Distractions: Digital devices and social media create unprecedented distractions that make deep spiritual conversations and sustained influence more difficult to maintain.

Religious Skepticism: Scandals involving Christian leaders and negative experiences with churches have created skepticism about organized religion that makes people resistant to Christian witness.

Tom Wilson, a businessman in Phoenix, learned to overcome modern witness challenges: "I was struggling with how to share my faith in a secular work environment where religious conversations were discouraged, and my colleagues were skeptical about Christianity. I learned that my most effective witness was demonstrating Christ's character consistently, integrity in business dealings, peace during stressful situations, and genuine care for coworkers' welfare.

This earned credibility that created opportunities for spiritual conversations when people noticed something different about my approach to work and relationships. I discovered that authenticity overcomes skepticism when people see faith that actually works in real-life circumstances."

CHAPTER 3:
Living As A Pentecost Person

Daily Life in Divine Power

Living as a Pentecost person means operating daily in the reality that the same Spirit who empowered the disciples lives within you and wants to demonstrate His presence and power through your ordinary circumstances and routine activities. This is not about dramatic spiritual manifestations in every moment but about supernatural enablement for natural responsibilities and divine guidance for daily decisions.

Morning Surrender: Begin each day by consciously yielding yourself to the Holy Spirit's control, asking for His guidance, and expecting Him to work through your activities and interactions throughout the day.

Constant Communication: Maintain ongoing conversation with God throughout your day, seeking His wisdom for decisions, asking for His help with challenges, and thanking Him for His presence and provision.

Spiritual Awareness: Stay alert to opportunities for ministry, divine appointments, and situations where God wants to demonstrate His power through your prayers, words, or actions.

Faith-Filled Responses: Approach challenges, opportunities, and unexpected circumstances with faith-filled responses that expect God to work rather than natural reactions based solely on human wisdom or emotion.

Love-Motivated Service: Look for ways to serve others throughout your day that demonstrate Christ's love and create opportunities for witness and ministry.

Scripture-Guided Thinking: Allow biblical truth to shape your thoughts, attitudes, and perspectives rather than being conformed to worldly thinking patterns.

Worship Lifestyle: Recognize God's presence and goodness in ordinary circumstances, maintaining an attitude of gratitude and praise that creates an atmosphere for His continued blessing.

Lisa Johnson, a mother and part-time office worker in Dallas, describes living as a Pentecost person: "I learned to start each day by asking the Holy Spirit to guide my activities and use me for His purposes. This simple change transformed everything. I became more sensitive to my children's emotional needs, more effective at work because I sought divine wisdom for problems, and more aware of opportunities to encourage neighbors and coworkers. Living as a Pentecost person doesn't require dramatic spiritual experiences every day, it means expecting God to work through ordinary activities in supernatural ways."

Developing Spiritual Sensitivity

One of the marks of authentic Pentecost living is increased spiritual sensitivity, the ability to discern God's voice, recognize His activity, and respond to spiritual realities that others might miss. This sensitivity develops through intentional cultivation and regular practice in listening to and cooperating with the Holy Spirit's leading.

Prayer Listening: Spend time in prayer, not just talking to God but waiting for His response, learning to recognize His voice through impressions, Scripture passages, and gentle conviction or peace about specific directions.

Scripture Meditation: Read the Bible not just for information but expecting God to speak personally to your current circumstances and needs through His written Word.

Circumstance Interpretation: Learn to see God's hand in your circumstances, recognizing His provision, protection, and guidance through events that might seem coincidental to others.

People Discernment: Develop the ability to sense people's spiritual condition, emotional needs, and openness to spiritual ministry, enabling you to respond appropriately to opportunities for witness and service.

Atmosphere Awareness: Become sensitive to spiritual atmospheres in different environments, recognizing when God's presence is particularly near or when spiritual warfare is affecting situations.

Gift Recognition: Discover and develop your spiritual gifts through practice and feedback, learning to recognize when the Holy Spirit wants to work through your particular abilities and calling.

Timing Sensitivity: Learn to discern God's timing for various activities and decisions, understanding when to move forward, when to wait, and when to step back from situations.

Michael Davis, an engineer in Denver, developed spiritual sensitivity through intentional practice: "I used to make decisions based purely on logic and analysis, but I began asking God for guidance and learning to recognize His voice through impressions and peace about certain directions. I started noticing when coworkers seemed discouraged or stressed and felt prompted to offer encouragement or prayer. I became more sensitive to my family's emotional and spiritual needs. This increased spiritual sensitivity made me more effective in every area of life because I was partnering with God instead of just relying on my own abilities."

Supernatural Ministry in Natural Settings

Pentecost people learn to minister in God's power within their natural environments rather than only in formal religious settings. This means bringing supernatural ministry to workplaces, neighborhoods, families, and social relationships through prayer, encouragement, practical service, and spiritual insight.

Workplace Ministry: Praying for colleagues' needs, offering biblical wisdom for work challenges, demonstrating Christ's character in business relationships, and looking for opportunities to share faith during natural conversations.

Family Ministry: Leading family prayers, providing spiritual guidance for children's challenges, creating home environments that welcome God's presence, and modeling faith-filled responses to family crises.

Neighborhood Ministry: Building relationships with neighbors that create opportunities for witness, offering practical help during difficult times, hosting gatherings that demonstrate Christian hospitality, and praying for community needs and challenges.

Social Ministry: Contributing hope and wisdom to social gatherings, supporting friends through personal crises, sharing testimonies of God's faithfulness during appropriate conversations, and demonstrating joy and peace that attract others to spiritual reality.

Service Ministry: Volunteering in community organizations where your spiritual gifts can benefit others, participating in disaster relief or charity work that demonstrates God's love practically, and using professional skills to serve people who cannot repay you.

Educational Ministry: Influencing schools, training programs, or educational settings through excellent performance and godly character that creates credibility for spiritual conversations and witness opportunities.

Jennifer Martinez, a marketing manager in Denver, learned to minister supernaturally in natural settings: "I realized that my office was my primary mission field, and that God had positioned me there to influence my colleagues for His kingdom. I began praying for coworkers by name, offering to help with personal and professional challenges, and looking for opportunities to demonstrate Christ's love through my work relationships. Several colleagues have come to faith through our workplace friendships, and our department has developed a reputation for teamwork and integrity that reflects kingdom values."

Building Spiritual Legacy

Pentecost people understand that their spiritual experience is not just for personal benefit but for building a legacy that influences future generations. They make decisions and investments that will strengthen faith and advance God's kingdom long after their earthly lives are complete.

Family Legacy: Raising children who experience authentic faith, creating family traditions that embed spiritual reality into ordinary life, and modeling relationships with God that inspire following generations to seek their own encounters with His Spirit.

Mentorship Legacy: Investing in younger believers who can carry on spiritual influence, sharing life experiences and spiritual lessons that help others avoid mistakes and grow more quickly in faith and ministry.

Ministry Legacy: Building ministries, organizations, or spiritual movements that will continue advancing God's kingdom beyond your direct involvement, creating structures and cultures that multiply your spiritual influence.

Financial Legacy: Using financial resources to support kingdom purposes, investing in eternal ventures rather than just temporal comfort, and teaching others biblical principles of stewardship and generosity.

Testimony Legacy: Recording and sharing your testimonies of God's faithfulness, creating written or recorded accounts of His work in your life that can encourage others long after you're in heaven.

Character Legacy: Developing a reputation for integrity, faithfulness, and love that influences how people think about Christianity and creates a platform for others to share faith more effectively.

Prayer Legacy: Establishing prayer commitments and intercession patterns that others can continue, creating spiritual covering for people and purposes that will benefit from ongoing prayer support.

Sarah Chen, now in her seventies, reflects on the spiritual legacy she has built: "When I began living as a Pentecost person forty years ago, I didn't think about legacy, I just wanted to experience more of God in my daily life. But over the years, I've seen how my spiritual choices influenced my children, my grandchildren, my coworkers, and my neighbors. My children are raising their own families with the expectation of God's presence and power. Former colleagues still contact me to pray about important decisions. Young people in our church ask me to mentor them because they've seen authentic faith lived out over decades. I realize that every choice to seek God more deeply, every act of faith, and every decision to prioritize spiritual reality over temporal comfort has created a legacy that will continue long after I'm with the Lord."

CHAPTER 4:
Your Personal Challenge

Honest Assessment of Current Reality

Before you can move forward into your full Pentecost inheritance, you must honestly assess where you are spiritually right now. This assessment is not meant to create condemnation but to establish a baseline from which you can measure growth and identify areas where God wants to work in your life.

Ask yourself these penetrating questions and answer them with complete honesty:

Spiritual Power: Do you regularly see God work through your prayers in ways that can only be explained by supernatural intervention, or do you pray primarily out of duty with limited expectation for dramatic answers?

Bold Witness: Are people regularly drawn to Christ through your influence, or do most people in your life remain unaware of your faith because it doesn't significantly affect how you live, work, or relate to others?

Divine Guidance: Do you receive clear direction from God for important decisions, or do you make most choices based purely on human wisdom, circumstances, and personal preferences?

Spiritual Gifts: Are you actively using spiritual gifts to minister to others and advance God's kingdom, or are you uncertain about your gifts and rarely exercise supernatural abilities in service to others?

Joy and Peace: Do you experience supernatural joy and peace that transcends your circumstances, or are you troubled by the same anxieties, frustrations, and discouragements that characterize non-believers?

Character Transformation: Are you becoming more like Christ in your attitudes, responses, and relationships through the Spirit's work in your life, or do you struggle with the same character issues year after year without significant change?

Spiritual Hunger: Do you have increasing hunger for more of God's presence and power in your life, or are you generally satisfied with your current level of spiritual experience?

Kingdom Impact: Are you making measurable contributions to advancing God's kingdom through your time, talents, and resources, or are you primarily focused on personal comfort and family security?

This honest assessment will help you identify specific areas where you need to seek God for greater spiritual empowerment and will create the holy dissatisfaction that motivates the pursuit of everything He has made available to you.

David Thompson, a teacher in Chicago, underwent this assessment process: "When I honestly evaluated my spiritual life, I realized I had been coasting for years. I wasn't seeing people come to faith through my influence, I rarely experienced clear answers to prayer, and I was struggling with the same character issues that had bothered me for a decade. This assessment created desperation for more of God, which motivated me to seek the Holy Spirit's fullness in ways I had never pursued before. The honest evaluation was painful but necessary for real spiritual progress."

Identifying Your Next Steps

Based on your honest assessment, you can identify specific areas where God wants to work in your life and develop practical steps for positioning yourself to receive more of His presence and power. These next steps should be specific, measurable, and focused on creating conditions that invite divine transformation.

Spiritual Disciplines: If your assessment reveals weakness in your relationship with God, commit to specific improvements in prayer, Bible study, worship, or fasting that will deepen your intimacy with Him and create space for His work in your life.

Faith Development: If you struggle with believing God for supernatural intervention, begin praying for smaller needs while building your confidence in His willingness and ability to work miraculously in your circumstances.

Character Growth: If you recognize persistent character issues, seek specific spiritual resources, accountability relationships, or ministry opportunities that will create pressure and support for continued growth in Christlike character.

Gift Discovery: If you're uncertain about your spiritual gifts, seek opportunities to minister to others in different contexts while paying attention to where you see supernatural fruit and effectiveness.

Witness Training: If you struggle with sharing your faith, seek training, mentorship, or practice opportunities that will develop your confidence and ability to communicate the Gospel effectively.

Ministry Involvement: If you're not actively serving in ways that advance God's kingdom, explore ministry opportunities that match your gifts, interests, and availability while challenging you to depend on God's power rather than just your natural abilities.

Community Connection: If you lack spiritual community and accountability, seek relationships with other believers who share your hunger for spiritual growth and can support your journey toward fullness in Christ.

Lifestyle Adjustment: If your schedule or priorities don't reflect spiritual values, make specific changes that demonstrate your commitment to seeking God's kingdom first and trusting Him to provide for other needs.

Creating an Action Plan

Spiritual transformation requires more than good intentions, it requires specific plans and concrete steps that move you from where you are to where God wants you to be. Your action plan should include both spiritual disciplines that position you for God's work and practical steps that demonstrate your commitment to change.

30-Day Spiritual Intensive: Commit to thirty days of intensified spiritual seeking through extended prayer, daily Scripture meditation, fasting, worship, and specific requests for the Holy Spirit's empowerment in your life.

Weekly Spiritual Goals: Establish weekly goals for spiritual growth, specific number of people you'll pray for, ministry opportunities you'll pursue, or spiritual disciplines you'll maintain consistently.

Monthly Ministry Challenges: Set monthly challenges that stretch your faith and require dependence on God's power, praying for healing, sharing your testimony, serving in new ways, or taking leadership in spiritual activities.

Quarterly Spiritual Assessments: Schedule regular evaluation of your spiritual progress, identifying areas of growth and continued need while adjusting your spiritual practices based on what you're learning about God's work in your life.

Annual Kingdom Commitments: Make yearly commitments to specific ministry involvement, financial giving, or service projects that advance God's kingdom while requiring faith and sacrifice on your part.

Accountability Partnerships: Establish relationships with other believers who will support, encourage, and hold you accountable for following through on your spiritual commitments and growth goals.

Learning Opportunities: Seek books, conferences, courses, or mentorship relationships that will expand your understanding of spiritual life and provide practical guidance for continued growth in faith and ministry.

Maria Gonzalez developed a comprehensive action plan after recognizing her spiritual needs:

"I realized I needed to move beyond casual Christianity to serious spiritual development. I committed to rising thirty minutes earlier each day for prayer and Bible reading, joined a small group for accountability and support, began volunteering in children's ministry to develop my gifts, and started asking God to use me supernaturally in my workplace relationships.

Within six months, I was experiencing answers to prayer, opportunities for witness, and spiritual growth that exceeded anything I had experienced in previous years of Christian life."

Overcoming Obstacles to Spiritual Growth

Every believer who seriously pursues their Pentecost inheritance will encounter obstacles designed to prevent spiritual breakthrough. Anticipating these challenges and preparing strategies for overcoming them is essential for maintaining momentum toward spiritual maturity and empowerment.

Time Pressures: Modern life's pace can crowd out spiritual priorities, making it difficult to maintain consistency in prayer, Bible study, or ministry involvement. Success requires ruthless elimination of less important activities and protection of time dedicated to spiritual growth.

Spiritual Opposition: Increased spiritual activity often triggers spiritual warfare that manifests through discouragement, conflict, unexpected obstacles, or temptations designed to derail your spiritual progress. Recognition and resistance of these attacks is crucial for continued growth.

Discouragement from Slow Progress: Spiritual growth usually occurs gradually rather than dramatically, and periods of apparent stagnation can create discouragement that tempts you to abandon spiritual disciplines or lower your expectations for God's work in your life.

Criticism from Others: Family members, friends, or church members who are comfortable with spiritual mediocrity may criticize your pursuit of deeper spiritual experience, labeling it as fanaticism or suggesting that you think you're better than others.

Personal Failure: Everyone experiences failures in spiritual discipline, lapses in faith, or mistakes in ministry that can create shame and temptation to abandon pursuit of spiritual growth rather than receiving forgiveness and continuing to seek God's grace.

Competing Priorities: Career advancement, family responsibilities, financial pressures, or other legitimate concerns can compete with spiritual priorities, requiring wisdom to maintain proper balance while not compromising your commitment to spiritual growth.

Doctrinal Confusion: Conflicting teaching about spiritual gifts, the Holy Spirit's work, or expectations for Christian living can create confusion that paralyzes spiritual progress rather than encouraging continued seeking of God's best for your life.

Tom Martinez overcame multiple obstacles in his spiritual journey: "I encountered resistance from family members who thought I was becoming too religious, workplace pressures that made spiritual priorities difficult to maintain, and personal failures that made me question whether spiritual growth was really possible. I learned that obstacles are normal parts of spiritual development and that persistence through difficult seasons often leads to the greatest breakthroughs. The key was not letting temporary setbacks become permanent defeats but continuing to seek God's grace for continued growth despite imperfect progress."

Making Your Commitment

Your Pentecost journey requires more than information or inspiration, it requires definite commitment to pursue everything God has made available to you regardless of cost, opposition, or personal inconvenience. This commitment becomes the foundation for all future spiritual growth and the source of strength when challenges threaten to derail your progress.

Your commitment should include several key elements:

Total Surrender: Yielding every area of your life to God's control, acknowledging His right to direct your decisions, relationships, resources, and priorities according to His purposes rather than your preferences.

Persistent Seeking: Committing to continue seeking God's fullness even when progress seems slow, circumstances are difficult, or others don't understand your spiritual hunger and pursuit.

Faithful Obedience: Agreeing to obey whatever God reveals to you through His Word, His Spirit, or godly counsel, even when obedience requires sacrifice, change, or stepping outside your comfort zones.

Sacrificial Service: Dedicating your time, talents, and resources to advancing God's kingdom rather than just pursuing personal comfort, security, or advancement.

Bold Witness: Committing to share your faith and demonstrate Christ's character regardless of others' responses or potential personal cost to your reputation or relationships.

Lifelong Learning: Agreeing to continue growing in spiritual knowledge, character, and ministry effectiveness throughout your life rather than settling for current levels of understanding or ability.

Community Accountability: Submitting yourself to spiritual authority and accountability relationships that can guide, correct, and encourage your continued spiritual development.

Write out your commitment in your own words, sign it, and date it as a covenant between you and God that can serve as a reminder during difficult seasons when you're tempted to settle for less than His best for your life.

Jennifer Park made her commitment after recognizing God's call on her life: "I wrote out a personal covenant with God that included specific commitments to daily prayer, regular Bible study, faithful church attendance, financial giving, and availability for ministry opportunities. I signed it during a weekend retreat and refer back to it whenever I'm tempted to compromise my spiritual priorities. That written commitment has kept me accountable to pursue God's best even when it would be easier to settle for spiritual mediocrity."

CHAPTER 5:
The Echo In Your Generation

Understanding Your Generational Assignment

Every generation faces unique challenges and opportunities that require specific expressions of Spirit-filled witness. Your generation's particular needs, cultural context, and spiritual hunger create your generational assignment, the specific ways God wants to use your life to impact the people and circumstances of your time period.

Understanding your generational assignment helps you focus your spiritual development and ministry efforts in directions that will have maximum impact for God's kingdom in your lifetime.

Current Cultural Challenges: Identify the specific moral, spiritual, social, and relational challenges that characterize your generation and consider how Spirit-filled believers can address these needs through supernatural wisdom, power, and love.

Technological Opportunities: Recognize how modern communication, transportation, and information technologies create unprecedented opportunities for Gospel advancement and spiritual influence that previous generations never had available.

Global Awareness: Your generation has more awareness of world conditions, international needs, and cross-cultural opportunities than any previous generation, creating unique responsibilities for global kingdom impact.

Educational Advantages: Higher levels of education and access to information create opportunities to engage intellectual and scientific communities with sophisticated presentations of Christian faith.

Economic Resources: Despite economic challenges, your generation has access to financial resources and economic opportunities that can be leveraged for kingdom purposes in ways that previous generations could not imagine.

Social Mobility: Modern societies offer unprecedented opportunities for believers to influence multiple social, professional, and cultural contexts throughout their lifetimes.

Spiritual Hunger: Despite secularization trends, many people in your generation have deep spiritual hunger that creates openness to authentic demonstrations of God's reality and power.

Sarah Martinez, a teacher in her thirties, recognized her generational assignment: "I realized that my generation faces unique challenges with technology addiction, social media pressure, and spiritual confusion that require new approaches to demonstrating authentic faith. God has positioned me to influence young people who are hungry for real relationships and genuine spiritual experience but who have been hurt by religious hypocrisy. My assignment is to show them what authentic Christianity looks like in contemporary contexts."

Becoming a Generational Game-Changer

Some believers are called to be generational game-changers, individuals whose spiritual influence creates significant shifts in how their generation thinks about God, approaches spiritual questions, or experiences kingdom reality. These game-changers often emerge from ordinary backgrounds but develop extraordinary spiritual influence through their availability to God's purposes.

Cultural Bridge-Builders: Believers who can communicate effectively between different cultural, generational, or ideological groups, helping people find common ground while maintaining biblical truth.

Intellectual Apologists: Christians who can engage academic, scientific, or philosophical communities with sophisticated defenses of biblical faith that address contemporary intellectual challenges to Christianity.

Artistic Influencers: Believers who work in entertainment, media, arts, or creative fields where they can influence cultural narratives and demonstrate kingdom values through excellent creative work.

Business Innovators: Christian entrepreneurs or executives who create business models that demonstrate kingdom principles while meeting practical needs and creating economic opportunities for others.

Ministry Pioneers: Believers who develop new approaches to evangelism, discipleship, or church life that effectively reach contemporary audiences with timeless spiritual truths.

Social Reformers: Christians who address social injustices, political challenges, or community needs through spiritual motivation and supernatural wisdom that creates lasting positive change.

Technology Leverage: Believers who use modern technologies creatively for kingdom purposes, finding innovative ways to share faith, build community, or serve human needs.

Michael Thompson, a software developer, became a generational game-changer through his technology skills: "I started using my programming abilities to create apps and websites that help people connect with spiritual resources, find Christian communities, and grow in their faith.

What began as a side project has become a ministry that reaches thousands of people worldwide. I realized that God wanted to use my professional skills and generational understanding of technology to advance His kingdom in ways that previous generations couldn't imagine."

Creating Movements vs. Following Trends

Spirit-filled believers in every generation have the opportunity to create spiritual movements that influence their culture rather than simply following secular trends or adapting to popular opinions. Creating movements requires vision, courage, and willingness to lead rather than just participate in what others have started.

Identifying Needs: Recognize specific spiritual, social, or practical needs in your generation that aren't being adequately addressed by existing religious or secular solutions.

Developing Solutions: Seek God's wisdom for approaches that address these needs in ways that demonstrate kingdom principles and create positive transformation.

Building Community: Gather other believers who share similar burdens for these needs and can contribute their gifts, resources, and influence on collaborative solutions.

Modeling Change: Start by making tangible changes in your own behavior that clearly show how your solutions work in real life. Instead of just talking about your ideas, put them into practice in everyday situations. This creates visible proof that your approach is effective and achievable. When others see these positive results firsthand, they become more inclined to adopt similar changes themselves. By embodying the transformation you propose, you set an influential example that encourages and inspires those around you to follow your lead.

Communicating Vision: Clearly express your vision to motivate others to join your cause. Explain its purpose in a way that connects with values and passions. Use relatable stories and examples to show what you want to achieve and why it matters. Invite people to see their role and how their skills can make a difference. Emphasize collaboration and that success needs everyone. Be honest about challenges but focus on opportunities for change. Inspire commitment by sharing clear steps to get involved. Keep the vision open so others can contribute ideas and energy. This approach will attract a committed, growing community for your cause.

Training Leaders: Develop other believers who can multiply the movement's impact by leading similar efforts in their own spheres of influence.

Creating Infrastructure: Establish organizations, systems, or resources that can sustain the movement beyond your direct involvement.

Measuring Impact: Track the movement's effectiveness in creating positive change and adjust strategies based on results and changing needs.

Lisa Johnson created a movement addressing her generation's need for an authentic community: "I recognized that many young families in our area felt isolated and overwhelmed by parenting challenges. I started hosting weekly gatherings in our home where parents could share struggles and support each other. This grew into a network of family support groups throughout our city that provide practical help and spiritual encouragement. What started as a response to personal need became a movement that has influenced hundreds of families and created models that other communities have adopted."

Your Legacy Echo

The echo of Pentecost that reaches you through two thousand years of church history is not meant to end with you, it's meant to be amplified through your life and passed on to future generations with even greater power and scope. Your spiritual legacy becomes part of the continuing echo that will influence believers long after you're in heaven.

Family Legacy: The spiritual influence you have on children, grandchildren, and extended family creates ripple effects that can influence generations of your family line toward stronger faith and more effective ministry.

Ministry Legacy: The people you disciple, the ministries you establish, and the spiritual influence you exert create ongoing impact that multiplies your kingdom contribution far beyond your lifetime.

Community Legacy: The transformation you create in your neighborhood, workplace, or social circles establishes patterns and relationships that continue advancing God's kingdom through others who carry on your influence.

Cultural Legacy: The contributions you make to art, business, education, politics, or other cultural spheres create lasting influence that shapes how future generations think about faith and values.

Written Legacy: Books, articles, testimonies, or other written materials you create can continue influencing people long after your earthly life is complete.

Institutional Legacy: Organizations, churches, schools, or other institutions you help establish or strengthen can continue advancing kingdom purposes for decades or centuries after your involvement ends.

Character Legacy: The reputation you develop for integrity, faithfulness, and love influences how people think about Christianity and creates a platform for others to share faith more effectively.

David Chen, now in his sixties, reflects on the legacy echo he hopes to create: "I want my life to amplify the Pentecost echo that reached me through faithful believers who influenced my spiritual development. I'm investing in young people who can carry kingdom influence into areas I'll never reach. I'm working to establish ministries that will continue long after I'm gone. I'm writing down testimonies of God's faithfulness that my children and grandchildren can treasure. I want the echo of Pentecost that transformed my life to sound even louder through the lives I influence for God's kingdom."

The Continuing Story

Your Pentecost journey is not just about personal spiritual experience, it's about becoming part of the continuing story that began in that Jerusalem upper room and will culminate when Christ returns to establish His kingdom on earth. You are living in the middle chapters of the greatest story ever told, and your choices about spiritual commitment will help determine how effectively the church fulfills its mission in your generation.

The same Spirit who fell on Pentecost continues to fall today. The same power that transformed the disciples continues to transform believers. The same fire that launched the early church continues to ignite hearts that are hungry for more of God. The same echo that has reverberated through twenty centuries of church history is sounding in your generation through believers who refuse to settle for spiritual mediocrity.

Your response to this echo will determine whether it grows stronger or weaker in your lifetime. Your commitment to your Pentecost inheritance will influence whether future generations receive this legacy with greater or diminished power.

Your faithfulness in living as a Spirit-filled witness will help determine whether the church in your generation successfully fulfills its mission to reach every people group with the Gospel.

The echo continues, but it needs your voice. The fire still burns, but it needs your heart as fuel. The story continues, but it needs your chapter to advance the plot toward its glorious conclusion.

Maria Rodriguez, after experiencing her own Pentecost transformation, became passionate about passing on this inheritance: "I realized that I'm not just receiving spiritual blessing for my own benefit, I'm a link in the chain that connects the first Pentecost to future generations of believers. My children are watching to see if Christianity really works in practical life. My neighbors are observing to see if faith makes a real difference. My generation is waiting to see if the church has the power to address contemporary challenges. The echo of Pentecost that changed my life must sound even louder through my influence on others."

Your Personal Pentecost Awaits

The journey that began with a curious observation of ancient history has brought you to this moment of personal decision. You have seen the evidence, understood the pattern, and discovered the inheritance that belongs to you as a believer in Jesus Christ. The question that remains is the same one that has faced every generation since that first Pentecost: What will you do with what you now know?

The echo of that first Pentecost morning is reverberating in your heart right now. The same Spirit who fell on those first disciples is hovering over your life, waiting for you to create the conditions that invite His fullness. The same power that transformed cowards into champions, doubters into defenders, and followers into leaders is available to transform whatever needs transformation in your circumstances.

You stand at the threshold of your own upper room experience. You may not feel ready, qualified, or worthy, neither did the disciples. You may not understand everything about how God works or what He might require of you, neither did those first believers.

You may have fears, doubts, or questions about stepping into supernatural living, so did every person who has ever experienced genuine spiritual empowerment.

But readiness comes through obedience, qualifications come through God's calling, worthiness comes through Christ's sacrifice, understanding comes through experience, and courage comes through faith. Everything you need for your Pentecost journey is already available to you through the Holy Spirit who lives within you and the promises God has made to every believer.

Your personal Pentecost may come dramatically in a moment of overwhelming encounter with God's presence, or it may unfold gradually as you consistently position yourself for His work in your life. It may be marked by supernatural manifestations that leave no doubt about divine intervention, or it may be characterized by quiet transformation that revolutionizes your character and effectiveness over time.

The form matters less than the reality. The method matters less than the result. The important thing is not how the Spirit fills you but that He fills you, not how He empowers you but that He empowers you, not how He uses you but that He uses you for His glory and the advancement of His kingdom.

Your generation needs believers who live in the reality of Pentecost power. Your family needs spiritual leaders who demonstrate an authentic relationship with God. Your workplace needs colleagues who operate in supernatural wisdom and love. Your community needs neighbors who serve with divine motivation and effectiveness.

The echo of Pentecost has been waiting for your voice. The fire has been waiting for your heart. The power has been waiting for your surrender. The inheritance has been waiting for your claim.

This is your moment. This is your invitation. This is your opportunity to step into everything God has prepared for you since before the foundation of the world.

The same Spirit who fell on Pentecost is ready to fall on your life. What will you do with this reality?

Your personal Pentecost awaits your response. The echo continues through you, starting now.

REFLECTION AND CLOSING PRAYER

Your Invitation to Fresh Empowerment

A Moment of Reflection

As you reach the end of this journey through the transforming fire of Pentecost, pause for a moment and let your heart absorb what you have discovered. You have witnessed the explosion of divine power that changed history in that Jerusalem upper room. You have traced the unbroken chain of believers who have carried this fire through twenty centuries of triumph and trial. You have seen how ordinary people became extraordinary demonstrations of God's reality when they opened their hearts to His Spirit's fullness.

More importantly, you have discovered that this same fire, this same Spirit, this same power, this same transformation, is not ancient history but present possibility. The God who breathed life into Adam's lungs, who filled Moses with courage to confront Pharaoh, who empowered David to face Goliath, who enabled the disciples to turn the world upside down, is the same God who lives within you right now.

The question that echoes through these pages is not academic or theoretical. It is deeply personal and urgently practical: What will you do with this reality?

You have seen what God can do through surrendered lives. You have learned the principles that position hearts for divine encounter. You have been shown the pathway from routine religion to authentic spiritual power. You have been invited to join the ranks of those whose lives become ongoing testimonies to the reality of the living God.

Now comes your moment of choice. Now comes your opportunity to move from observer to participant, from admirer to experiencer, from student to practitioner of the supernatural life that Jesus made available to every believer.

Your heart may be stirred with holy hunger for more of God. Your spirit may be resonating with the testimonies you have read, creating a deep longing for similar encounters with divine power. Your mind may be convinced that God wants to work through your life in ways you have never experienced before.

But hunger must lead to seeking. Longing must result in surrender. Conviction must produce commitment. The fire of God is waiting to fall on your life, but it only burns in hearts that are prepared to be consumed.

Your Personal Prayer Invitation

This is your invitation to prayer, not merely to say words, but to open your heart completely to the God who wants to fill you, transform you, and work through you in supernatural ways. This is your opportunity to pray the prayer that could change everything, the prayer that positions you for your own Pentecost experience.

If your heart is hungry for more of God than you have ever experienced, if you are tired of settling for spiritual mediocrity when spiritual power is available, if you sense the Holy Spirit drawing you toward deeper surrender and greater empowerment, then this prayer is for you.

Find a quiet place where you can be alone with God. Kneel if you are able, as a physical expression of your heart's submission. Open your hands as a symbol of your willingness to receive whatever God wants to give you. Quiet your mind from distractions and focus your attention on the presence of the One who loves you more than you can imagine.

Then, from the depths of your heart, pray these words, not as a formula to follow but as an expression of your genuine hunger for everything God has made available to you:

A Prayer for Fresh Empowerment

Heavenly Father,

I come before You with a heart that is hungry for more of You than I have ever experienced. I confess that I have been settling for spiritual mediocrity when You have made spiritual power available to me. I acknowledge that I have been living far below the inheritance You purchased for me through the death and resurrection of Jesus Christ.

I thank You that the same Spirit who fell on Pentecost lives within me today. I thank You that the same power that transformed the disciples is available to transform me. I thank You that Your fire still burns, and Your presence is still available to fill hearts that are truly surrendered to You.

Lord Jesus, I surrender my life completely to You. I give You my dreams and my fears, my strengths and my weaknesses, my past, and my future. I hold nothing back from Your control. Take every area of my life and use it for Your glory and the advancement of Your kingdom.

Holy Spirit, I invite You to fill me completely. Come into every corner of my heart, every area of my life, every relationship, and responsibility. I want to experience Your presence not just occasionally but continually. I want to walk in Your power, not just during church services but throughout every ordinary day.

Fill me with boldness to share the Gospel with everyone You bring into my path. Give me supernatural love for people I find difficult to love naturally. Grant me wisdom that exceeds my natural understanding for every decision I face. Empower me to pray prayers that move Your heart and change circumstances.

Use my hands to bring healing to the sick. Use my words to bring comfort to the hurting and hope to the discouraged. Use my life to demonstrate Your reality to people who have never seen authentic Christianity lived out in practical ways.

I ask You to break every barrier that has kept me from experiencing Your fullness, fear, pride, doubt, busyness, compromise, or anything else that has hindered Your work in my life. Remove whatever needs to be removed, change whatever needs to be changed, and add whatever needs to be added to make me the kind of person You can use for Your purposes.

Lord, I don't just want to be saved, I want to be empowered. I don't just want to go to heaven someday, I want to bring heaven to earth today. I don't just want to have religion, I want to have a relationship that transforms everything about how I live.

Give me a testimony that brings glory to Your name. Let my life become evidence that You are still working potently in our generation. Use me to influence others toward deeper faith and more authentic spiritual experience.

I pray for a fresh outpouring of Your Spirit not just on my life but on my family, my church, my community, and my generation. Let the fire that falls on my heart spread to every person You've positioned within my sphere of influence.

I make this prayer not based on my worthiness but based on Your promises. Not because I deserve Your power but because Jesus has made it available to every believer. Not because I am qualified but because You are faithful to work through surrendered hearts.

Holy Spirit, come and fill me now. Come and empower me today. Come and use me for Your glory, starting in this moment and continuing for the rest of my life.

In the mighty name of Jesus Christ, who baptizes with the Holy Spirit and fire, I pray with faith and expectation.

Amen.

After Your Prayer

Having prayed this prayer with sincere faith, now walk forward in confident expectation that God has heard you and will respond according to His perfect will and timing. You have positioned yourself for divine encounter, opened your heart to supernatural transformation, and invited the Holy Spirit to work in your life in unprecedented ways.

Your Pentecost experience may begin immediately with a profound sense of God's presence, peace that transcends understanding, joy that bubbles up from your spirit, or boldness to share your faith that you have never experienced before. Or it may unfold gradually over days and weeks as you consistently live in surrender to God's will and expectation of His power.

However, God chooses to work in your life, remain faithful to the surrender you have made. Continue seeking Him daily through prayer, Scripture reading, and worship. Look for opportunities to step out in faith and allow Him to work through you. Stay connected with other believers who can encourage your spiritual growth and hold you accountable to live in the reality of what you have asked God to do.

Most importantly, remember that this prayer is not the end of your spiritual journey but the beginning of a new chapter in your relationship with God. You have opened your heart to transformation that will continue throughout your lifetime as you learn to walk more closely with the Holy Spirit and cooperate more fully with His work in your life.

The same God who answered the prayers of believers throughout history is faithful to answer your prayer as well. The same Spirit who has empowered ordinary people to live extraordinary lives is ready to empower you. The same fire that has burned through twenty centuries of church history is ready to burn brightly in your heart.

Your Pentecost journey has begun. Your transformation from routine to alive is underway. Your life as a Spirit-filled witness starts now.

To God be the glory, great things He has done and will do through your surrendered life. May the fire fall fresh on your heart today and burn brightly for His glory until Jesus comes again.

"But you shall receive power when the Holy Spirit has come upon you; and you shall be witnesses to Me in Jerusalem, and in all Judea and Samaria, and to the end of the earth." - Acts 1:8

The promise is for you. The power is available. The fire is falling.

Receive it today.

REFERENCES

- Biblical References from various bible translations such as New International Version (NIV), New King James Version (NKJV), English Standard Version (ESV)

- Historical recounting of events like the Moravian prayer movement, Great Awakenings, Azusa Street Revival, and citations of William Carey's pamphlets, mission histories, and personal journals: Moravian prayer movement, Great Awakenings, Azusa Street Revival: Carey, W. (1792). *An Enquiry into the Obligations of Christians to Use Means for the Conversion of the Heathens*

- Professional Journals: References to church historians: LaTourette, K. S. (1937). A History of the Expansion of Christianity.

- Online Materials & Modern Movements: Mentions of organizations (24-7 Prayer Movement, International House of Prayer, Taizé Community) and approaches such as prayer walking and digital prayer networks. International House of Prayer. (n.d.). Retrieved from https://www.ihopkc.org.

- Quotes and Testimonies: Embedded quotes from historical figures and contemporary Christians, sometimes attributed narratively and sometimes with reference to their work or roles.

Echoes of Pentecost isn't just a book about history—it's a gateway to experiencing the same transformative power that ignited the early Church. Authored by John Chacko, this work is a powerful call to embrace the fullness of the Holy Spirit and step into a life defined by courage, conviction, and divine strength.

Through a mix of biblical teachings, personal reflections, and inspiring historical examples, John reveals how the Pentecostal experience can ignite a new level of spiritual life in every believer. You are not reading about a past moment—you are discovering your own inheritance as a child of God, filled with His Spirit and ready to walk in His power.

Whether you are seeking personal revival or longing to see God move in your church or community, Echoes of Pentecost will challenge you to believe that the same fire that fell on the disciples is still available today. Will you answer the call to live as a Spirit-filled witness?

The time is now.

JOHN CHACKO

$24.99
ISBN 979-8-9938038-0-7

www.ingramcontent.com/pod-product-compliance
Lightning Source LLC
Chambersburg PA
CBHW072001150426
43194CB00008B/952